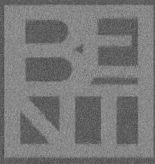

bent street

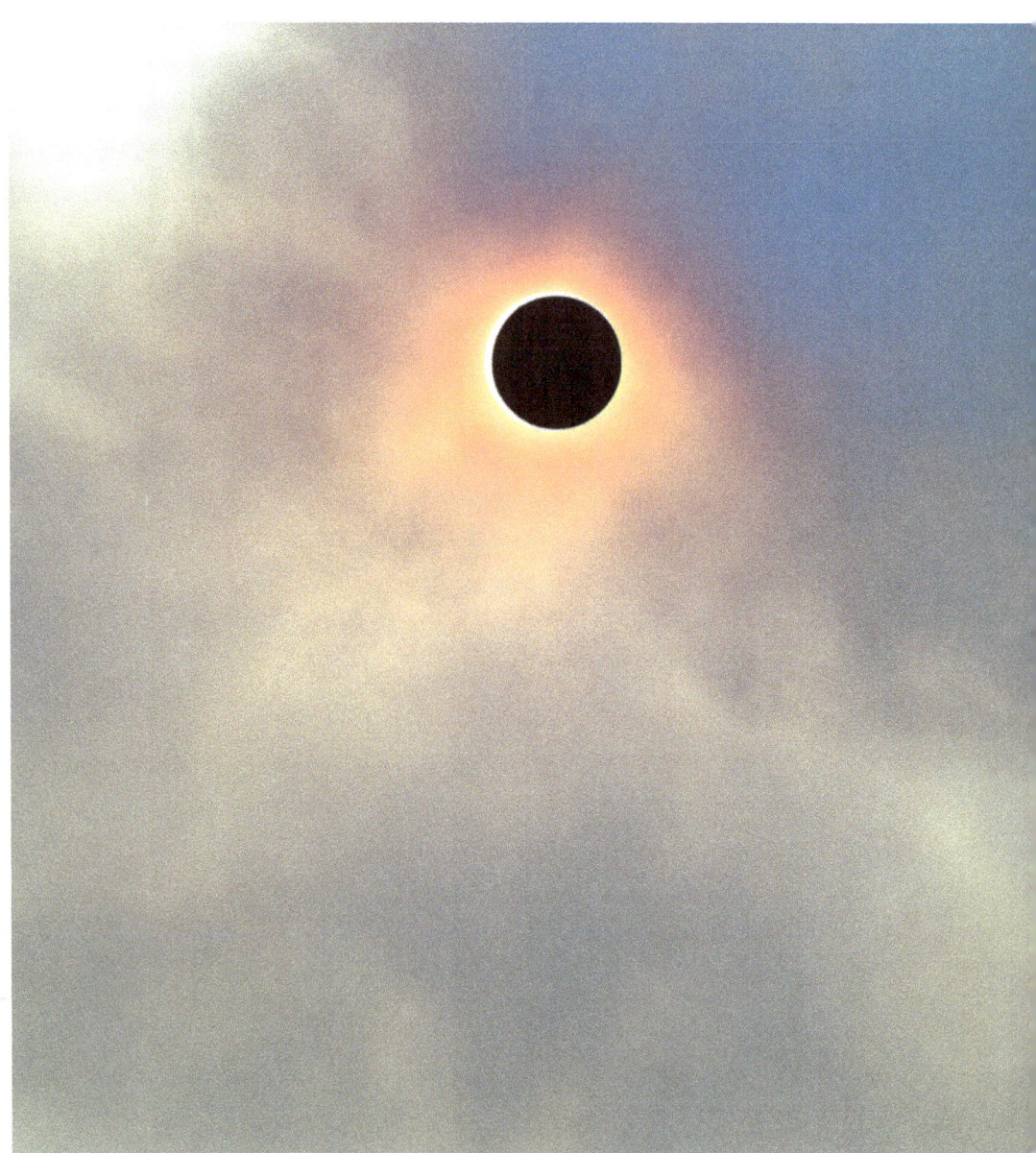

Gordon Thompson—*2020*

bent street

4.2 2020

Bent Street: Australian LGBTIQA+ Arts, Writing & Ideas

Edited by: Tiffany Jones

Clouds of Magellan Press | Melbourne

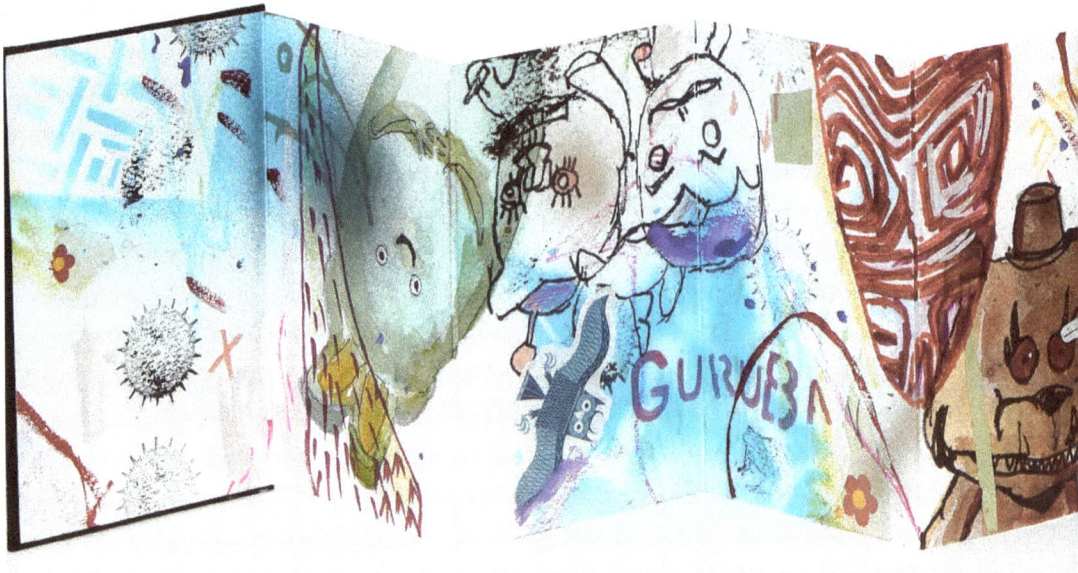

Bent Street: Australian LGBTIQA+ Arts, Writing & Ideas is published twice yearly by Clouds of Magellan Press, Melbourne. www.cloudsofmagellanpress.net

bentstreet.net

ISSN 2652-659X (Print)
ISBN: (paperback) 978-0-6487469-8-0
ISBN: (ebook) 978-0-6487469-9-7

Series Editor-in-Chief: Tiffany Jones
Editorial Advisor: Dennis Altman
Contributing Editors: Ashley Sievwright, Gordon Thompson

Logo: Andrew Liu | Design: Gordon Thompson

Publication and distribution, Lightning Source, through eBook Alchemy. ebookalchemy.com

Cover: Kiss My Apocalypse—Mel Simpson

Special thanks to Henry von Doussa, Margie Fischer, Geoff Allshorn, Helen Bell, Guy James Whitworth, Andrew Farrell, Amber Karanikolas

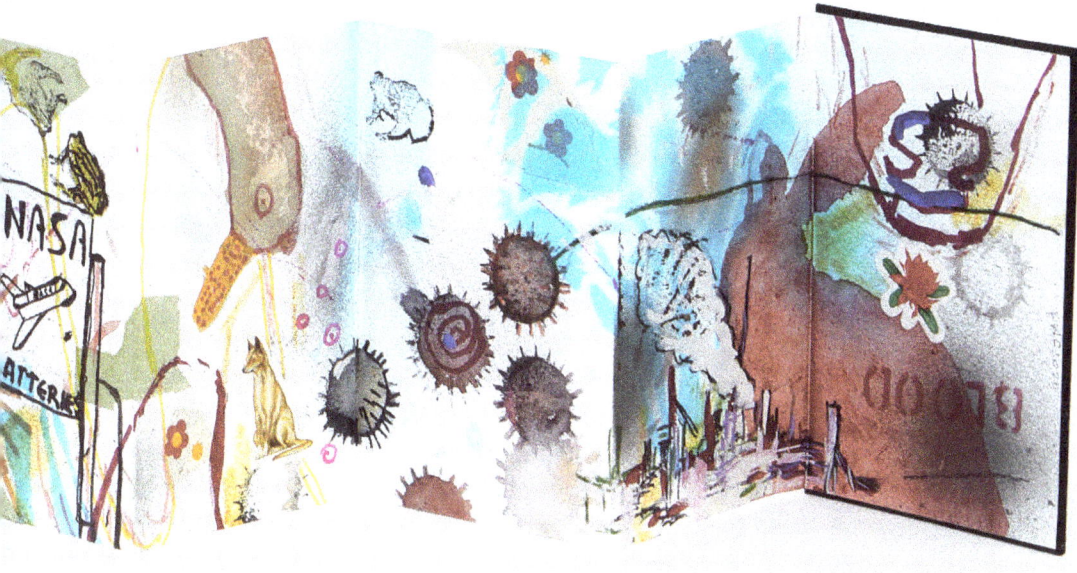

Peter Waples-Crowe—*Book 1,* mixed media on Orihon books 15 x 100 cm

Acknowledgement

Bent Street acknowledges the Traditional Custodians of country throughout Australia and their connections to land, sea and community. We pay our respect to their Elders past, present and emerging, and extend that respect to all Aboriginal and Torres Strait Islander peoples.

CONTENTS

THE YEAR IN QUEER

ESSAYS

POETRY

FICTION

Artists and image makers, not listed in the contents above, whose work appear in this edition of *bent street* include:
Neika Lehman, Isabella Whāwhai Waru, Caleb Thaiday, and Jazz Mooney (pp. 14-16); Derek Jarman (pp. 130-139); Howard Sooley (p. 132); Luke David (pp 18, 21); Peter Casamento (pp. 76, 78); Gordon Thompson (frontmatter, p.132). All images used with permission.

INTRODUCTION
Tiffany Jones

As I welcome you back to *Bent Street*, I wonder, where is it that we as the LGBTIQ+ and allied communities can credibly, consistently congregate beyond our creative contributions? The many disasters of the year 2020 saw rural and remote LGBTIQ+ communities chased from their towns and homes by flames and floods as the threats of climate change intensified, leaving some important community halls and meet-up sites in ashes and mud. The dominance of meet-up technologies taking over real-world gatherings have seen suburban and urban commercial queer venues reduced to queer nights, and then to single rounds of queer drinks, and even a clink-of-a-drink against a computer screen from separate locations. The widespread COVID-19 pandemic lock-down restrictions have left our school and university-based queer rooms emptied; our protests over a plethora of anti-LGBTIQA+ bills relatively unpeopled or intensely policed; our art shows unseen and our music unheard.

Accordingly, this year *Bent Street* serves as an interstitial space for meeting to discuss the sites available to us; our sense of separation from each-other; our concerns about the uses and misuses of lockdowns and community iconography; and a host of other apocalyptic topics. As our assurance in the security of our old worlds and ways end, our contributors show we need to rethink our connecting and creating modes anew.

Tiffany Jones—Editor
November 2020

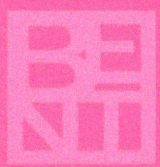

THE YEAR IN QUEER

INTERVIEWS, TALKS, OPINION, MEMOIR, EXPERIENCE, COMMUNITY

RECOMMENDED BY KERRY
Sam Elkin

I'd just started my first year of uni in 2001 when I became aware of the Harry Potter phenomenon. I had not had a happy childhood and was desperate to enter adulthood. At the time I understood this to involve drinking copious amounts of cask wine smuggled into the Court Hotel, struggling to comprehend excerpts of Judith Butler's *Gender Trouble: Feminism and the Subversion of Identity*, and having noisy sex with my housemates in dilapidated weatherboard houses in Northbridge. Due to this, a book about a boy wizard held little appeal at the time, and my frankly pretentious resolve not to read the series grew at roughly the same pace as the global literary juggernaut.

But the Hogwarts universe proved impossible to avoid. After moving to Melbourne in 2001 to escape the conservatism of Perth, I got a job at a discount bookshop near the Queen Victoria Market. It also delivered a discount on my legal minimum wages, but without family to support I was desperate for a job and I naively hoped that it would be my first of many glamourous roles in the publishing industry. That soon wore off when I found that my weekends were taken up with me selling endless copies of the dreaded Potter series to tourists, broken up by the occasional sale of *The Da Vinci Code*, which I felt equally snooty towards.

After years of being a Potter-refusenik, I broke my own rule on a supposedly romantic trip to the Grampians with my lover, who seemed permanently annoyed at me for one reason or another. She suggested that we watch *Harry Potter and the Prisoner of Azkaban*, the only DVD on the shelf of our cheap motel. My cultured opposition gave way to my desire to not cause further offence and we sat down to watch the movie from opposite sides of the couch while sharing a joint. As the artful cinematography rolled over the palatial Hogwarts college, I was unwillingly taken back to memories of my own humbler high school, full of homophobic teachers, taunting bullies, negligent guidance counsellors, and psychotically unwell friends.

The pot, paired with wind banging on the motel windows, the terrifying scenes of dementors sucking the joy out of everyone and the ongoing mystery of what exactly I had done to piss off my girlfriend, sent me into a tailspin of paranoia, and I soon tiptoed off to bed, where I was beset by grotesque nightmares of demons and all the horrors of high school.

My next experience of Rowling's work was in 2015 after I'd just turned 30. My birthday came with something of an epiphany; that I hadn't willingly run away from my family at all, but that I'd had to walk away after a lifetime of put-downs and neglectful treatment because I was queer and gender non-conforming. I marvelled at how my mind could hide the bleedingly obvious from itself. I immediately resolved never to return to Perth, and to focus on supporting the people in my life that were able to support me back, wherever I might find them.

But, family dynamics are a dark and powerful force. Later that year my brother's unhappy marriage to his childhood sweetheart finally came to an end after he stopped making any effort to hide the affair he was having with a younger woman from the next town over. My Mum, far from rebuking my brother for his emotionally dishonest behaviour, leapt to his defence and suggested to me that I might make my brother feel better by taking him and his children on a nice beach holiday. Why I was required at this moment was not clear to me, since he hadn't said more than a few words to me since we were teenagers. Did my older brother actually want to build some sort of meaningful relationship with me after all these years? It turned out the answer was no. He just wanted me to pay for his kids to go on holiday. Nursing my resentment at being allocated the dual role of benefactor and babysitter for older brother's progeny, I first did what I knew best; and began to drink my feelings. We were in Margaret River after all.

But, as the days went on, I decided to stop moping and to focus on developing a relationship with my ten-year-old niece and nephew, who I'd always found a delight to be around. Sitting at the campsite I listened to their cheerful banter about the Harry Potter series and saw for the first time the appeal of being able to lose yourself in another world where true friendships blossom and magic really happens. They were aghast when I admitted I hadn't actually read the books and had no idea what they were on about. I promised them I'd read them when I got back to Melbourne, so that we could have a more stimulating back and forth next time I saw them. I went as far as taking a series of online tests on the plane home to find out which Harry Potter house I would belong to (Gryffindor) and the Harry Potter character I was most like (Dolores Umbridge), but didn't manage to crack onto the actual books.

So, when JK Rowling's comment about her opposition to trans rights first came out on Twitter, I must admit that it wasn't initially personal for me. My first response was that I was relieved to finally have a bullet-proof excuse for having not read Harry Potter. For a person who has lived a life marked by discrimination and fear of exclusion, JK Rowling's views are sadly not new or surprising. As far as I could tell, her arguments were the same as those that Janice Raymond espoused in *The Transsexual Empire: The Making of the She-Male* from the 1970s, which arguably did more to justify anti-transgender sentiment than any book previously written. Their viewpoint is basically that transgender women are in fact men in drag who want to either symbolically annihilate women, or else to cause women literal harm by sexually assaulting them in public toilets.

These views cause real life harm, both at an individual level, and by providing the political ammunition conservatives need to work to curtail our collective rights. In the last three years we've sat through the assault on the Safe Schools program; been described, by the Prime Minister as 'Gender Whisperers' who need to be kept well away from children; and been trotted out as the 'boy in a dress' bogeyman during the marriage equality debate.

When I saw legions of trans and gender diverse Harry Potter fans writing heart wrenching essays about how betrayed they felt, having found a haven from their troubles in that magical world, I did feel more than a pang of regret on their behalf. It seemed bizarre to me that someone who had made billions of dollars on stories of secret, hidden teenage truths, magic potions and transmogrification would have such a bee in her bonnet about the small minority of people who identified as transgender.

And JK Rowling's hatred came closer to home last week when I was outside my local bookshop, wandering the streets to kill time during something like the eighth month of Melbourne's COVID-19 lockdown. I noticed that *Troubled Blood*, the new instalment of Rowling's detective series, was pride of place in the front window. I immediately felt a pang of anger and frustration. Peering closer into the shopwindow, I noticed a red love-heart stuck to the front of the book that said 'recommended by Kerry'.

I felt bitterly disappointed that my local bookshop would tout Rowling's new book with apparent disregard of the offence that her negative views on trans rights law reform have caused to the trans and gender diverse community. I wondered if they were aware of the controversy that this new book has caused in featuring a male serial killer who dresses in women's clothing in order to lure women to their deaths.

It's tiring spending your life feeling outraged though, so instead of calling the shop or taking a photo and posting it online, I tried to just let it go and go back to playing the *What would I buy off of this shelf if this shop was actually open?* game.

But my unease at seeing that red love-heart stuck to the work of a person, who has preached hate about people like me, ate at me. When I got home, I went online to see whether this controversy was actually widely known about, or whether it was just my tiny section of the internet that was taking about the issue ad nauseum. I soon decided that my bookshop would have definitely known about the furore, which depressed me. I felt some relief when I saw that Roxanne Gay, Margaret Atwood and Stephen King signed an open letter expressing support for trans and gender diverse people in response to Rowling's comments. I must've read just about every Stephen

King novel in high school, and I felt somewhat heartened to know that my first favourite writer was on my side.

The lives of trans and gender non-conforming people are both as interesting and as boring as everyone else's, so why shouldn't they serve as inspiration for great fiction? I live in hope of a time when I'll see even more of my trans and gender diverse friends and colleagues publish *their* representations of our lives. But I've also noted with interest the new crop of books featuring trans and gender diverse characters that cisgender authors like Craig Silvey have written, and I have no doubt that we will see many more in the next few years. I personally have no issue with cisgender authors writing trans characters, as long as they do a good job and don't resort to tired, offensive stereotypes, or use us to push agendas like JK Rowling has, or by dwelling endlessly on cliched depictions of our supposed trauma.

Life keeps rolling on. Seemingly overnight my niece and nephew have transformed into precocious teenagers and are no longer interested in the Harry Potter universe. I'm giddy with relief that I no longer have a single reason to engage with the franchise. I also won't be reading *Troubled Blood*, or Silvey's *Honeybee* either. I'll hold out for the release of my trans writer friends' books, as I just think they'll be more interesting. Hopefully, they'll also make it into the front window of my local bookshop with a big recommendation from Kerry.

Sam is a writer, radio maker and community lawyer living in Melbourne's west. Sam is a Wheeler Centre Next Chapter recipient, and their essays have been published online in *Overland* and *Archer* Magazine. You can download Sam's new podcast Transdemic: Trans and Gender Diverse Experiences of the Pandemic wherever you get your podcasts.

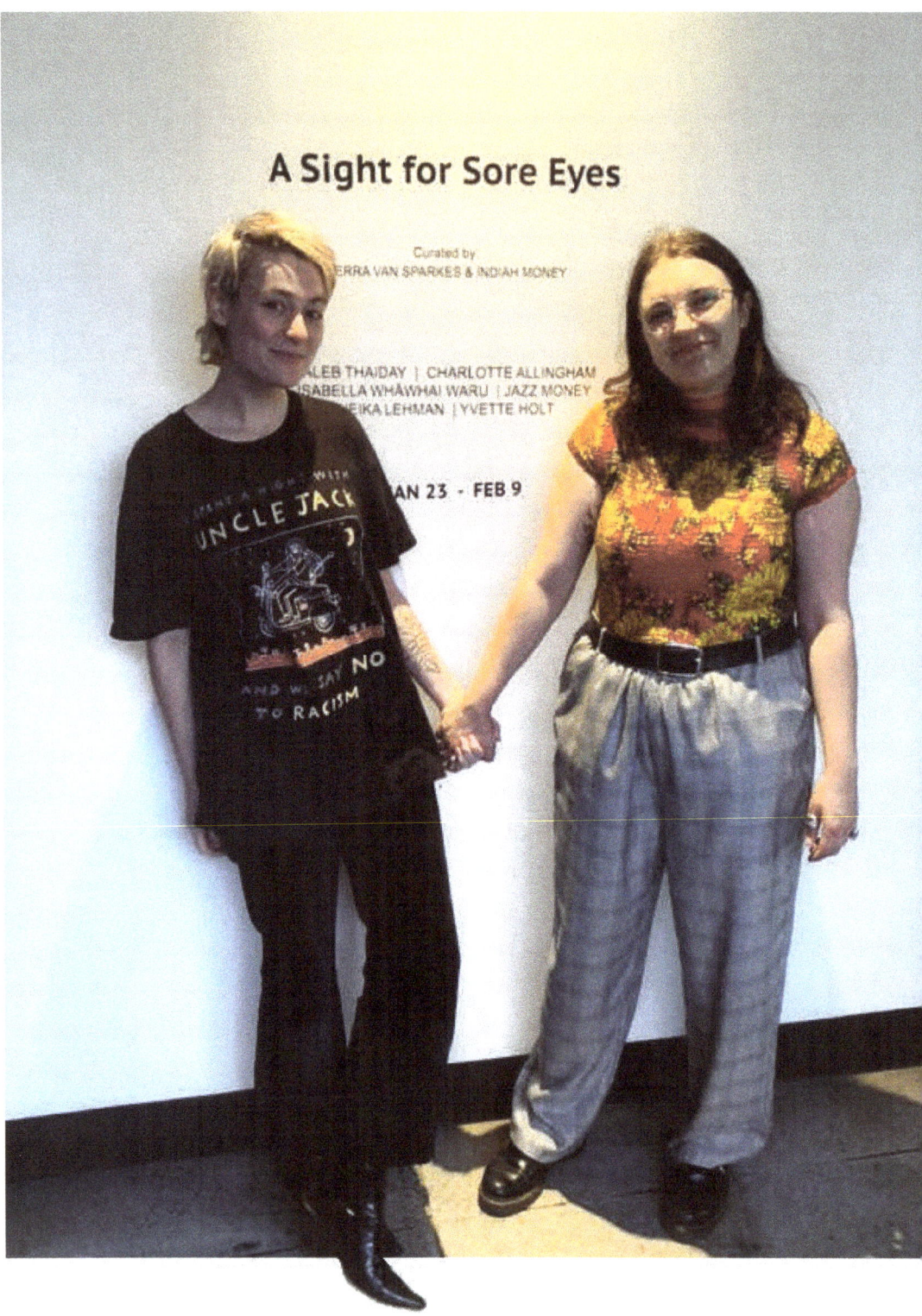

A SIGHT FOR SORE EYES
Indiah Money

A SIGHT FOR SORE EYES AT BLAK DOT
GALLERY 23 JANUARY—9 FEBRUARY 2020.
CO-CURATED BY KULIN COUNTRY-BASED
ARTISTS, PIBBULMAN NOONGAR VISUAL
ARTIST PIERRA VAN SPARKES, AND
WIRADJURI WRITER AND VISUAL ARTIST
INDIAH MONEY. ARTISTS EXHIBITING
INCLUDED: ISABELLA WHĀWHAI WARU,
CALEB THAIDAY, CHARLOTTE ALLINGHAM,
JAZZ MONEY, NEIKA LEHMAN, AND
YVETTE HOLT.

OPPOSITE: Wiradjuri writer and visual artist Indiah Money (l) with Pibbulman Noongar visual artist Pierra Van Sparkes

It feels surreal that the show Pierra and I put on was only in late January of 2020. It's been a year of natural disasters. At the time of us putting together our exhibition, many people across the continent had been devastated by bush fires that consumed so much. While the show wasn't directly paying homage to this, the fires that burnt rapidly were very present in our minds.

Our eyes are sore but in a good way. While smoke has been getting in and making them tight with ash and death; we're able to make sight of what good is to come. We have our eyes set on a future that we can create. For us. By us.

What do you see? Is it a place, person, a story? Is it coming, has it been? Tell us what you're longing for, sib. Share your sight as we share this sanctuary.

For Midsumma 2020, Pierra Van Sparkes and I co-curated an exhibition that took place on the stolen lands of the Woi Wurrung people at Blak Dot gallery, Brunswick, Melbourne. We are both Aboriginal, queer artists that love our communities and wanted to create an exhibition for space to be held

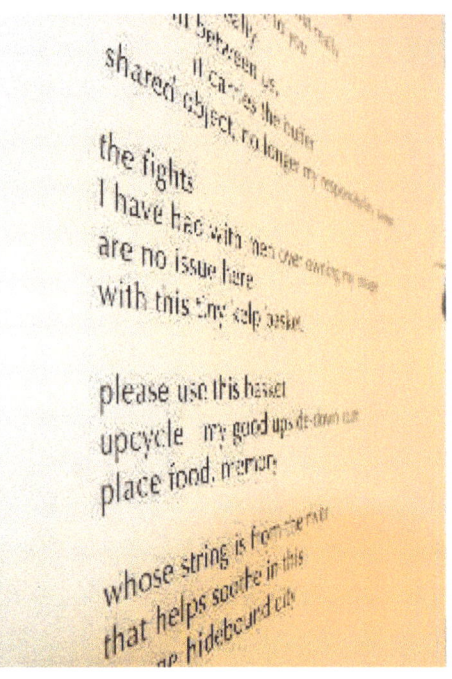

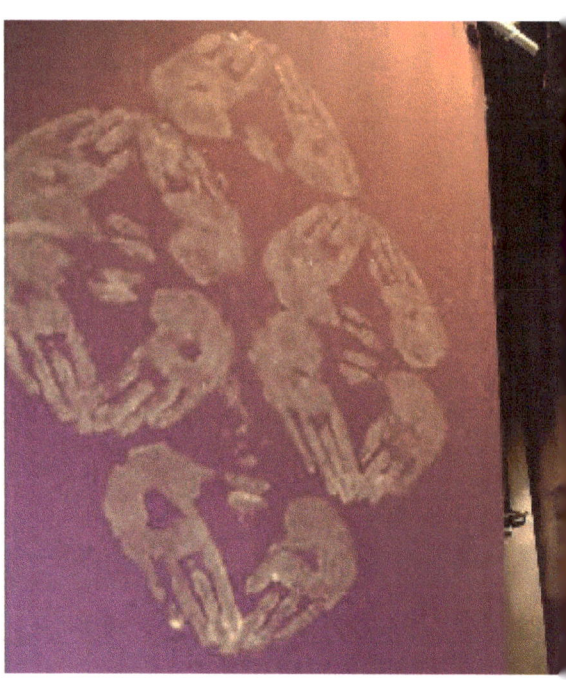

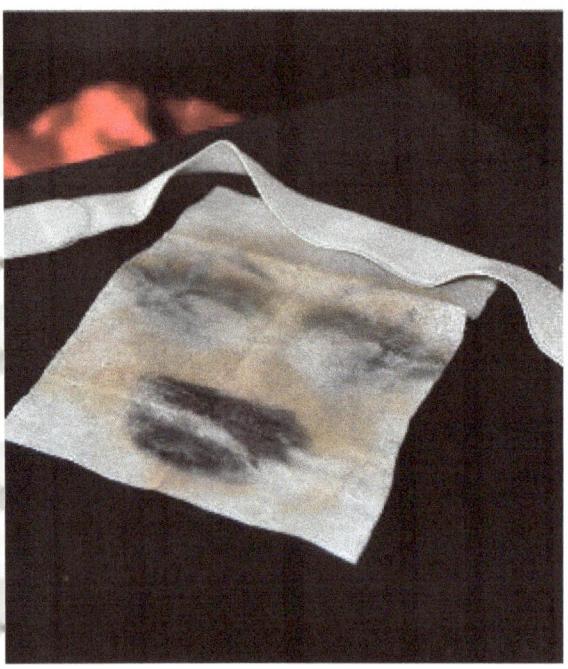

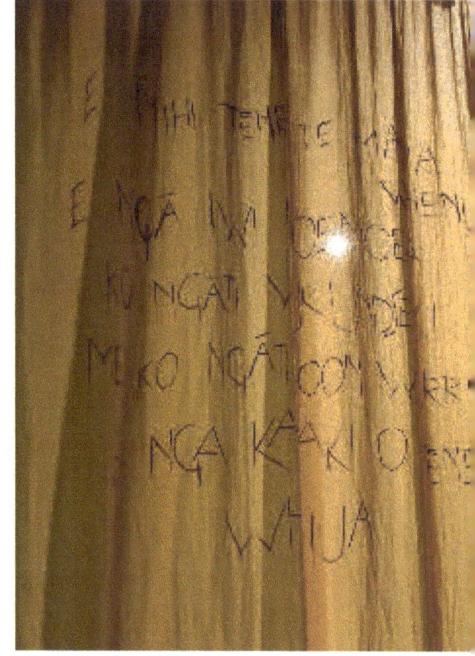

(Top left) Neika Lehman—*Heartbreak Hotel*; (Top and bottom right) Isabella Whāwhai Waru—*The capacity for growth*; (bottom left) Caleb Thaiday—*When the Music Fades*

by queer First Nation artists, for other queer First Nation artists. It was important for the exhibition to be intergenerational in paying respects to queer mob who paved the way for us to exist in the capacity we can today. These artists brought different aspects to the show such as digital print work, installations, poetry, video and sound work.

Queer mob have always existed. The gender binary as we know it today is a colonial weapon. Heteronormativity is supremacist tool that doesn't exist. We are queer and we are deadly.

Water Song

welcome to the waters
old friend welcome me
back into your loving
embrace that I've met
before
but before wasn't the
right time
no
it was in a public
puddle and the light
shone in ways that
were more predictable

small body kissing tiles
big colours
then big arms stole
you away from me
sweet water
welcome me into the
numbing state of
a reliable constant
and we can dance slow
whispering shivers on my skin
now we can
nourish together
feed one another
flourish in ways that
change and grow
together
just us and all our
friends

family
ancestors
we can become one
after all these years
of being birthed by you
cared for by you
just your stones
caressing softened flesh
now back home
in a place of comfort
familiarity
stones smooth
from the running water
fast pace
wearing them away
almost soft   — *Indiah Money*

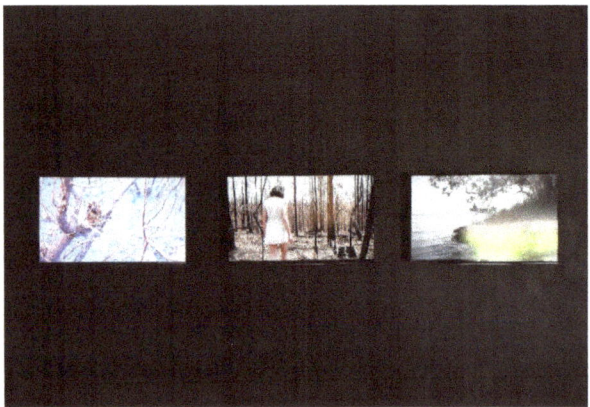

ABOVE: Jazz Money—*This Healing Land*

OPPOSITE PAGE: Charlotte Allingham—*Here to Stay*

Indiah Money is a queer Wiradjuri non-binary person who was raised on Kulin Nations and continues to reside there. Indiah's practice includes visual art, written work, installations, performance art and more. These are done with strong recurring themes of colonialism, assimilation, skin colour, gender, mental illness, sexuality, climate change, stolen generations, identity as well as critiquing the Eurocentric western idealised structure that each person in Australia is forced to maintain.

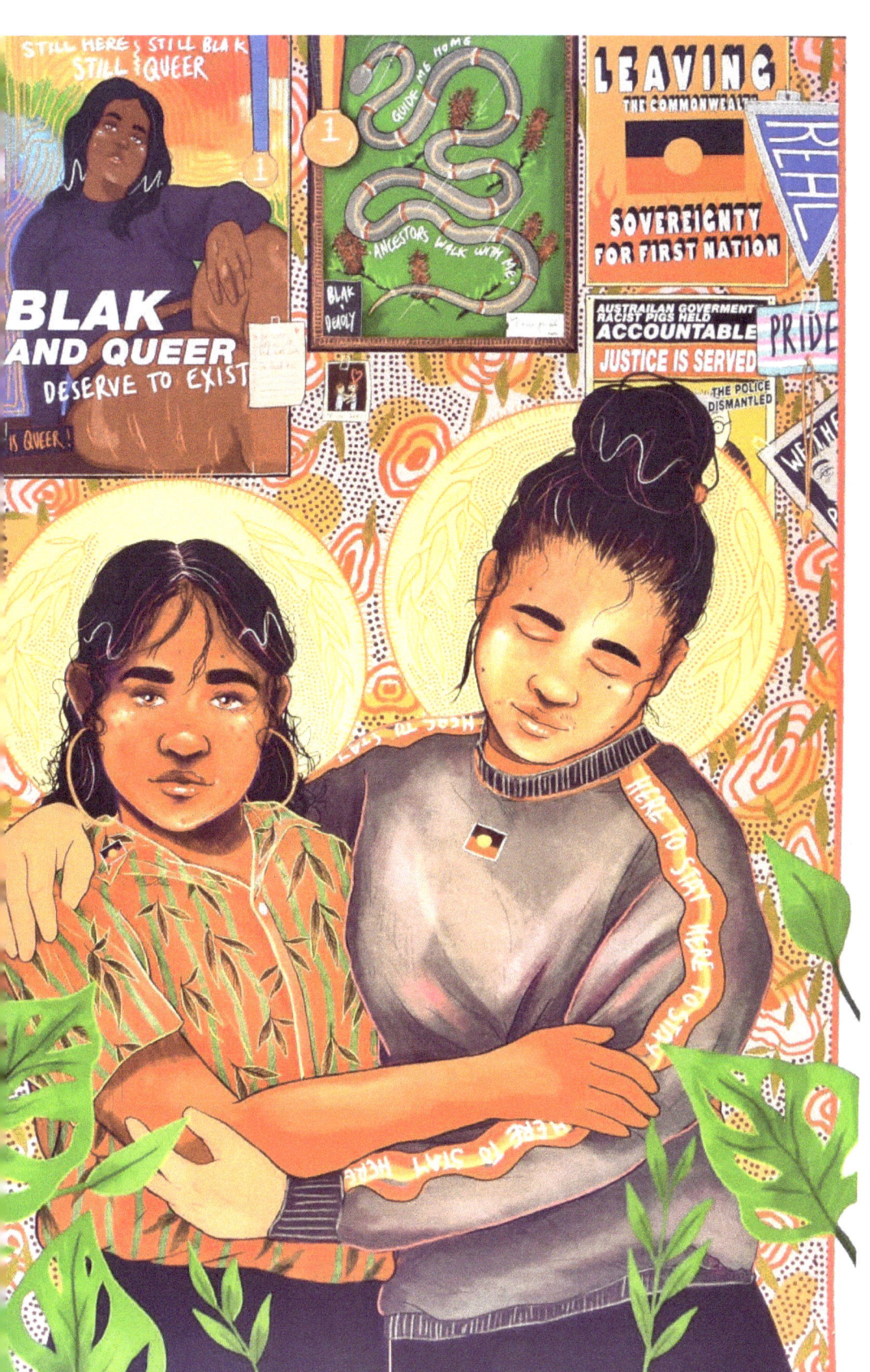

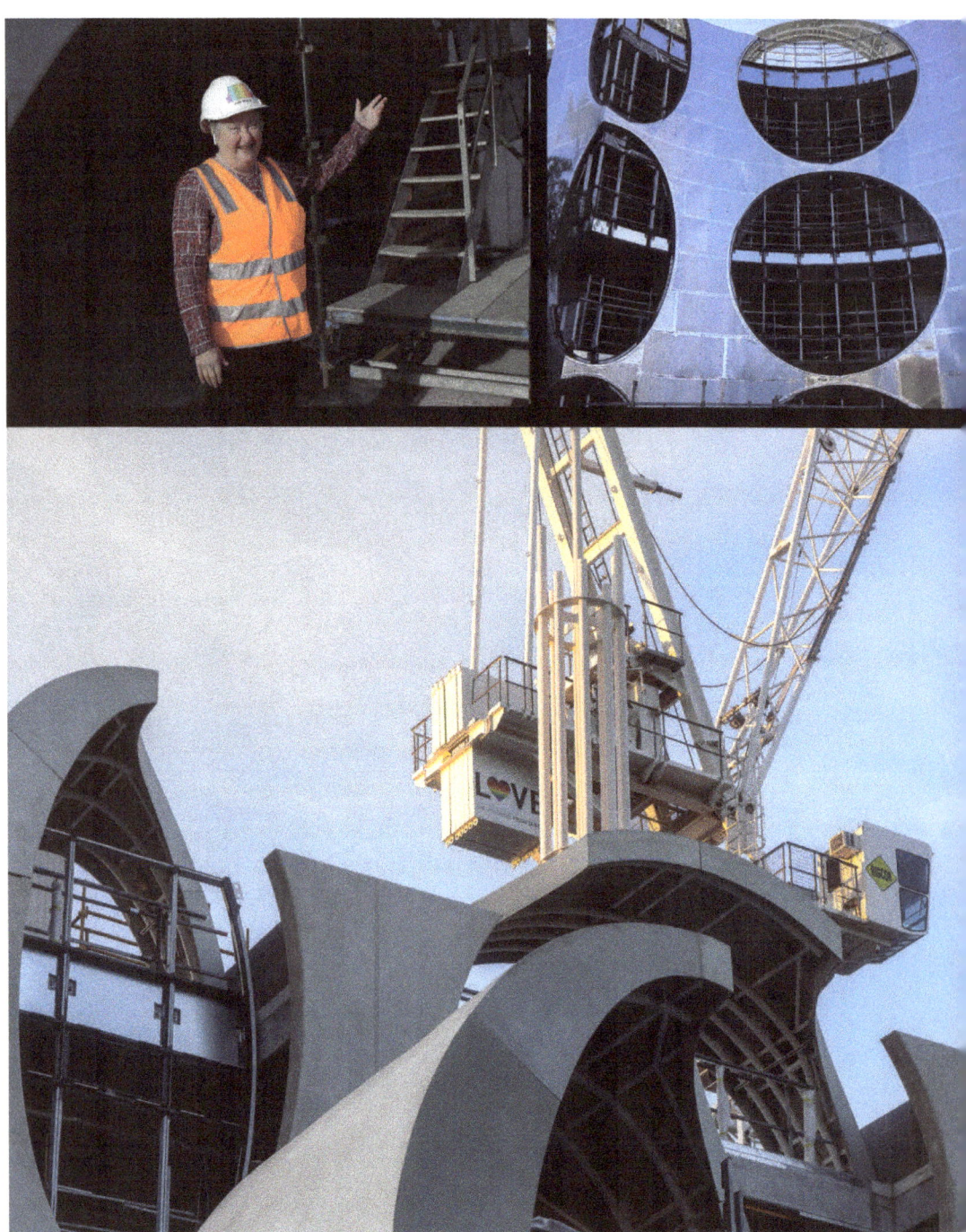

Jude Munro, top left | exteriors, Pride Centre | images: Luke David

PRIDE CENTRE
Jude Munro

Bent Street spoke with Jude Munro, Chair of the Pride Centre, located in the Melbourne beachside suburb of St Kilda. The Centre is scheduled to open at the end of 2020.

Jude—thanks for taking the time to speak with *Bent Street*. A Pride Centre could mean a lot of things to many, but what does this Pride Centre mean for you?

For me, the Pride Centre is a visible and tangible 'Coming Out' of the whole LGBTI+ community. The wider community can't ignore its presence and what it signifies. And the Centre will be a beacon of hope for LGBTI+ people who live in countries quite close to Australia, who don't enjoy the same rights as us.

The Centre is also a capital investment, which, over time will give us a base to raise funds to make other investments on behalf of the LGBTI+ community. So, I can imagine supported accommodation for young, homeless LGBTI + community members, and the Pride Centre might be able to assist in kicking off the capital required to get that happening. There is potential for a transformation of this section of Fitzroy Street St Kilda into a San Francisco-esque Castro quarter for Melbourne's LGBTI + community.

So the Centre is about possibilities—we have a desire to make the Pride Centre greater than the parts of our community taken individually, through the opportunities to collaborate through their physical presence in the one building.

Tell us about some of the groups and organisations that will be located within the Pride Centre.

We will have a number of organisations permanently tenanted at the Pride Centre. So, Hares and Hyenas bookshop who network widely across the rainbow community and run interesting discussion evenings and workshops, they will be based on the Ground Floor. There is the internationally significant Australian Lesbian and Gay Archives, and the Pride Centre administration will be housed on the Mezzanine floor.

JOY 94.9 FM radio which has about 300 volunteers a week and broadcasts to Melbourne, and digitally has a worldwide audience. JOY 94.9 FM broadcasts selected programs to 75 community radio stations across Australia giving them access to LGBTI programming. JOY will be based on the first floor of the Pride Centre.

Melbourne Queer Film Festival, Australian Multicultural GLBTI Council, Koorie Pride Network, Transgender Victoria, Switchboard and Star Health (rainbow-ticked local primary health) will all have their administration based at the Pride Centre on the first, second and third floors.

Then there is Minus18 which runs formals for young people in Adelaide, Sydney and Melbourne, who will be based on the first floor.

Monash Gender Clinic and Thorne Harbour Health will offer a variety of counselling, allied health and medical services from the third floor of the Centre. In addition, we expect to run everything from Pilates in the morning to live theatre and performances in the evenings at the Theatrette.

The Centre will be jumping.

Jude, how did you come to be involved with the Pride Centre?

I was asked to chair the board back in July 2016. When I was asked by Ro Allen, on behalf of the State Government back in July 2016, it was a request I jumped at, and I couldn't refuse because for me it was 44 years on from co-founding Gay Lib back in 1972, and there are awesome things you get asked to do that you just have to say yes to.

Tell us a little bit about the architectural competition for the Centre.

Professor Dimity Reed prepared the architectural brief after extensive consultation with our future tenants. We then ran a national architectural competition from September 2017 supported by the Royal Australian Institute of Architects. This led to a blind shortlisting of four top entries and the Architectural Competition was won by a combined entry from Grant Amon, and James Brierly both St Kilda based architects, with James' firm also having a Shanghai base.

COMING OUT IS CRUCIAL TO OUR ACCEPTANCE OF OURSELVES AND OUR OWN SELF CONFIDENCE AS LESBIANS, GAYS, BISEXUALS, TRANS AND INTERSEX PEOPLE. BEING OUT THERE, INCLUDING AS A PRIDE CENTRE, IS THE OPPOSITE OF US BEING HIDDEN. A PRIDE CENTRE UNDERPINS SOCIETY'S ACCEPTANCE OF ITS OWN DIVERSITY. IT LIES AT THE HEART OF A COHESIVE SOCIETY

—JUDE MUNRO

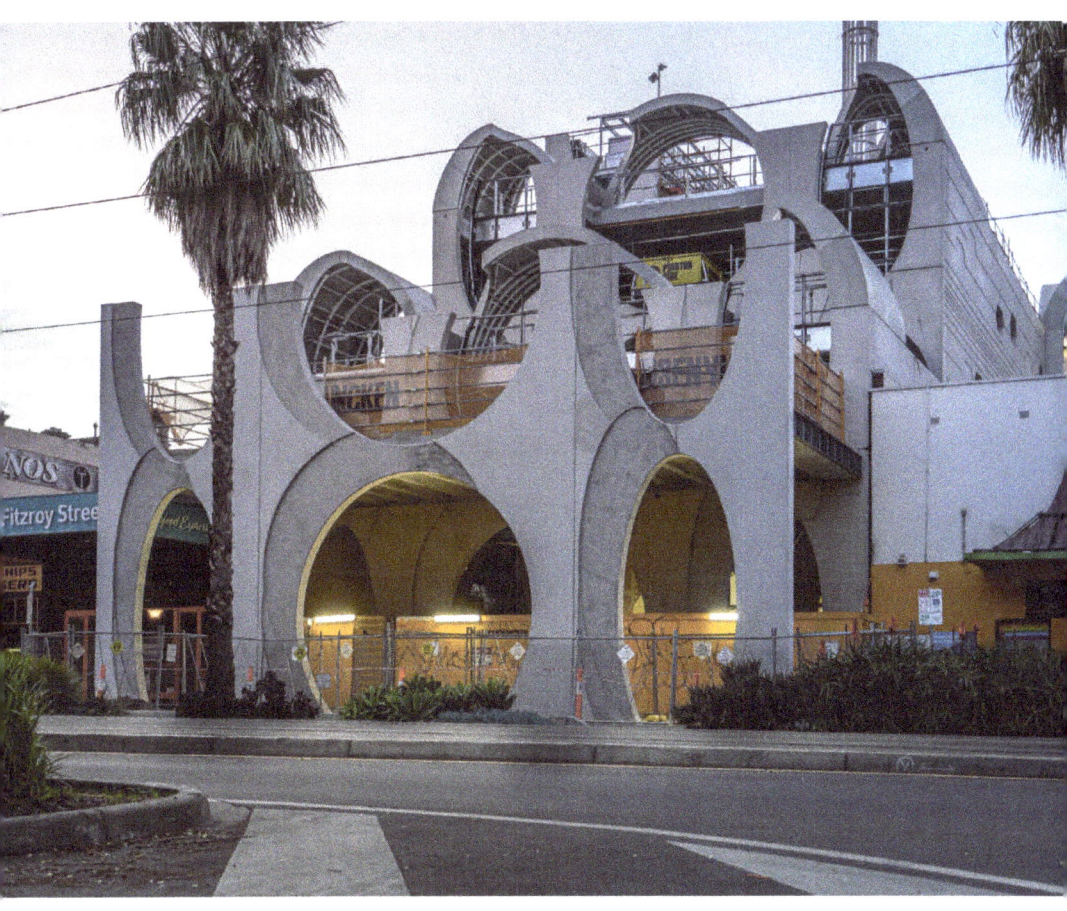

Pride Centre | image: Luke David

What are some of the architectural characteristics of the new building?

The building is inspired by a number of themes and motifs, with no one theme dominating. The first is the striking use of the beehive, and the honeycomb of light that runs from the front to the rear of the building. The second is the use of the motif of the eggshell and the breaking through of the egg to allow new life to emerge and 'come out'. This eggshell gives the shape of the Central atrium. It will end up being inscribed by local Aboriginal people in the tradition of ancient emu egg etchings. The third influence is the St Kilda neo-Moorish influence, derived from Spain (La Mezquita, Cordoba) and Morocco. The fourth motif that plays into the building is the tradition of Melbourne's laneways and arcades evident in the first floor shopfronts. The building has a magnificent double height portico and is awe-inspiring in its design.

There have been stacks of challenges. Almost everything has been difficult, but nonetheless a solution has always emerged from the difficulties. We have had a skill-based board that has thought through every difficulty and, in my words, 'kept marching on'. We have managed to persuade others to contribute the finances, we've run fundraisers, we have had lots of pro bono support—it must now be close to $2M in pro bono or low bono support. We've raised $1M through the founders fund and close to $1M in philanthropic fund raising.

Practical completion of the Pride Centre is now the 18 December 2020 and we are expecting the first of our resident organisations to move in the New Year. Hansen Yuncken have paid attention to the detailing and high finish required in the building. The Pride Centre is iconic and will be an international beacon of hope.

Jude Munro AO was one of the founding members of the Gay Lib movement in Melbourne in the early 1970s and was awarded the Order of Australia in 2010 for distinguished service to local government.

OPPOSITE: Firdhan Aria Wijaya—*Solidarity*

Firdhan Aria Wijaya is currently working at a university in Central Java as a lecturer and researcher. He is fascinated with Halberstam's work on failure and the intersection of food justice and sexual diversity issues.

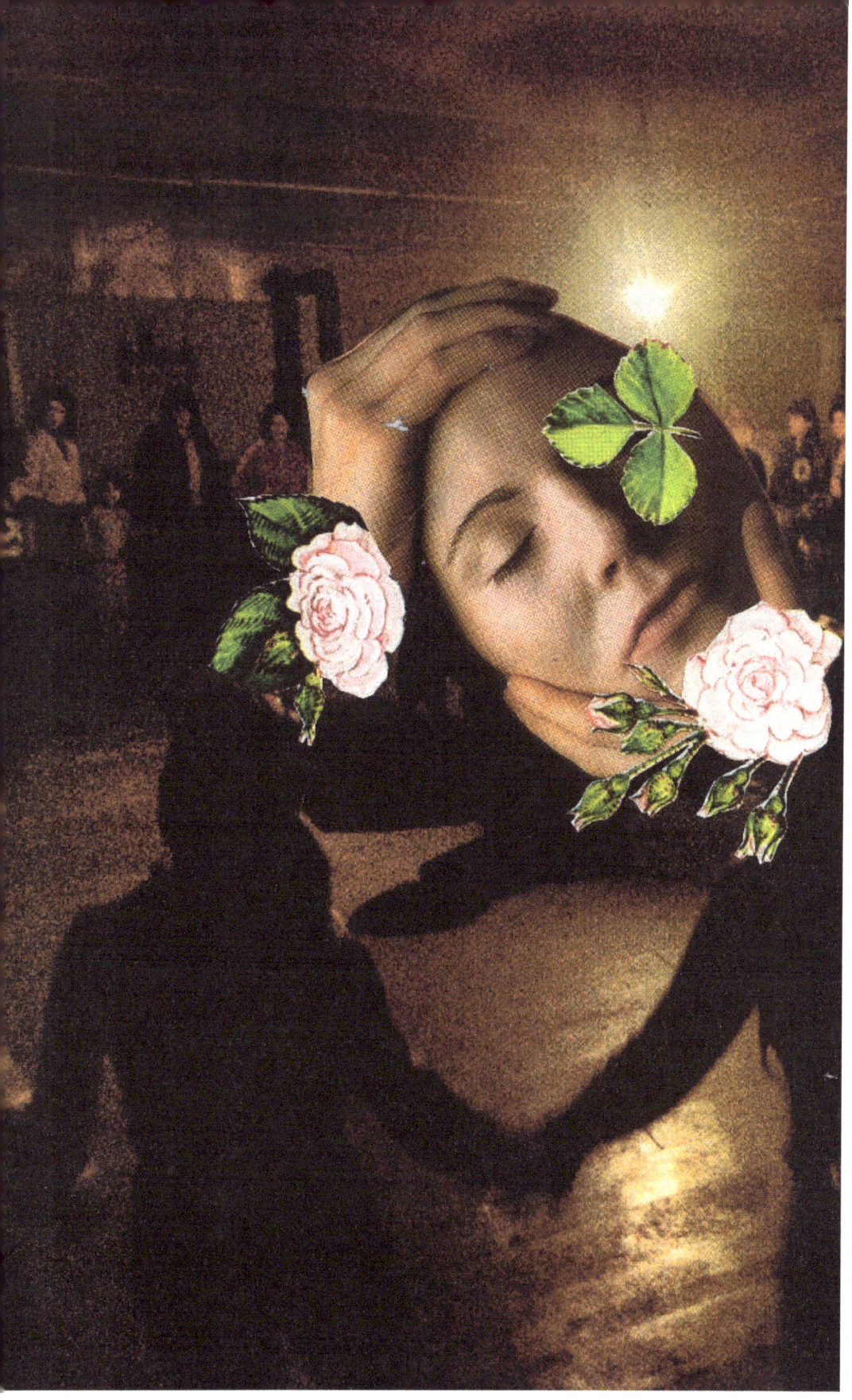

CASH, HANDSHAKES, AND CROWDED TRAINS
Steph Amir

As Melbourne descends into COVID-19 lockdown, Steph Amir sees the lines blurring between mental health and illness.

'The medical establishment is trolling me,' my friend Josh says with a groan. It is mid-March 2020 and we are scrolling through Facebook feeds full of articles featuring desperate plea from doctors, epidemiologists and government officials: *Wash your hands! Don't touch surfaces that might be contaminated! Stay home if you're sick!*

Given the rising rates of COVID-19 around the world, it is excellent advice. It was also the exact opposite of what he and I have been told in the preceding months and years. Doctors, psychologists, books, podcasts and online learning modules all had similar messages: stop washing your hands; touch those public bathroom doors with your bare skin; and if you start to worry about a sickly-looking colleague, stay right there next to them.

It's called Exposure-Response Prevention and is standard practice for the treatment of people with obsessive-compulsive disorder (OCD).

The seminal and arguably most popular guide for managing OCD is a book called '*Brain Lock*' by American psychiatrist Jeffrey Schwartz. In it, Schwartz explains that rigorous handwashing and other compulsions have no value. Among other things he describes them as false, inappropriate, bizarre, senseless, irrational, abnormal, worthless, foolish and silly.

Other books about OCD treatment make similar claims, with some authors explaining that even the patients themselves usually know that behaviours like frequent and rigorous handwashing make no sense. The bible of psychiatry—the DSM-5—specifies that practitioners should differentiate between OCD patients who have 'good or fair insight' and those with 'absent insight or delusional beliefs'. Presumably for those with an obsession around contamination, a patient in the former category may agree that their determined handwashing is unfounded, while someone in the latter may say that their careful handwashing is perfectly fine, thank you very much.

And yet here we are, being strictly instructed to wash our hands for at least twenty seconds, all the way to our wrists, with warm water and soap. The Premier of Victoria suggests singing the first verse of 'Dancing Queen' by ABBA to ourselves to get the timing right.

It makes me wonder: if less than twenty seconds is insufficient, at what point does the washing of hands become inappropriate, bizarre, abnormal or silly? Thirty seconds? Sixty? It's not a rhetorical question for someone working hard to fight the monster that OCD can become. It's a very real decision that must be made to balance the risk of physical illness with the risk of increased mental illness symptoms, because once someone with OCD becomes accustomed to a particular ritual, it can be very difficult to stop.

The next week in an office bathroom I watch someone lather their hands into a frenzy, and this sign of crisis unexpectedly makes me feel comforted, knowing that the doors of public bathrooms are a bit less disgusting during the pandemic than they usually are.

It's an odd experience to transition from being stuck in my own individual world of fear to suddenly being part of a fearful crowd. Pressing buttons for the lifts with my knuckle and for pedestrian lights with my elbow is no longer unusual because everyone else is doing the same. Suddenly others are seeing the world as I do, and avoiding the same things: cash, handshakes, crowded trains. They are horrified to realise that if they use their phone with potentially contaminated hands, then wash their hands carefully, they can't touch their phone again without getting potentially re-contaminated. Welcome to my world.

When my OCD was at its worst, I'd become angry at all the ways that day-to-day life required people to put themselves at risk. 'What kind of *masochist* invented networking functions?!' I once ranted to my therapist. 'You're expected to shake everyone's hand and *then* eat canapes! Whyyyyy?!'

This kind of anger sometimes led to fantasies of all the contagion-prevention measures I'd take if social convention allowed, and how clean and safe everything would be. Yet reality is brought into focus as I take my daughter to the library and the swimming pool for the last time before council services close across Melbourne. Both were places that have made me feel fearful in the past as I imagined all the sticky fingers touching the books and sweaty bodies in the pool before me, but faced with the reality of my OCD-dream coming true, I desperately mourn the loss of these places. I make a promise to the atheist gods that when the COVID-19 pandemic passes and public places re-opened, I won't let my fear overshadow the joy of public libraries and swimming pools ever again.

Most people with OCD work hard to present as 'normal', hiding their compulsions and staying silent about their obsessions for fear of judgement or discrimination, so it's hard not to smile at the irony when people ask if I've washed my hands, or express concern that I'm not being cautious enough.

As we enter lockdown, I overhear snippets of conversations as I pass people on my daily walk. They discuss whether it's necessary to disinfect groceries, how long it's safe to share a room with someone before they could breathe enough to infect you, agreeing that churches are safer than gyms but what about schools?

The constant assessment of risk is a big part of OCD, as is frantically seeking information in the hope it will provide reassurance that everything will be okay. I think of this as I attend yet another meeting on Zoom with the window slightly minimised so that I can keep pressing 'refresh' on *The Guardian* live updates page to see the daily tally of new cases as soon as it's published. '278' my colleague says suddenly, looking up from her phone. My screen refreshes to report 278 new cases.

I'm not the only one lying awake at night, my mind reeling. News articles report that anxiety is on the rise, and by July the weight of extended lockdown in Melbourne is driving people to breaking point. A woman I've never met calls me about a routine administrative matter then mentions her children and bursts into tears. 'I'm just so tired, Steph,' she sobs. 'It's too hard having to work and home-school every day. I don't know how to go on.'

It's the second time in two weeks that a stranger has cried to me on the phone and it pushes me towards action, checking in more vigilantly on my friends and family. I share resources and stories, and gently guide people with anxiety symptoms towards professional supports. I notice some friends do the same, especially those with experience of mental illness. The chronic fear caused by uncertainty—and the shock at the many ways that it can impact a person's mind, body, and day-to-day life—is new to many people this year, but not to those who were living with illnesses like anxiety or OCD before COVID-19 emerged. The tricks and tools we've learnt and developed turn out to be quite useful in a global pandemic.

I also lie awake and think about all the things I will do when the pandemic is over. I think about going to concerts and hugging my friends and hanging out in other people's lounge-rooms. This pandemic highlighted to us all the extent to which humans—including myself—crave physical proximity. Most of us need human touch and connection. We want to be part of a roaring crowd. We want to run or sing or dance together.

In September, my partner is horribly sick for weeks so I'm trying to look after her fulltime while juggling two jobs and solo-parenting our three-year-old with limited access to childcare in Stage 4 lockdown. I don't have to worry much about contamination because we're barely allowed to leave the house anyway, but the stress and sheer volume of work causes OCD symptoms to manifest in the form of frightening, violent or disgusting images flashing in my mind's eye (referred to by psychologists as 'intrusive thoughts'). Meanwhile, friends and family from Sydney and Canberra share idyllic photos of holidays and brunch dates.

The clinically-proven strategy to reduce the impact of intrusive OCD thoughts is to accept them rather than trying to stop them, but I'm too tired to follow the recommended approach, so I ignore the tiger snake slithering through my thoughts and distract myself with work. In my Facebook feed, people across Melbourne make a similar choice, telling interstaters to quit it with their sunny cheerfulness, and then clocking up their twelfth hour of screen-time that day to binge-watch something on Netflix or attend an online event. Self-improvement will have to wait; we're too busy trying to survive.

Now it's early October and restrictions in Melbourne are slowly being eased. We can sit in a park, with our masked faces turned towards the sunshine, or a friend 1.5m away. I could go for a swim if my local pool wasn't booked out completely every day.

Public toilets still have signs about handwashing, installed in March or April, but they now seem archaic. But when we all return to offices, restaurants, cinemas and yoga classes—and when the vaccine arrives and the risk of COVID-19 fades—will everyone return to their former habits, leaving OCD-folk alone in the bathroom to wash their hands for the full twenty seconds, thirty or sixty seconds? Or will some people retain a preference for avoiding cash, handshakes and crowded trains? Are they 'abnormal' too, or rationally taking steps to reduce the risk of future illnesses? The answer is of course subjective, variable across time and place, and in a constant state of flux.

We don't yet know when the pandemic will end, but in the interim I'll try to keep my handwashing within the normal-for-a-pandemic range. '*See that girl, watch that scene, digging the dancing queen ...*'

Steph Amir is a current social scientist and former politician, zoologist and nachos-seller. She has been actively involved in the LGBTIQ community for many years including as a radio presenter and on the Board of Directors at JOY 94.9, Program Manager for Safe Schools Coalition Australia, inaugural Co-Convenor of Queer Greens Victoria, and Chair of the Sex, Sexuality and Gender Diversity community advisory committee at the City of Darebin. Her writing has previously been published in Bent Street, Archer and Melbourne City of Literature.

FOLLOWING PAGE: Mel Simpson—*Carol*

Mel Simpson has exhibited in solo and group shows in Queensland, New South Wales and Victoria, including shows for Midsumma at galleries such as Gasworks, 69 Smith Street and Red Gallery. More recently she has started her own independent illustration business, Kittenpants Studios. Mel's images grace our cover, and are found throughout the pages of *Bent Street 4.2*

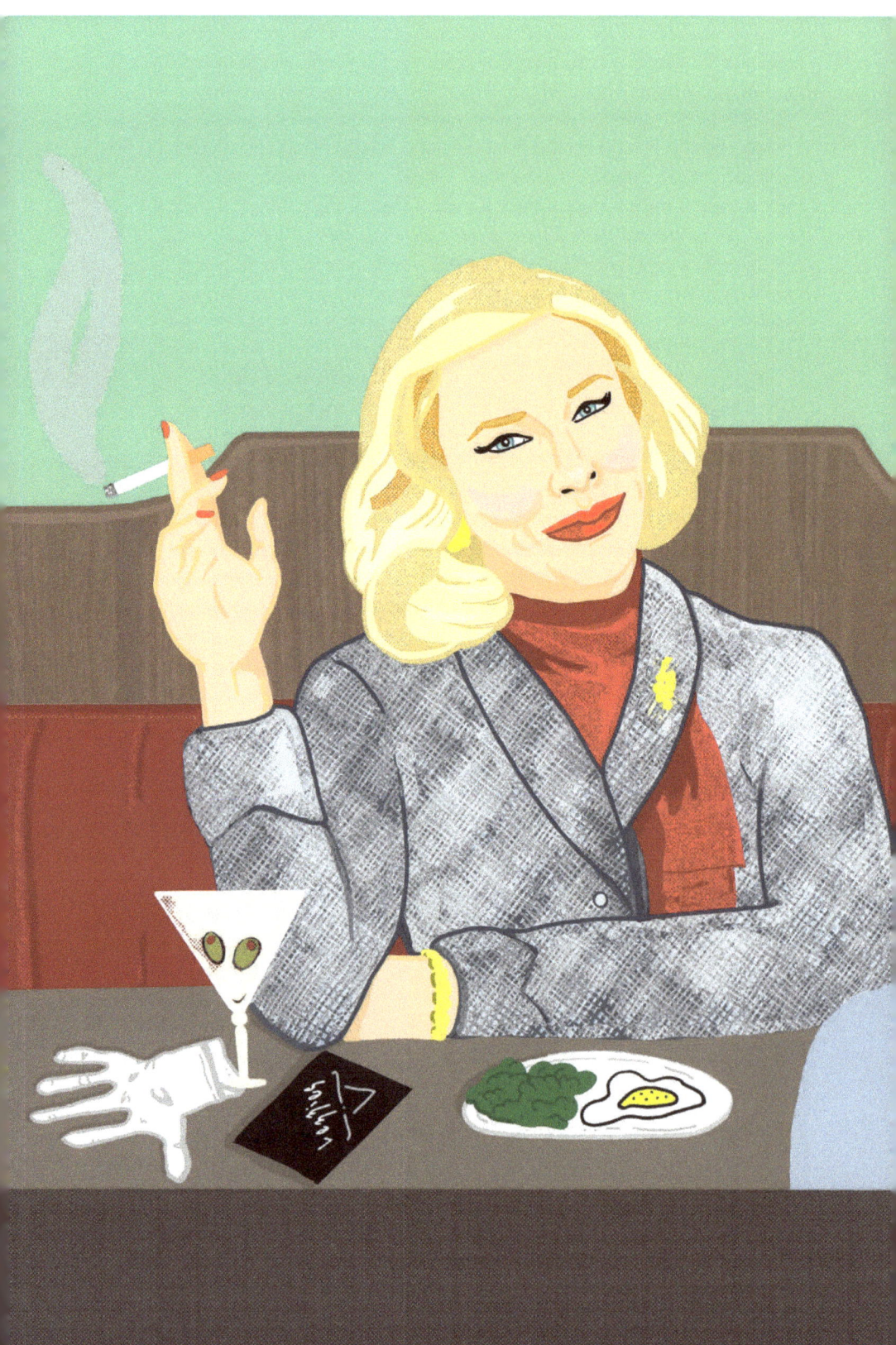

DÉJÀ VU DIARY
Jean Taylor

Jean Taylor continues her diary of lockdown begun in Bent Street 4.1. *We pick up the trail once again in June …*

Monday 29 June Just back from a twenty minute walk to Methven Park where all the tall trees are holding up the sky with their bare branches, along the irregular bluestone laneways where I felt a physical connection with my Irish father's family who moved from rural Donaghadee to the city of Belfast in 1915 and my Scottish great grandmother who arrived by boat from Leith Scotland in 1882 and lived in Richmond and Northcote and finally Brunswick East, just three streets away from where I live now. In fact I walked past my great grandmother's old house in Jarvie Street, and back along the laneways where I feel at home, all urban grunge, tags and small single-fronted houses and tiny gardens competing for space with the three bins, for rubbish, green waste, and recycling.

Tuesday 30 June Daniel Andrews says there have been 233 new cases of Covid-19 detected in Victoria since last Thursday, 64 of those were in the past 24 hours.

Wednesday 1 July Tonight at 11.59 the ten postcodes, of which ours, 3057, is not one, although we're within spitting distance of Brunswick West, 3055, which is, go into stage three lockdown.

Thursday 2 July All I really want to do today, I decided again this morning, is to live companionably with Ardy, do the final corrections to a book I wrote in '79/'80, *A Trios Travels, Trials and Tribulations on the Overland Route From Melbourne to Istanbul in 1977*, and see whatever else eventuates before sitting on the couch with Ardy this evening to watch our regular TV show, *The Project* and *Celebrity Gogglebox USA,* and the next episode of either or both of our on-going Netflix shows, *After Life* and *Grace and Frankie.* Being able to see my grandchildren and my lesbian friends from time to time, knowing they're all out there, is a comfort.

Saturday 4 July Sixty-six new cases in Victoria because security guards, who were in contact with infected returned travellers while in quarantine in a hotel in Melbourne, took it back to the north west suburbs where it's been a bush fire out of control ever since, from postcode 3012 to 3064 where 300,000 people most of whom through no fault of their own are now in Stage 3 Lockdown and 'going it alone'. It's increasingly unlikely that any state, let alone Queensland, is going to open its borders anytime soon to anyone from Victoria, so goodness knows when I'll be able to get to Cairns to see my daughter and her family.

Sunday 5 July One of the better pieces of news is that according to a COVID-19 Epidemiology Report for Aboriginal and Torres Strait Islander people: Sixty-nine cases (0.8%) have been reported in Aboriginal and Torres Strait Islander persons since the start of the epidemic in Australia, almost half of whom had been infected overseas and the majority lived in large cities. No cases among Aboriginal and Torres Strait Islander persons have been notified from remote or very remote areas of Australia ... and no fatalities have been reported. All because the Aboriginal communities, in conjunction with the government, acted quickly to protect themselves.

Tuesday 7 July A five-day lockdown of 3,000 mainly migrant people in nine high rise towers, 'vertical cruise ships', while they're being tested, which some people are seeing as racist. Not too surprisingly, NSW will temporarily close the border with Victoria at midnight tonight, the first time this particular border's been closed for over 100 years.

This afternoon, Premier Daniel Andrews announced a stage three Lockdown for the whole of metropolitan Melbourne as well as Mitchell Shire in the north for the next six weeks starting at midnight tomorrow, Wednesday, because there were 191 new cases today, 69 of which were the infected residents in the Towers, which totals 772 active cases altogether, 35 of whom are in hospital and nine in Intensive Care. Once the intensive testing of all the residents in the nine Towers has been completed and appropriate measures taken for their ongoing welfare they'll go into Stage 3 Lockdown like the rest of us.

Cafe and restaurants will close again and go back to takeaway only. No more films, plays, swimming pools, libraries, bookshops or art galleries, but it was business as usual on-line and being the middle of NAIDOC week I enjoyed Lou Bennett's interview about her illustrious music career with Tiddas and The Black Arm Band.

Wednesday 8 July (final day before stage three lockdown in Melbourne from midnight) Not happy about going back into Lockdown, even though I can see with the spikes of infections in the ten postcodes and the nine Towers, that it has probably got completely out of hand and calls for drastic measures.

However, with the sun shining and our last day of 'freedom', and knowing I wouldn't see the three grandchildren for six weeks if I didn't go later this afternoon, Ardy and I drove to Carlton, the tram still being a bit too dangerous. We parked just before Elgin Street, put on our masks, mine was a scarf, and arm-in-arm we toddled up Lygon Street to Readings Bookshop. I waited in a queue till someone came out, used the hand sanitiser at the entrance, went in to admire my four books on the shelf, *The Archives Trilogy* plus the latest, *What Are Dykes Doing: Collected Non-Fiction*, (turned front cover out, much to my delight), and bought Aileen Morton-Robinson's *Talkin' Up to the White Woman: Indigenous Women and Feminism*, with my gift voucher. I waited on the bench under the tree outside till Ardy returned from her visit to the Kathleen Syme Library with an armful of the books she'd borrowed. And since the Nova Cinema had closed at midday for the duration and because Brunetti's was only doing take-away we went to Trotters Bistro for coffees and cake sitting outside with our backs soaking up the bright sunshine.

Friday 10 July I put the following on Facebook today: While the actual National Aboriginal and Islander Day Observance Committee Week has sensibly been postponed to November, this is to wish all Aboriginal and Torres Strait Islander people a very productive, politically active and celebratory virtual NAIDOC with many thanks for all the interesting and entertaining events online for the benefit of us all to learn from and show our respect to the creative, vibrant, talented and hard-working Indigenous people here in Australia.

Sunday 12 July It is so long since I sent the COVID-19 article to US-based radical feminist journal, *Rain and Thunder*, that when I got the rejection I had to print it out to see what I'd written. I can see why it was rejected because it was wishy-washy personal stuff, I forget I need to be fiercely radical feminist focused and politically oriented if I want to be published in *R&T*.

Wednesday 15 July Another day another Zoom at 11am with Jamie Lowe, Michael Mansell and Professor Megan Davis, in conversation with the Australia Institute's Richard Denniss, as part of the National Treaties Summit, which shows how complicated the concepts of Sovereignty and Treaty are in terms of coming up with a workable legal solution.

I fixed the corrections and emailed both The Circus Women's Memorial Bench and the Victorian Women's Liberation and Lesbian Feminist Archives blurbs for Heritage 100 to the Australian Lesbian and Gay Archives. I also emailed the article, The Best Laid Plans Gang Apt to go Astray or Why We're No Longer 'All in This Together,' plus the Fruit of the Backyard Monstera photo to the Matrix Guild News.

The PM's boast that 'we're all Melbournians now' rang a bit hollow in the light of footage of him watching the Sharks lose badly, and then the Queensland Premier Annastacia Palaszczuk boasting that as the AFL teams and their families had moved to Brisbane to train and play, that the Grand Final would also be played up there as well. No solidarity whatsoever, it seems to me, let alone 'we're all in this together.' And I'm not even a footy fan.

Friday 17 July Yesterday it was announced that Wiradjuri writer, Tara June Winch, won the Miles Franklin award for her novel, *The Yield*, great news! And there were 428 new cases of COVID-19 in Victoria, another daily record.

Saturday 18 July Wow! Two hours on the Moreland Reconciliation Network Anti-Racism group Zoom this morning was more familiar and I felt more confident about speaking out and felt invigorated by the discussions, this is only my second meeting with this group, but now it looks like it's going to turn into a *Me & White Supremacy* by Layla F Saad Book Circle because everyone is keen on that idea.

Then the *Four Corners* episode with Stan Grant, 'I Can't Breathe', about the destructive racism in the US and Australia and making connections between what happens to the Aboriginal people and the African Americans in terms of the murderous and brutal cultures of both countries that continue to cause harm on a daily basis.

As a final entertainment for the afternoon, even though I attended the premier of the play in Melbourne in 2010, I watched *Jack Charles versus The Crown* by Ilbijerri Theatre Company filmed at Belvoir Theatre 2011 and showing free on YouTube as part of the Arts Centre's NAIDOC week's virtual Program July 2020.

Thursday 23 July The third week of stage 3 lockdown has now morphed into Stage 4, with the introduction of the compulsory wearing of masks. Not too surprisingly, given another 374 new cases and three deaths on Tuesday, and 484 new cases and two more deaths on Wednesday, bringing the total number of deaths in Victoria to 44. These consist of mainly the elderly with more cases and deaths likely with the virus spreading and 383 residents testing positive in Aged Care facilities, and 69 in one of the facilities alone.

Friday 24 July A productive working day, I didn't do too much, but I got a lot done. I got up to correcting page 52 of a 60-page transcript of an interview with me by a PhD student who is researching the herstory of the Women's Liberation Movement in Melbourne, and also did a bit more knitting of the cover for my 60-page book of words and photos, ISO Lockdown for the forthcoming Counihan Gallery Summer Show.

Given masks are now compulsory I did the right thing and wore a mask when I went for a walk through Methven park this afternoon, but found it very difficult to breathe and my glasses kept fogging up all the time. It's a damned nuisance, but I don't want to be seen as one of those who are resisting wearing any face covering out of sheer bloodymindedness, so will persevere with it.

Saturday 25 July What's happening in Melbourne is not good at all: 300 new cases and seven deaths, the Victorian toll now 56, as announced last night, the highest in Australia. Forty schools have closed for deep cleaning, 101 people have been fined for disobeying the regulations; and Dutton had another go at the Tamil family of four, with two young children who were born in Australia and have a home waiting for them in Biloela Queensland, (and the mother in a Perth Hospital with severe abdominal pain), for wasting taxpayers' money by being detained indefinitely on Christmas Island. Talk about victim blaming, the man's mad!

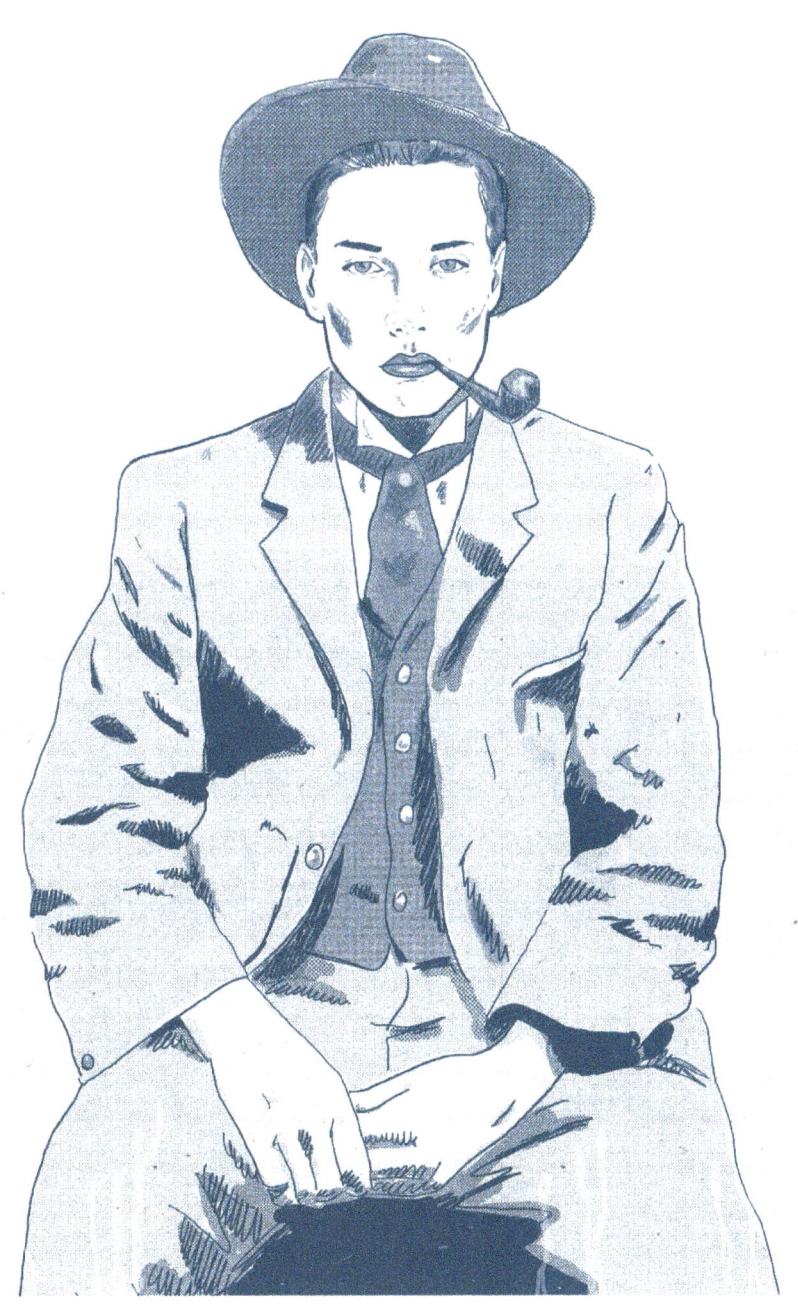

Mel Simpson—*A Quiet Afternoon in Blue*

The statistics reveal another 357 cases and five deaths as well as double figures of COVID-9 in Geelong and Colac and the news announced that Bunnings sausage sizzles have opened again in SA, WA and Queensland. Why it is that Melbourne, The Most Liveable City in the World for several years in a row not so long ago, is now the most dangerously virus-ridden city in Australia?

Monday 27 July We enjoyed watching the Women's Circus's free show on Facebook yesterday afternoon, *Ghosts* in Shed 14, performed by friends we recognised and directed by Andrea Lemon in 2003. I was a founding member of the Women's Circus in 1991, performed in their first five shows and afterwards supported all their annual shows by volunteering with the front of house team.

Wednesday 29 July Aged Care is descending into crisis with 804 cases and 45 deaths. Eighty-seven facilities have known outbreaks, 99.4% of cases in privately owned and run facilities. Andrews said he wouldn't put his mother in one, having a return shot at the PM whose job it is to make sure that all of the 822 Residential Aged Care facilities in Victoria are adequately funded and run efficiently. One private facility alone has 80 cases, whereas there are only five cases in all of the state-run facilities.

According to online information: *The Commonwealth government is responsible for the Aged Care system in Australia. Aged Care falls under the* Department of Health. The Commonwealth Government is responsible for the provision of residential Aged Care services in Victoria.

So much for Morrison blaming Andrews when according to online reports into Residential Aged Care in Victoria, it was discovered there were no government regulations about staff-to-resident ratios, no requirement that at least one registered nurse needed to be on duty at all times, and no properly recognised training qualifications were required to work in a nursing home. It's no wonder that the under-qualified, over-worked, under-paid staff working across several of the large privately-owned Aged Care facilities in any one week were unable to curb the PANdemIC when it hit with a vengeance. But while the staff survived, many of the residents in their 80s and 90s did not.

Thursday 30 July Up and at the laptop by 10am, we relaxed on the couch and watched the Koorie Heritage Trust's Zoom event of Nornie Bero from the Torres Strait and Mabu Mabu Café, making three dampers, (pumpkin for brekky, wattle seed for afternoon tea and salt bush and pepper berries for dinner), and eating them hot out of the oven with lashings of butter and golden syrup.

Saturday 1 August *The Saturday Age*: The stats for Victoria are very grim and somewhat alarming: Confirmed cases, 10,577 and 113 deaths, far more than any other state, more than double that of NSW; nationally there 16,906 cases overall, 5,983 active and 197 deaths; world total 17,303,253 confirmed cases and 673, 284 deaths and 10,137,875 people recovered. All of which is the reason I'm not in Cairns celebrating my grandson's 24th birthday today, as planned.

Sunday 2 August As there were another 671 cases and seven deaths overnight, from tonight there's an 8pm–5am Curfew, and Greater Melbourne is in a State of Disaster in Stage 4 lockdown: only one person to do shopping per household per day, any travel restricted to a radius of five km, all schools closed except for special needs and essential services, takeaway still allowed, exercise for an hour and compulsory mask wearing, with regional Victoria in stage 3 lockdown.

Wednesday 5 August It seems we had an existential dilemma this morning trying to adhere to the new regulations, with me going for a drive this afternoon to buy grog and out again this evening to pick up takeaway burgers from Brunswick East for dinner. But I'll combine my exercise time with picking up the takeaway. Another good thing, after Ardy had told me to make a twist on the elastic loops on my mask, I have been able to breathe a lot better and my glasses don't fog up at all.

I'm so enamoured of Zoom these days that I watched two yesterday, including At Risk: Older Women Facing Homeless in Australia. Now up to my favourite, book 8, called *1222*, of the Hanne Wilhelmsen series by Anne Holt and it has been an absolute pleasure to be rereading these books in chronological order.

Over 700 new cases today, a total of 13,035 active cases in Victoria, and fifteen deaths including a man in his 30s. Andrews reiterated that all the new restrictions were painful and difficult but necessary with 250,000 workers affected by the closures of businesses, 155 fines and many more warnings issued by the cops to people breaching the stage four lockdown regulations and grandparents are advised not to mind their grandchildren.

Friday 7 August Rather too 'down' today to be productive but I did add to this Diary as usual. The Anti-racism Book Circle Journal is also almost up-to-date, and while the questions are not designed for Australia I've just adjusted them to write about my complicity in racism towards Indigenous people here. The biggest thing is that I finalised the first draft, with photos and script, 60 pages in all, of the ISO Book for the Counihan's Summer Show, so that was a good thing,

Saturday 8 August The *Bent Street 4.1, Love From a Distance: Intimacy and Technology in Time of COVID-19* anthology was in the PO Box this morning and not only does it look great but Ardy says my contribution, Dark POMO, based on extracts from my COVID-19 Diary reads well. The editor has kindly asked me to do more of the same as a follow-on in the next edition at the end of the year.

I am buoyed by the warmer weather this morning and the promise from the weather person of more to come this week in the region of 15 to 17 degrees, which is a lot better after all the icy cold temperatures and the bitter wind the past few days. And in this mood, I opened the Zoom and we all got stuck onto the first introductory session of the *Me & White Supremacy* Book Circle discussion which went extremely well.

Monday 10 August One thousand health care workers are now COVID-19 positive and apparently while we have a stockpile of masks and sanitiser and all the rest of the necessary equipment, they're not being distributed to hospitals where they're needed most. Five million infections in the US and Trump wants his head on Mt Rushmore alongside the other four presidents … That could be arranged.

Wednesday 12 August *The New York Times* Coronavirus Update 11 August 2020: Russia announced today that it has approved a vaccine for the coronavirus, the first country in the world to do so. But the claim has been met with international skepticism because the vaccine has not been thoroughly tested …

While the Melbourne Writers Festival Zoom event, Are You Paying Attention?, featuring six Australian womyn writers, Jess Hill, Michelle Law, Leah Jing McIntosh, Favel Parrett, Ellen van Neerven, and Alison Whittaker hosted by Jamila Rizvi and supported by the Office for Women, was extremely well done, it just wasn't the same as being in Fed Square and mingling with everyone and joining the long queues and hanging out and generally feeling like I am part of a community of writers.

Thursday 13 August Unfortunately, after 100 COVID-free days, there were fourteen new infections in Auckland and seventeen altogether in Aotearoa New Zealand,

Saturday 15 August As I returned from buying *The Saturday Age*, followed by a short walk (the arthritis in the second toe on my right foot is very painful at the moment), I was astounded as I crossed Lygon Street, which is always busy with the usual Saturday morning shopping stream of cars, that there was not a single car in sight in either direction.

Sunday 16 August *The Sunday Project:* There were 279 new cases and sixteen deaths, fourteen in Aged Care and the stage four lockdown had been extended by another four weeks taking Melburnians up to Monday 12 October before there's even any consideration of relief from the restrictions.

Monday 17 August Typed up my day 6 anti-racism homework in the Journal, did a few more of the corrections to my other novel written 1986-1993, *In Sisterhood, In Struggle*, and emailed Let's Not Kid Ourselves, We're No Longer ALL In This Together, off to my lesbian community and even went for a quick walk late in the day, before I heated Ardy's chicken curry leftovers with steamed veggies and a salad to try and calm my agitated and overly stimulated mood, which was to no avail because I made several more mistakes: after printing out the pages of the ISO book wrongly, I had to pull out some of my crocheting as well as knitting because I'd used the wrong wool.

Wednesday 19 August I read bits from several books I have on the go at the moment while I have my coffee: first, one of the backlog copies of *Spectrum; followed by Sinister Wisdom* #117, *Lesbians in the City* edited by Erika Abad for the lesbian stories and poetry. Third, *Bent Street 4.1*, reading the lesbian contributions first. *Fourth Me & White Supremacy* by Layla F Saad, homework for the Anti-racism Reconciliation group. Fifth, a start on Aileen Morton-Robinson's *Talkin' Up to the White Woman*, and finally *Offline* by Anne Holt, something light to finish off before I meditate for an hour. These books change as the days go on depending on what is on offer.

Another day another Zoom and this time an Australian lesbian film, *Ellie and Abbie (& Ellie's Dead Aunt),* part of the limited online Melbourne International Film Festival, which we thoroughly enjoyed for its quirky home-grown humour and its inclusion of lesbian-feminist politics in Sydney in the 1970s.

Sunday 23 August On this wet and cold Sunday we had bacon and eggs inside with the gas fire on while we watched episode four of the Danish comedy drama series on Netflix, *Rita*, and afterwards played a game of Banarama, I had halva and coffee for arvo tea and over dinner we watched *The Sunday Project*. There were 208 new cases and seventeen deaths to bring it to a total of 415 deaths compared to four new cases in NSW and two in Queensland; the vaccine when it arrives eventually will be free and a 'no jab no play' policy might be used in certain instances; a dancer on *The Masked Singer* tested positive with several others becoming infected, so everyone has gone into quarantine and the final episode put on hold; a Click for Vic has started as online support for Victorian businesses.

Monday 24 August Heard back from BookPOD this morning that as printers were considered an essential service the Long Breast Press Travel book could be done and dusted by the end of the year. Our previous idea for our collective LBP photo on the back cover has been knocked sideways by COVID-19 but I emailed the others with the novel suggestion that we could do individual photos of ourselves wearing masks!

Tuesday 25 August This is odd I know, but over the past few days I've felt a kind of calmness at the core of me, as if I've settled into and have now accepted life the way it is and that to keep myself safe I just have to stay at home and wear a mask if I go out for exercise. I'm comparatively well-off financially on the Old Age pension, I live in a small comfy house and it's not as if I don't have enough at home to amuse myself between my writing work, Zoom, the ISO and LBP books, the anti-racism group, umpteen books to read, TV shows, Netflix and my darling Ardy for company.

In fact, there's a certain pride in us Melburnians managing to get ourselves through Stage 4 lockdown in the State of Disaster without too much bother and fuss. Every time I go out with my mask on and see everyone else with their masks on I feel there's a sense of community because WE really are all in this together, in a way the rest of Australia is not.

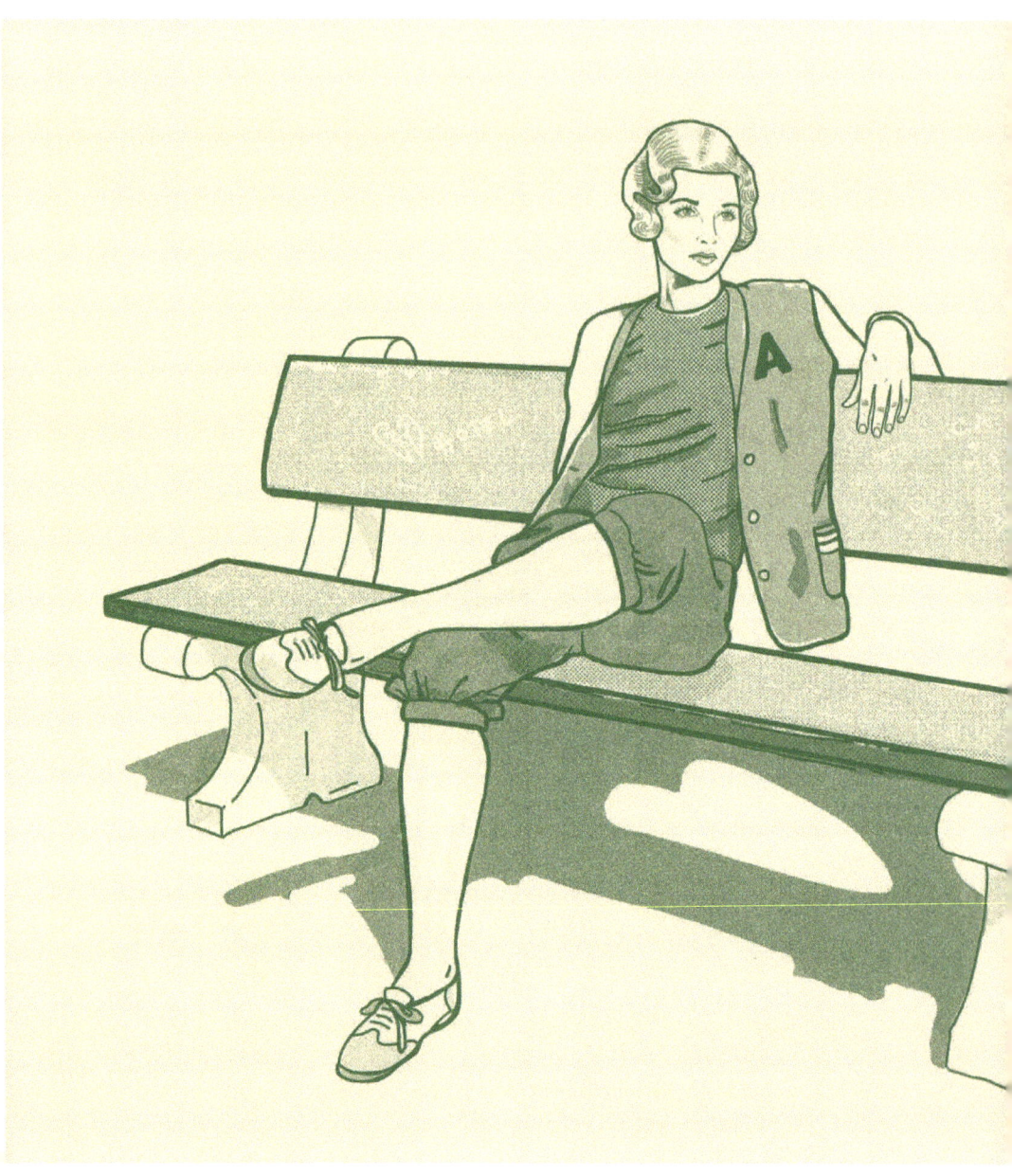

Mel Simpson—*Benched Again*

Saturday 29 August I cut my hair first thing, one of the advantages of doing this since the age of 16, before I went out and bought *The Saturday Age* and walked further than I have lately. I'll mainly be sitting on the verandah today with 19 degrees predicted and no wind, having lunch and doing a bit of this, the knitted cover, and a bit of that, answering emails, having already ordered Sheila Jeffreys' autobiography, *Trigger Warning: My Lesbian Feminist Life*, online from Spinifex, which will be delivered hot off the press shortly, as well as *Born Still: A Memoir of Grief* by Janet Fraser.

Over another delicious Lebanese takeaway meal from Tete Mona we watched a lesbian film on Netflix, *Good Kisser*, about a lesbian threesome that didn't go according to plan, not too surprisingly, and with a definite feel of a stage play with all the exits and entrances and a gay neighbour in the back bungalow and a lesbian taxi driver to add to the mix.

The Saturday Age: The hotel quarantine inquiry is still front page news with lot of mismanagement as far as social distancing and sanitiser are concerned; more family violence during lockdown; '*Victorians more resilient than nation may realise, Community support for the second lockdown remains at remarkably high levels despite blame-shifting between Morrison and Andrews*'; Naked City by John Sylvester: '*Time to admit our national shame, the sorry truth is that every week, a woman is killed by her partner… Police deal with a family violence victim every six minutes,*' (never mind that radical feminists have been screaming about this for decades and are well aware of this national disgraceful and violent male truth); there were 113 new cases and eighteen deaths bringing the death toll to 496 in Victoria and 583 death nationally and 831,615 deaths world-wide, 180,844 of those in the US.

Monday 31 August The start of the fifth week of stage 4 lockdown and settling at the computer to get this COVID-19 Diary up to date. Ardy told me over the weekend that she is really really missing being able to go to Libraries not only to borrow books but to browse and hang out and also she is missing her weekly volunteering at the University of Melbourne Archives and ALGA, where she felt she was making a significant contribution towards lesbian community and culture. Whereas I think that Ardy doing the food shopping and creating some amazing signature dishes for our dinners in the evening are both vital aspects for our wellbeing.

Made a start on the next article for *Rain & Thunder* #75 about Nursing Homes in the 1960s and the deaths in Residential Aged Care facilities during COVID-19 in 2020 and then answered the questions in Layla's book for Week two Day thirteen.

Wednesday 2 September A notice about *Brazen Hussies* (the film) popped up in my inbox and there's no doubt now that there's definitely a heavy emphasis on middle class womyn, and it looks as if it bears little resemblance to the grassroots WLM as I experienced it.

After spending a great deal of the afternoon in the back yard soaking up the warmth of a 23 degree day with no need for a cardie while sewing the knitted cover onto the ISO book and taking my washing out of the drier and folding it, by 6.15pm I was onto the Wheeler Centre site to watch and listen to Aileen Morton-Robinson, who wrote *Talkin' Up to the White Woman*, being interviewed and was utterly impressed as Aileen discussed her late-in-life academic career and her take on racism and life from a Quandamooka women's point of view.

Friday 4 September An interview on Zoom at 11am about The Rise and Fall of Lesbian Nation with the lesbian writer and herstorian, Lillian Faderman, who wrote many award-winning books including: *Odd Girls and Twilight Lovers: A History of Lesbian Life in Twentieth-Century America* (1991). Lillian covered all the main aspects of radical lesbian-feminist cultural and political pursuits during the 1970s and 1980s and into the early 1990s, all much the same as happened here in Australia, albeit on a smaller scale.

Saturday 5 September Another day, another two Zooms with three down and one to go tomorrow which will make six Zooms altogether this week, a record. But first, the fortnightly two-hour anti-racism Book Circle discussion with Moreland Reconciliation at 10.30am.

The Saturday Age reported that the general population in Melbourne is largely COVID-19 free and 'it is largely healthcare and Aged Care workers getting sick… Of Victoria's 2060 active cases yesterday, 993 were related to Aged Care and 297 were amongst health care workers—between them about 63 percent of the total.' With 19,415 confirmed cases and 650 deaths, most of those in Aged Care, Victoria has had an enormous number of cases and deaths compared to the rest of the country: a total number of 6,722 cases and a total of 87 deaths in the rest of the states.

At 7pm, the launch from London of Sheila Jeffrey's autobiography, *Trigger Warning: My Lesbian Feminist Life*, was well done and I found all three speakers, Sheila, Linda and Renate and the interviewer, Jo, made for a lively and interesting session.

Sunday 6 September Up and at the computer by 7am for a June Mazer Lesbian Archives session from West Hollywood with Katherine V Forest, *Curious Wine*, (1983) and the Kate Delafield Mysteries including *Murder At The Nightwood Bar* (1987), but it was definitely worth it to see and hear Katherine read from her latest Kate Delafield-in-progress which was intriguing.

I was pleased when a cardboard box was delivered to the front door, imagining it was from Spinifex with the two books I'd ordered, but even more delighted and surprised when I opened it to find a Care Package Hamper from my daughter in Cairns, on top of the bunch of yellow roses she'd sent a couple of days ago, full of edible goodies to let us know they were thinking of us down here in house-bound and plague-ridden Melbourne.

For financial reasons there is pressure on Daniel Andrews to start opening the state and easing the restrictions for Melbourne but the plan that the Premier announced this afternoon sees the Stage 4 Lockdown extended for another couple of weeks with slight easing of restrictions, curfew at 9pm, two hours of exercise and a designated visit if living on your own and nothing more till 28 September when pools will open up again and I might get to visit my grandchildren for the first time in about twelve weeks!!!

Tuesday 8 September After a lot of concentration and perseverance I finally completed and submitted online the Summer Show application for the 60-page story book of words and photos, now called *ISO Lockdown in Naarm / Birraranga in the Grip of the COVID-19 PANdemIC*, which clears my desk for all the other things, like the Long Breast Press book, and the articles for *Bent Street, Rain & Thunder* and *Matrix Guild News*.

Saturday 12 September Another red-letter day, I emailed all the details, the photos, the graphic and the blurbs for the Cover of LBP's *Walking to the Edge* to BookPOD to design us a fantastic cover, as usual. Then emailed my article, (without a title, I've just noticed), with a photo of my old thongs nailed to the side fence above the strip of garden in the backyard, for laughs. A rainy cold Saturday afternoon and just spent a delightful hour and a half watching two episodes of the Danish series *Witch Hunt* and now off to hunt and gather our takeaway Thai dinner from Thaila Thai.

Sunday 13 September I was in the middle of doing the dinner dishes before watching the Cathy Freeman doco about her running career, culminating in winning the gold medal for the 400 metres at the Sydney Olympics in 2000 which was excellent, when my granddaughter rang to let me know that she'd colour-printed the photos for the ISO Book which is good news.

Tuesday 15 September Just as it seems as if the pandemic is under control, with people doing the right social distancing plus mask thing, there is a spike in infections, in Sydney, mainly, at this stage, because the commonwealth government wants it to be capitalistic business as usual to restore the economy, when it's perfectly obvious from what is happening in countries like India and Brazil that COVID-19 is still out there and as infectious as always and that the slightest mistake, as happened here in Victoria, can spark another resurgence of the virus.

Wednesday 16 September I finished reading Aileen Morton-Robinson's *Talkin' Up to the White Woman* and can feel a review or two coming on because this is an extremely important book for lesbian-feminists in particular to read.

I was thoroughly impressed by the Wheeler Centre event hosted by Amy McQuire, a Darumbal and South Sea Islander woman from Rockhampton, who questioned lawyer and human rights advocate Nyadol Nyuon, author of All Our *Relations*, Canadian Tanya Talaga of Polish and Ojibwe descent who wrote *Seven Fallen Feathers*, and the African American author of *White Negroes*, Lauren Michele Jackson. All of them womyn activists who know absolutely from their lived experience the terrible effects of racism and are doing their darndest to change the social conditions in their respective

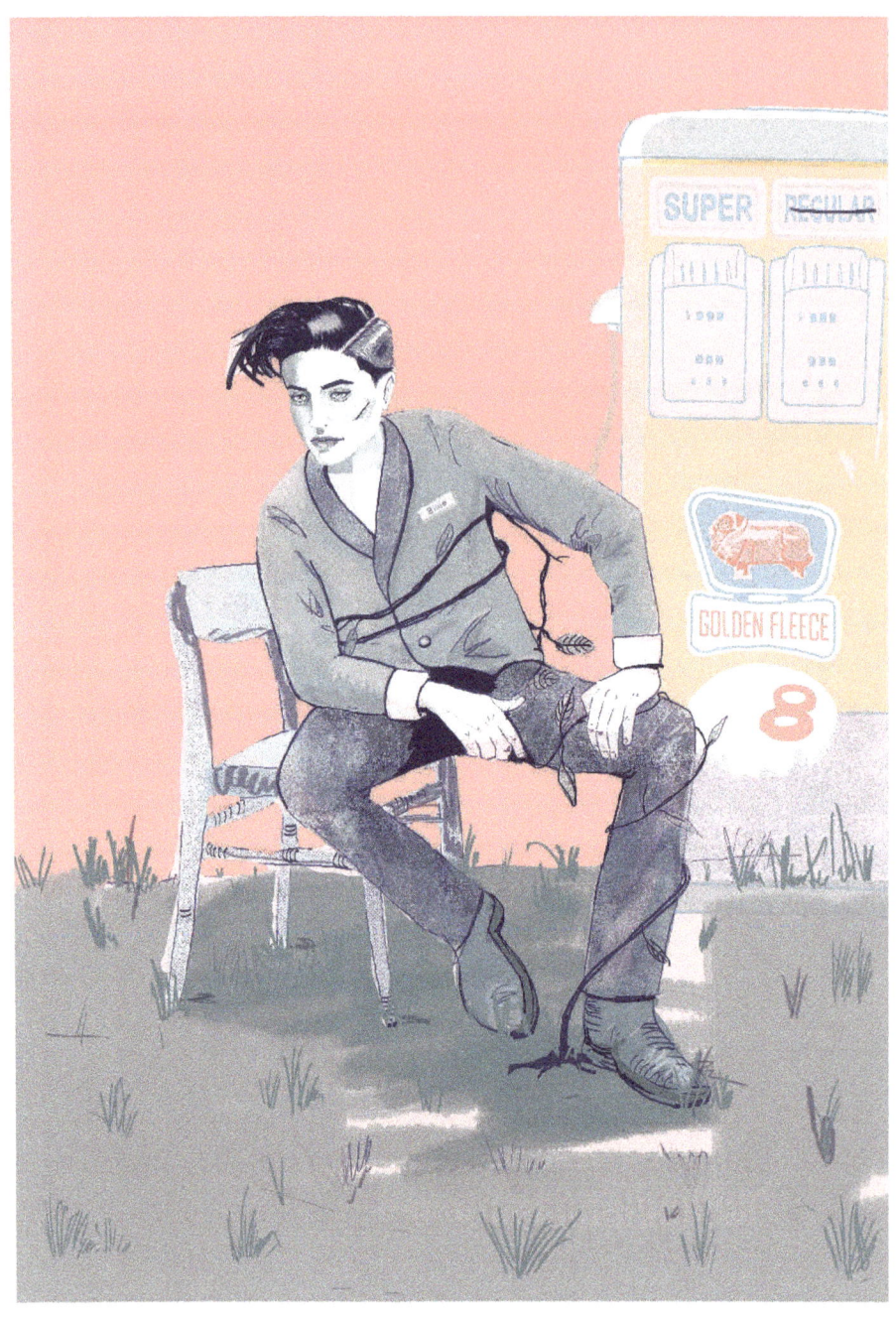

Mel Simpson—*Billie*

countries but also know that these terrible conditions are not going to change anytime soon.

Thursday 17 September *The Project*: Some returning travellers are complaining about having to be in an hotel room for the fourteen day quarantine and how terrible it is and how they can't go outside and the takeaways are terrible, with no understanding or compassion that the reason Melbourne has been in stage four lockdown for months is because of travellers like these being careless and not respecting the strict quarantine rules and passing the virus out into the community. Shut the fuck up, I yelled at the TV screen, and suck it up like the rest of us are doing.

Friday 18 September The *New York Times* Coronavirus Update 17 September 2020: India has reported 97,894 new virus cases, its highest one-day increase. With 5.1 million confirmed cases, or 378 per 100,000 people, the country has the world's second-highest caseload, after the U.S.

A bit stunned and very disappointed that after all the work I put into the ISO book, the Counihan Gallery, for good and obvious reasons, is making the whole Summer Show a virtual one. But that's the new normal life in Melbourne until such time as a vaccine is available, and in the meantime ...

Jean Taylor
Wurundjeri Woiwurrung country Bulleke-bek Naarm

Jean Taylor is a radical lesbian feminist writer, publisher and activist who lives on Wurundjeri Woiwurrung country in Bulleke-bek Naarm. More of Jean's written work can be found on www.dykebooks.com and her activist work is included in the Victorian Women's Liberation and Lesbian Feminist Archives which is stored at the University of Melbourne Archives.

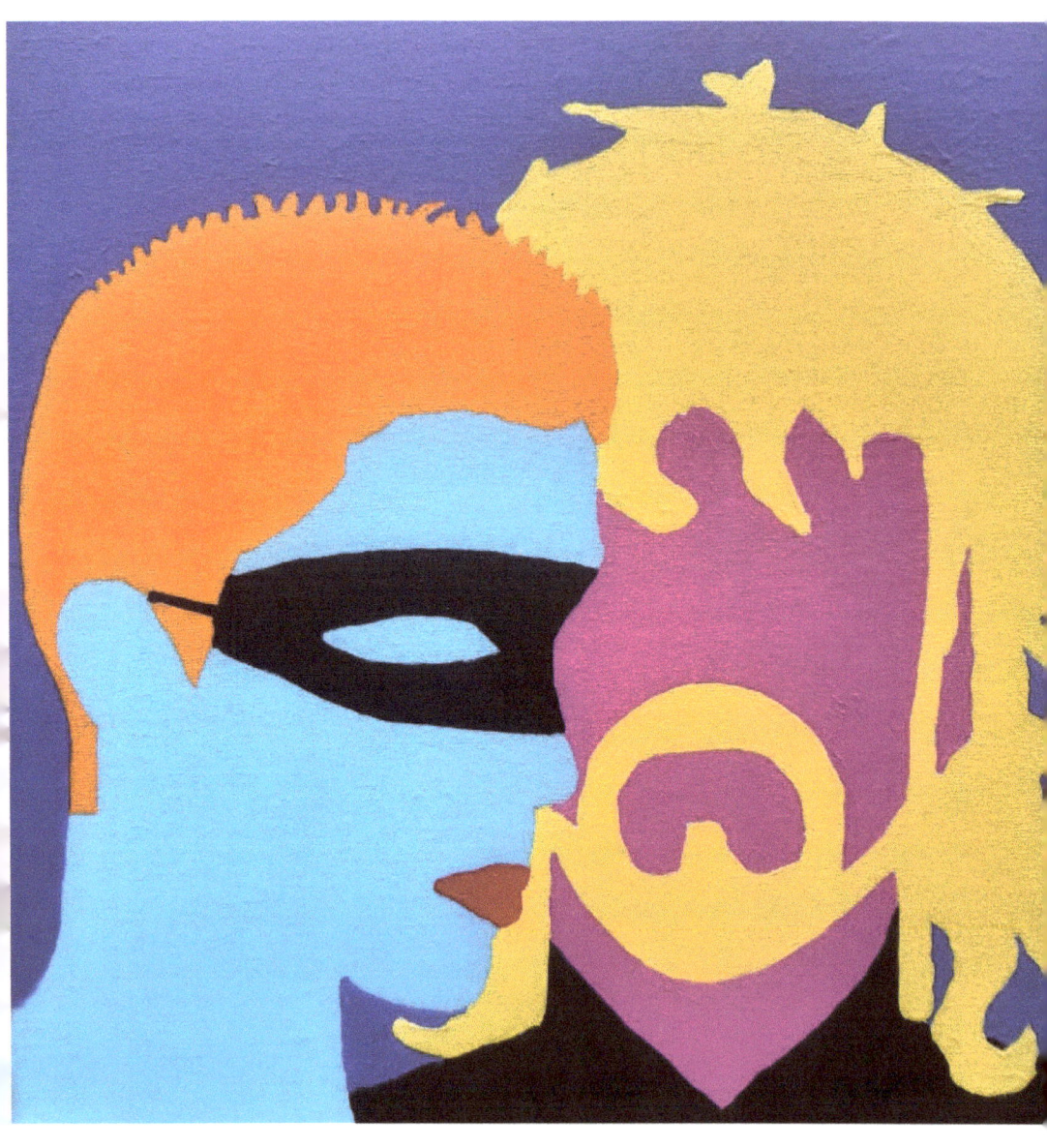

Andrew McNamara—*Eurhythmics*

FACETIME
Andrew McNamara

Andrew, tell us about these images ...

It's a project I started and finished during Lockdown in Melbourne. The focus was musical bands that could be identified without seeing their facial features. This meant that they needed a certain level of fame and a somewhat unique physical appearance. An iconic photo pose that people would recognise also helped. The Trio made up of Dolly Parton, Emmylou Harris and Linda Ronstadt missed the cut because they weren't recognisable enough!

I notice you didn't include the Rolling Stones ...

Most bands that are made up of four or five men wearing casual clothes with messy hair can't be identified without facial details—even a very famous band like the Rolling Stones looks just like other bands when seen without facial features. I also wanted the bands included to be known for being teams, where the sum is greater than the parts. This led me towards bands that kept the same members for an extended period, that wouldn't be the same if one person was missing. For example, that's why Split Enz missed the cut—they changed from seven to six to five members at various times.

Did lockdown inspire this project?

The main impact of lockdown was that the day before Stage 4 lockdown was to start, I raced out and bought 19 canvasses. Then I started painting a few different things, and I really liked a painting that I completed of Abba, and so I continued with the theme.

For our non-queer readers, could you identify the queer elements in the project? For instance, they might be expecting a picture of The Village People ...?

The queerest part of the project might be that with the Eurythmics, I painted Annie Lennox blue in a mask attempting to make her as masculine as possible, and I painted Dave Stewart pink with flouncy yellow hair trying to make him a bit feminine. As I was doing the paintings, I had a changing list of about a dozen bands in contention for the next painting. U2's Joshua Tree cover was an option. Blondie's Parallel Lines. And the Village People—but after painting the Spice Girls, a band where the members have strong individual characters and outfits, I felt that the Village People were too similar!

I'm actually a little disappointed that the project hasn't come out a bit queerer. I guess I didn't plan it but just went with the flow.

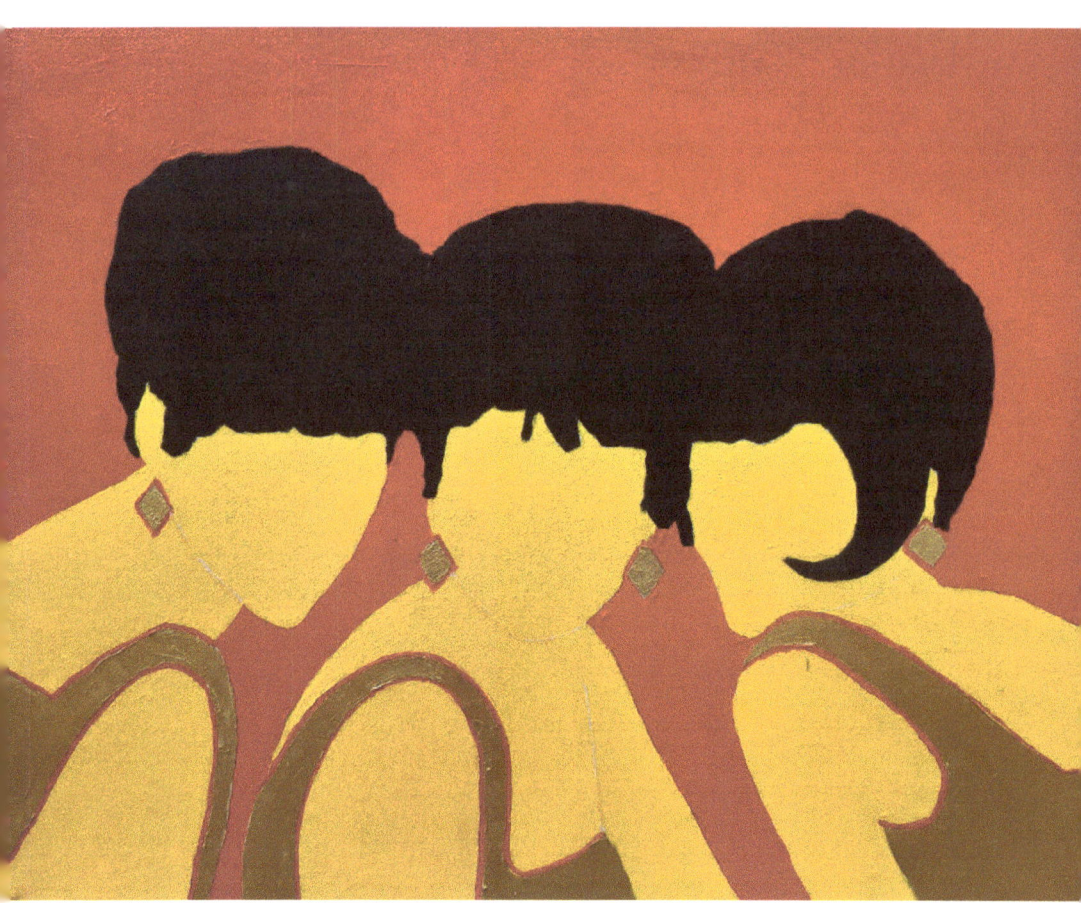

Andrew McNamara—*The Supremes*

Andrew McNamara paints and draws for pleasure, writes a bit, makes furniture, has been a selector for a film festival, has produced/directed/hosted loads of community TV, and for the past fifteen years has presented the radio show *Three Chords and the Truth* on JOY 94.9.

LONDON LOCKDOWN
Jodie Hare

As summer begins to bloom and the days become longer, the lack of intimacy in my days seems magnified. I am waiting for the sticky touch of a loved one's arms as we embrace one another at the beginning and end of an outing. The further I get from the last instance of touch, the less real my existence feels. How can I be sure I'm still here when the only person validating my tangible existence is me ...? I am missing the regular signs of other's lives in the world I inhabit. The small shop by my house allows two customers in at a time, and as I stand in the frozen food isle and let the sweat on my forehead be cooled by the freezers, I wonder, are we the last survivors of this world? Will the day come when we have to fight for the last pack of sausage rolls? It's not likely, but all of a sudden it feels like a real possibility. Having often felt secluded from the connection of others, to see others turn the other way or slightly widen the gap between us feels personal—even when I know it's not. How can our relationships with others be understood when every bid we make for connection is rejected on the basis of self-preservation? And how can we continue to remind ourselves of that when our brains begin to rewrite the narrative as a personal failure?

As someone who entered lockdown single, my friend asked me whether I would continue my quest for dates despite the new limits on shared spaces. I considered the idea; thought about the possibility that this time could be spent texting a woman with whom I had intense day long conversationssa, uninterrupted by the journey to University or nights in the pub with friends. The unlimited time would give us the chance to delve so deeply into the enquiries of each other's lives that when quarantine ended there would be nothing that we didn't know about the other person. But is this really true? Can I claim to know someone whose arms I haven't felt around me, or whose perfume I can't recognise in a crowded room? Do I want to build something so deeply with someone whose fingers I haven't felt entwined between mine, just to suddenly meet in the real world on an undetermined date in the distant future and find that actually being in my presence doesn't illicit the same curiosity they felt for the words I type behind my screen? For me personally, the short answer is no, not really. My heart is simply too fragile to hold up against 'unprecedented' circumstances. So, what does that mean for me? Is my love life over for the foreseeable future? How will I know when it's safe to try again? Will I ever lose that anxiety? Will I come out of this brutal lockdown and find that every queer woman in London has gotten engaged over FaceTime?

Having long identified as a part of a group that Hannah Gadsby dubs 'the quiet gays,' I have already come to depend on technology for my dating experience. With London's LGBTQIA+ scene limited mostly to a small handful of pubs and clubs (and that one lesbian bar that's the size of a shoebox!), if you're a socially anxious person who prefers a quiet night in a restaurant to a 3 day bender, it's hard to find areas where you can meet other people from the community. For this reason, amongst others, my dating life always begins online, whether it be a swipe or a DM slide, there is always virtual talk before there is in-real-life talk. My straight friends constantly warn me of the dangers of this, meeting dangerous people, being catfished, connection being stilted. But what are my alternatives? I hold privilege as a straight-passing lesbian, and this makes the 'you will meet someone in person!' advice difficult. Foregoing the tattooing of 'hi, I'm gay' on my forehead, it's difficult to present myself as available to women rather than men. This invisibility is a small annoyance I have had to come to terms with. Even when I'm in designated queer spaces I feel anxious that I'll be perceived as the straight friend that tagged along, but this is not a worry for me online—I don't feel that pressure because I can plaster rainbow flags over any and every space I virtually inhabit.

I try to explain to my straight friend that the dating landscape shifts once you begin to search out experiences that aren't heterosexual. I don't necessarily love that most of my interactions begin online, I often wonder how the experience would change were I to meet someone accidentally, if it would be more natural or less anxiety inducing. But online dating also allows me to quickly surpass those whose views I don't share, or whose relationship needs don't match mine, and it will always be easier to send a quick 'hello' message than to approach someone in public. I hope that over time London's queer spaces will diversify and I won't have to feel disheartened every time I redownload Tinder, but for the current moment, this is where potential intimacy lingers.

Jodie Hare is a Postgraduate student currently working towards an MA in Modern Languages, Literature and Culture at King's College London.

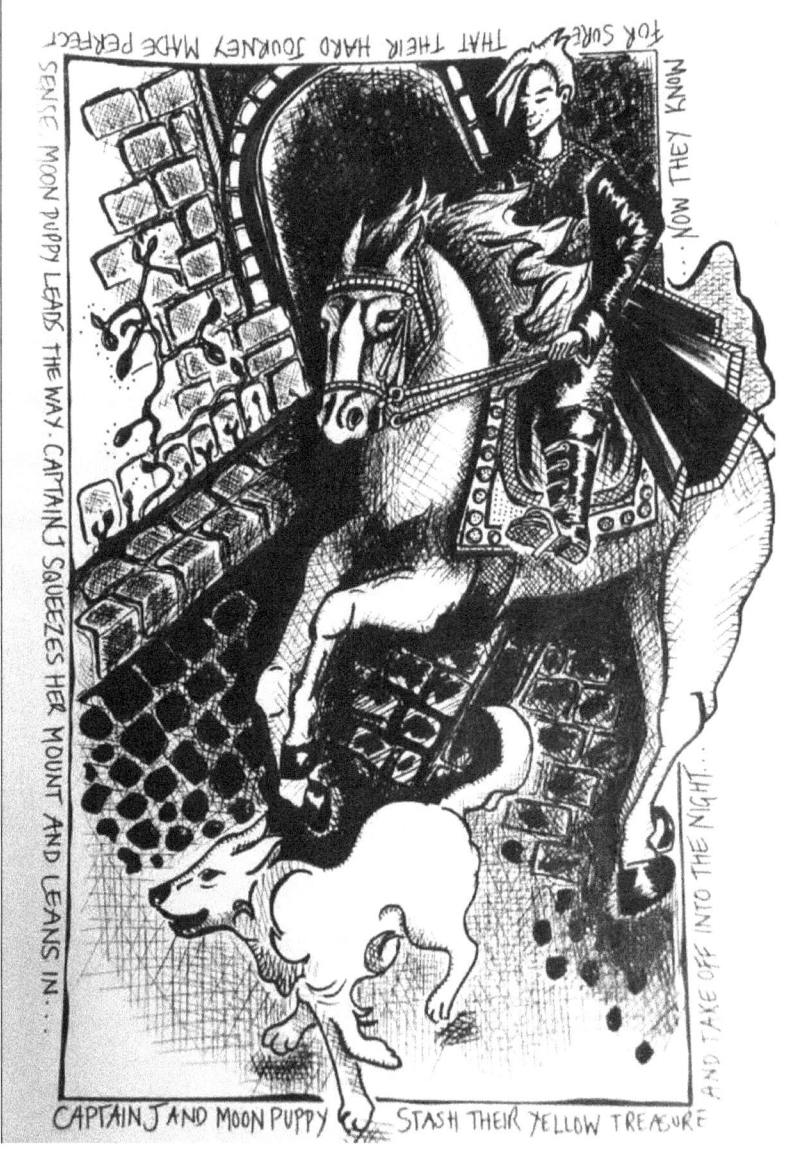

Jennifer Power—*Captain J*

Jennifer Power is a Senior Research Fellow at the Australian Research Centre in Sex, Health and Society at La Trobe University. Her research is focused on HIV, sexual and reproductive health and fertility, LGBTI health and wellbeing, and the impact of new technologies on sex and intimacy.

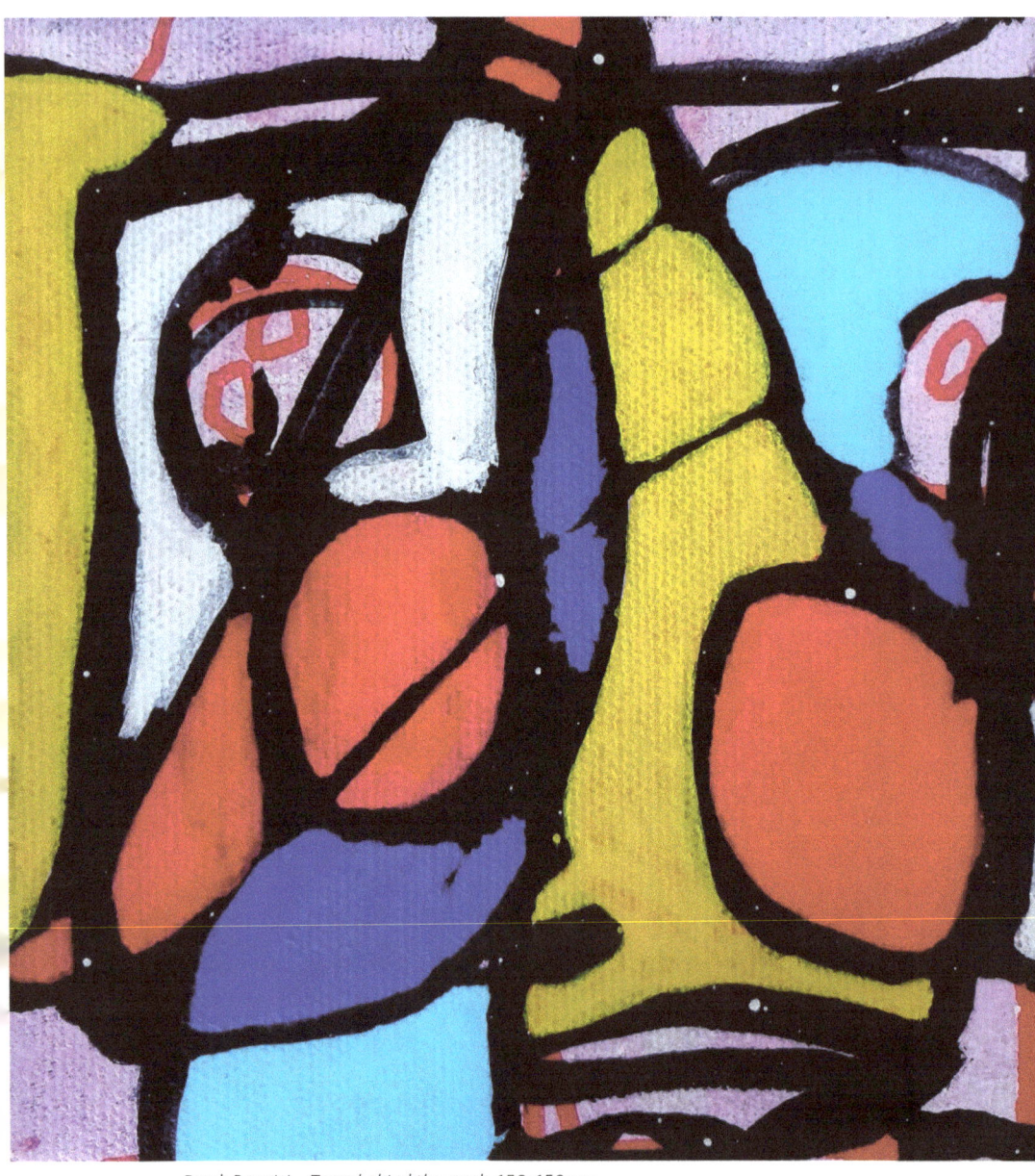

Frank Bonnici—*Tears behind the mask,* 150x150mm

Frank Bonnici is a Melbourne based artist and life model. His artistic interest is in denaturalising the body to show how it is socially produced and understood. Line work is fundamental to both his aesthetic approach and as a metaphor of dis/connection. Many of his works focus on the human figure and are made at Last Peek Studio in Thornbury

2020: THE YEAR IN QUEER
Tiffany Jones

In 2020 a series of disasters took place around the world. These disasters were exacerbated by issues of climate change, geopolitical tensions and incompetent government responses.

However they were also challenged by the Queer communities—organisations and individuals—participating in non-government funded relief efforts. These efforts were not tied to the usual political hierarchies and conservative priorities of aid in general for sustaining the world order 'as it was'. The relief given was instead more disruptive and sometimes social, comical, musical, financial or based on alternative ideas about 'relief' … and how the world could re-form, after the disasters.

This article with weblinks to videos mentioned can be found at bentstreet.net

JANUARY

In January a series of subversive news articles in the alternative and Queer press circulated, poking fun at homophobic responses from parts of the far right religious fringe to the 'Australian apocalypse'. The 'Australian Apocalypse' was used by both the alternative and Queer press to loosely refer to these extremists' framings of the intense floods Australia experienced in January 2020, as well as the devastating fires, as the punishments of an angry God. The trope held that such extremists viewed the series of disasters as direct smiting by an angry God for Australia's recent legalisation of same sex marriage. In part this framing was tied to religious discrimination in the ongoing 2020 push for the Religious Freedom Bills. As Cam Smith from *The Chaser* noted in his seminal satirical piece:

> BREAKING: Australian government repeals gay marriage in attempt to stop natural disasters … Asked whether it might be climate change behind a majority of the freak weather events, given scientists predicted it would cause this exact outcome over 20 years ago, Morrison said that 'so called Climate Change' was just wild superstition, and he would not be making laws based around the fringe beliefs of a crazy cult. In unrelated news, the Religious Discrimination Bill is expected to be passed by the parliament early next week.

FEBRUARY

k.d. lang is a Canadian dykon pop and country music vocalist of remarkable talent. She is increasingly given the honorific 'K-Daddy Lang' by her Queer fans; honouring her fathering of butch self-determination in the public eye against all advice and odds in the mainstream music and media industry of the 1980s during the global HIV pandemic. To fathom what K-Daddy put up with in the earlier years, one need only (re-)watch her 1980s and even early 1990s interviews on Youtube. A bright-eyed and colourfully dressed young lang talks about how she channels Elvis or Patsy Cline, eats a vegetarian diet, prefers to date women and enjoys wearing short hair and boots … themes found in fairly standard tropes for contemporary lesbians or women generally now, but often directly labelled 'eccentric', 'bizarre', 'freaky' or 'hoopla' by her interviewers (here's looking at you, Jack Webster from *BCTV Webster)*. lang's ironic, honest but generously warm responses in the face of gender biased and sometimes directly homophobic attitudes that she was so far ahead of, are both an absolute pleasure and a pain to watch. Part of the pain is given the persistent or increased grip of these attitudes in some quarters to this day.

K-Daddy has long owned a special relationship with Australia. In

response to the extreme bush fire season, Daddy lang joined comedian Celeste Barber's *Fire Fight Australia* concert to benefit Australian bushfire relief. Daddy Lang gave a matchless rendering of Leonard Cohen's 'Hallelujah' to a sold-out crowd at ANZ Stadium in Sydney Olympic Park alongside a range of many other performers. Her haunting performance brought the audience to a standstill.

MARCH

OutRight Action International is a New York, non-government organisation focussed on rights-based pragmatic interventions for LGBTIQ+ people. As COVID-19 continued to spread around the world, Outright distinguished its own response sharply from the US Trump Administration with its early and diversified recognitions of the increased impacts of COVID-19 on marginal international populations. In mid-March, OutRight launched the *OutRight TV* video and podcast series bringing to light stories of LGBTIQ people and allies from across the globe interviewed on the issues they faced around COVID-19: experiences, feelings, challenges … mixed in with funny sock-puppet play, anxieties about growing police states and shutting down of LGBTIQ+ bars, and soul-sustaining gossip about favourite trending Lebanese drag queen videos moving onto Instagram and Youtube!

OutRight COVID-19 Global LGBTIQ Emergency Fund, a more materially oriented measure in collaboration with founding partners Calvin Klein, Inc., Microsoft Corp. and the Dunn Family Charitable Foundation, had, by the end of March, raised $130,000 from individuals keen to support the LGBTIQ+ community globally with emergency financial resources to organizations around the world serving people impacted by COVID-19, and to document and respond to the impacts of the crisis on LGBTIQ communities. Outright's Executive Director Jessica Stern introduced these new measures with the statement:

> LGBTIQ people already experience barriers to access to health, high levels of domestic and family violence, and scapegoating for crises such as the COVID-19 pandemic. Now, LGBTIQ people are also cut off from community centers and gatherings where we can be ourselves, feel supported, and safe. Our friends and partners tell us they are also facing income loss, food scarcity, homelessness, and more.

APRIL

In April social and physical distancing measures and health-based school exclusions spread more widely across a range of countries around the world; though in an *ad hoc* way complicating their effectiveness. These policies were an attempt to 'slow down the curve' of charts plotting increased COVID-19 reports by nation, relieving or attempting to prevent the inevitable over-burden on healthcare systems (and related loss of life) that the quicker spread of the virus would engender.

A late April New Orleans event 'Cyber-distancing' showcased local drag artists online via zoom and in Chicago, Mini Pearl Necklace took to Twitch with 11 performers for a show they called 'Notta Contact Sport'.

Similarly, Transgender Ugandan activist Victor Mukasa released the first episode of The Victor Mukasa show on Spotify, a Queer African show. The show offered a source of news, lifestyle, history, business, politics, organizing, entertainment with an African Queer core. The introductory episodes tell Mukasa's own story including his experiences of police assaults and harassment over his work with Sexual Minorities Uganda, and subsequent work on lawsuits.

MAY

Across Australia (and the globe!) many LGBTIQ+ people and supporters joined *Queer Love In*. Together from their homes, they sang, danced, laughed and even drew peacocks as they—with LGBTIQ+ pioneers, leaders, celebrities and frontline workers—reflected on paths from the past and future for Australian LGBTIQ+ equality. Participants donated almost $10,000 to support Equality Australia's work and LGBTIQ+ artists doing it tough through COVID-19 restrictions on their work. A recap on participants' favourite bits can be viewed on Equality Australia's facebook page—including contributions from IndigLez, intersex rights advocate Stephanie Lum, lawyer Anna Brown, comedian Joel Creasey, Olympian Ian Thorpe and many others. Equality Australia also launched a report (Equality Australia, 2020) and an online repository of COVID-19 related supports for LGBTIQ+ people on their webpage (equalityaustralia.org.au).

In Poland, the LGBTIQ+ community faced recurrent and increasing abuse under right-wing governance and social discourse perpetuated by the presiding conservative Law and Justice party (PiS), often being cast as part of a so-called 'homosexual plague' (Campbell, 2020). This notion was especially spurred on in the discriminatory comments made by Polish religious leaders in the Polish Catholic Church's attempt at revival. This included for example in various public remarks by Krakow's Archbishop Marek Jedraszewski, who had labelled Poland as embattled under a 'rainbow plague' of LGBTIQ+ rights campaigners/ everyday citizens he conflated also absurdly with all-powerful cruel past Polish communist leaders (Duffy, 2020). Gay-identifying men Dawid Mycek and Jakub Kwiecinski from Warsaw Poland, who had married in Portugal and seen this increase of homophobia across recent years especially from the ruling party's encouragements in 2020. They decided that they should rebel against this notion of LGBTIQ+ people as plagues or plague-spreading, and subvert the dominant leadership's discourse on their identities. They developed a public activism and aid movement, specifically representing LGBTIQ+ people as helping cure a real 'plague': COVID 19. The two husbands filmed themselves as they gave away hundreds of free rainbow face masks they had made, to aid people in protecting themselves from the fast-spreading coronavirus on the streets of the northerly urban area Gdansk. At the time Poland had reported over 10K cases and around 500 deaths; wearing a mask was required in public places. The two men also used the opportunity to encourage a show of pride from the Poles, and raise awareness of the difficulties faced by the LGBTIQ+ community in being misrepresented as a disease in their country. The video 'Rozdajemy tęczowe maski' was uploaded online to Facebook and viewed millions of times, global versions of the video in different languages also went viral. The two received over 80 death threats reportedly by the end of April; but continued promoting their actions regardless for the LGBTIQ+ community and for local Polish citizens' health.

On the eve of the International Day Against Homophobia, Transphobia and Biphobia (IDAHOBIT) on 17 May 2020, a group of United Nations and international human rights experts made a fierce statement calling on countries and stakeholders to urgently account for the impact of COVID-19 on LGBTIIQ+ people (OHCHR, 2020). Especially when designing, implementing and evaluating the measures to combat the pandemic. The statement acknowledged the increased poverty and homelessness experienced by the group, and how the pandemic created a context conducive to increased persecution including some nations:

- enacting measures which intentionally target LGBT persons under the guise of public health
- proposing legislation to deny transgender and gender diverse persons of their legal recognition
- reporting increased hate speech explicitly or implicitly inciting violence against LGBT persons as on the rise
- displaying discourse by prominent political or religious leaders blaming the pandemic on the existence of LGBT persons in the community
- using increased surveillance and other digital technologies enacted to track COVID-19 carriers for infringing privacy and exacerbating stigma.

JUNE

In June the Trump administration was rolling back protections for trans and gender diverse folks, with the Department of Health enabling a crisis of discrimination against trans folks seeking healthcare. However in a landmark decision mid-June, the Supreme Court voted 6-3 that workplace discrimination based on sexuality and gender identity is a form of sex discrimination, and protected by Title VII of the Civil Rights Act of 1964. US LGBTIQ+ advocacy group and media watchdog GLAAD President Sarah Kate Ellis made a statement: 'Victories like this don't happen in a vacuum. (…) This morning's ruling by the Supreme Court to uphold employment protections for LGBTQ people gives us hope that as a country we can unite for the common good and continue the fight for LGBTQ acceptance.'

Immediately, LGBTIQ+ advocates in Western Australia called on Premier Mark McGowan to reassess problematic state laws, and Tasmanian advocate Rodney Croome called on Scott Morrison to abandon his Religious Discrimination Bills, in light of the US Supreme Court's decision (Hill, 2020).

JULY

Kalen Allen, a celebrity personality from the Ellen Show, was one of the grand marshals for the first-ever Global Black Gay Pride, which was a virtual 12 hour global experience taking place on Friday, July 10th, 2020. This inaugural event was not be the usual pride celebration, but described as 'a riot'! As a movement, organisers of Global Black Gay Men Connect (GBGMC, founded in 2018, an activist-led non-profit organization registered in New York—globalbgmc.org) stated that they 'believe that our core issues are at a make-or-break moment, and together we need solutions bold enough to meet the greatest challenges of our lifetime, and big enough to bring world leaders and all of us to get it done'. As a collective, GBGMC fosters an activist-led movement with the goal of building local power to intervene in discrimination and violence inflicted on Black Gay communities and men wherever they live. Organisers state that they strive to facilitate intentional involvement by engaging Black gay men across the world and developing their capacity to rapidly intervene on human rights issues surrounding mental and physical health, police brutality, immigration, and general wellbeing.

AUGUST

In May a United Nations report was prepared on the disastrous impacts of faith-based conversion therapies used to change LGBTIQA+ people to fit heteronormative cisgender binary sex ideals; with information on the health crises they comprised presented to the human rights commission in June (United Nations, 2020). Legislative studies found Brazil, Ecuador, Malta, and Taiwan banned conversion therapy nationally; whilst Canada, Spain and the US had some localised restrictions and began debating them further (Bishop, 2019; UN, 2020). This move was reflected in a variety of bans in bills or inquiries around bills emerging at the state level in Australia, with aid from a variety of academic, community and legal queer representatives towards the end of 2020:

- Queensland's parliament outlawed conversion practices by health service providers and set aside funding to identify supports for survivors using the *Health Legislation Amendment Bill 2019* (QLD Government, 2020) in August.
- The Australian Capital Territory's parliament outlawed paid or unpaid formal and informal conversion practices for both children and adults, focusing on the intent of the 'practitioner' and including unprecedented affirmation of the psychological equality of LGBTQA+ individuals in the *Sexuality and Gender Identity Conversion*

Practices Bill 2020 (ACT Minister for Social Inclusion and Equality & ACT Minister for Justice Consumer Affairs and Road Safety, 2020)

- Victoria's Premier made a commitment to outlaw conversion practices (Carey, 2019), investigating across the end of the year.
- South Australia's Labor Opposition signalled it would introduce a private members bill in 2020 (Richards & Skujins, 2020); and
- The Tasmanian Law Reform Institute began conducting an inquiry into Tasmanian legislation in the area (Hill, 2019).
- Tasmania's Law Reform Institute is inquiring into local legislation (Hill, 2019); and
- Western Australia's Health Minister will assess the effectiveness of incoming Federal health regulation strategies towards legislation (WA Parliamentary Council, 2020).

SEPTEMBER

Over 2020 and as Melbourne's restrictions lengthened, the particular multi-generational and gender-based implications for 'who would mind the kids' and 'who would school the kids' during lockdowns were borne out in problematic ways in many households with children. Feminists were concerned about the return to the old problem of the traditional expectation of reliance on female role-related childcare in many homes; such issues were particularly exacerbated in the US, which was one of the few Western democracies not providing free childcare. One study found that US mothers with young children reduced their work hours four to five times more than fathers—consequently the gender gap in work hours had grown by 20–50 per cent (Collins, Landivar, Ruppanner, & Scarborough, 2020). The UK, Australia, Sweden and many other democratic countries had some government-funded childcare supply available. LGBTIQ+ parents and guardians of children and young people have always presented a difference to heteronormative 'Mum-as-child-minder/educator only' demands; though it is notable that many parents in LGBTIQ+ studies are more often cisgender middleclass lesbians who may face some additional gender-based pressures around ideals for mothers and work engagement (Mann & Jones, 2019). From the child-minding roles of fafafine in Samoa to the co-parenting of two or more dads in relationships right through to gender diverse family 'village' communities who provide different types of role modelling and education for kids, LGBTIQ+ people were both family and educative faculty to their shared children and those of loved ones in their networks across 2020. There were also implications for those LGBTIQ+ people stuck at home with unsupportive families and housemates.

OCTOBER

As the year closed, across contexts the freedom to protest faced significant challenges that some activists argue come from the misuse of COVID-19 restrictions to contain legitimate peaceful protests, and thus to contain dissent against government actions and inactions. There were for example police crackdowns against LGBTIQ+ pride parades in the Philippines (Thoreson, 2020), and against blank protest signs in Hong Kong (Bradsher, 2020), and against the Black Lives Matter (BLM) movement in the US and in nations like Sri Lanka and Australia (Kumarasinghe, 2020; Moore, 2020; Wax-Thibodeaux, Elfrink, Armus, & Peiser, 2020), to name but a few examples... leading various advocates, journalists, academics and politicians to question whether the freedom to fight various rights incursions was *itself* under particular threat in many locations in 2020 where a slide into authoritarianism had already taken place or was potentially in process. In Sydney during October arrests and $1,000 fines were issued by police at a Community Action for Rainbow Rights' protest against Mark Latham's introduction of a proposed amendment bill to parliament restricting support for LGBTIQ+ topics and people in schools (Hayman, 2020). Key speakers such as Member for Parliament Jenny Leong were ultimately unable to speak at the event, and took to social media such as Facebook and other locations to share concerns about limitations being imposed on not only the education system's supports for the LGBTIQ+ community, but on the free non-violent and socially distant expression of dissent itself.

In sum, the internet—though doubtless a highly problematic tool for the LGBTIQ+ community—has nonetheless provided possibilities to speak out; share funding, support and connection and voice political dissent when *many other avenues* and *physical venues* became unavailable this year... whether due to pandemic restrictions, financial closures or police interventions. As 2021 beckons, the LGBTIQ+ community will continue to need to (re)consider how specialised disaster relief for members can be ensured by the community itself, as mass unemployment and more restrictive governments redirect past support elsewhere. Shared spaces—once somewhat reinforced through commercial viability or institutional offerings—may continue to be reimagined using online and networked environments overcoming the obstacles of our times. Finally a close watch should be kept on misuse of disasters themselves as means for attacking the community, and its voice.

References

ACT Minister for Social Inclusion and Equality, & ACT Minister for Justice Consumer Affairs and Road Safety. (2020). *Sexuality and Gender Identity Conversion Practices Bill 2020*. Canberra: Australian Capital Territory Government and ACT Parliamentary Counsel's Office

Bradsher, K. (2020). Under the Cover of Corona Virus Hong Kong Cracks Down on Protesters. *The New York Times*,. Retrieved from https://www.nytimes.com/2020/04/21/world/asia/coronavirus-hong-kong-protests.html

Campbell, E. (2020). Poland's government is leading a Catholic revival. It has minorities and liberals worried. *ABC News*,. Retrieved from https://www.abc.net.au/news/2020-04-28/poland-catholic-church-revival-lgbt-rights/12180704

Carey, A. (2019). Victoria to ban gay conversion therapy. *The Age*,. Retrieved from https://www.theage.com.au/national/victoria/victoria-to-ban-gay-conversion-therapy-20190203-p50vdn.html?link_id=4&can_id=ac2b07a77286b0fcaba82d673345c2e2&source=email-its-time-to-end-lgbtq-conversion-practices-2&email_referrer=email_891137___subject_1218954&email_subject=update-on-ending-conversion-practices

Collins, C., Landivar, L., Ruppanner, L., & Scarborough, W. (2020). COVID-19 and the gender gap in work hours. *Feminist Frontiers, Onlinefirst*. Retrieved from https://onlinelibrary.wiley.com/doi/10.1111/gwao.12506

Duffy, N. (2020). Archbishop claims a 'rainbow plague' is afflicting Poland. *Pink News*,. Retrieved from https://www.pinknews.co.uk/2019/08/02/archbishop-claims-rainbow-plague-afflicting-poland/

Equality Australia. (2020). *LGBTIQ+ COMMUNITIES AND COVID-19: A report on the impacts of COVID-19 on Australian LGBTIQ+ communities and building a strong response*. Retrieved from Melbourne:

Hayman, R. (2020). NSW Police make arrest and issue $1,000 fines at banned Sydney rally protesting anti-transgender bill. *ABC News*,. Retrieved from https://www.abc.net.au/news/2020-10-10/nsw-arrests-made-at-sydney-protest-anti-transgender-bill/12751208

Hill, L. A. (2019). Tasmanian Law Reform Institute to conduct inquiry into conversion practice. *Out in Perth*,. Retrieved from https://www.outinperth.com/tasmanian-law-reform-institute-to-conduct-inquiry-into-conversion-practice/?link_id=6&can_id=ac2b07a77286b0fcaba82d673345c2e2&source=email-its-time-to-end-lgbtq-conversion-practices-2&email_referrer=email_891137___subject_1218954&email_subject=update-on-ending-conversion-practices

Hill, L. A. (2020). US Supreme Court rules against LGBTIQ+ workplace discrimination. *Out in Perth,*. Retrieved from https://www.outinperth.com/us-supreme-court-rules-against-lgbtiq-workplace-discrimination/

Kumarasinghe, K. (2020). Sri Lanka Cracks Down on Black Lives Matter Solidarity Protest: A protest against police brutality in the U.S. is met with police brutality in Colombo. *The Diplomat,*. Retrieved from https://thediplomat.com/2020/06/sri-lanka-cracks-down-on-black-lives-matter-solidarity-protest/

Mann, T., & Jones, T. (2019). What LGBT Parents Want in Schools. In *Bent Street* (Vol. 3, pp. 151-162). Melbourne: Clouds of Magellan.

Moore, C. (2020). Australian Black Lives Matter protesters are set for a showdown with the police after cops call for weekend demonstration to be BANNED. *Daily Mail,*. Retrieved from https://www.dailymail.co.uk/news/article-8390671/Gladys-cracks-NSW-asks-Supreme-Court-BAN-protest.html

OHCHR, U. N. (2020). Statement by human rights experts on the International Day against Homophobia, Transphobia and Biphobia. Retrieved from https://www.ohchr.org/EN/NewsEvents/Pages/DisplayNews.aspx?NewsID=25884&LangID=E

QLD Government. (2020). *Health Legislation Amendment Bill 2019*. Brisbane: Queensland Government and Parliamentary Counsel

Richards, S., & Skujins, A. (2020). SA move to outlaw conversion therapy. *InDaily,*. Retrieved from https://indaily.com.au/news/2020/07/16/sa-move-to-outlaw-conversion-therapy/?link_id=5&can_id=ac2b07a77286b0fcaba82d673345c2e2&source=email-its-time-to-end-lgbtq-conversion-practices-2&email_referrer=email_891137___subject_1218954&email_subject=update-on-ending-conversion-practices

Thoreson, R. (2020). Philippines Police Crack Down on LGBT Protest: Covid-19 Pandemic Should Not Be Used to Silence Dissent. Retrieved from https://www.hrw.org/news/2020/06/29/philippines-police-crack-down-lgbt-protest

United Nations. (2020). *Report on conversion therapy*. Geneva: United Nations Human Rights Office of the High Commissioner.

WA Parliamentary Council. (2020). McGowan Government Election Commitments. *Hansard*, p1497c-1516a. Retrieved from https://www.parliament.wa.gov.au/Hansard/Hansard.nsf/0/0c7df2e4032e8f2548258531002809a2/$FILE/C40%20S1%2020200318%20p1497c-1516a.pdf

Wax-Thibodeaux, E., Elfrink, T., Armus, T., & Peiser, J. (2020). Protests: Barr slams Black Lives Matter, accuses the left of 'tearing down the system'. *The Washington Post,*. Retrieved from https://www.washingtonpost.com/nation/2020/08/10/protests-live-updates/

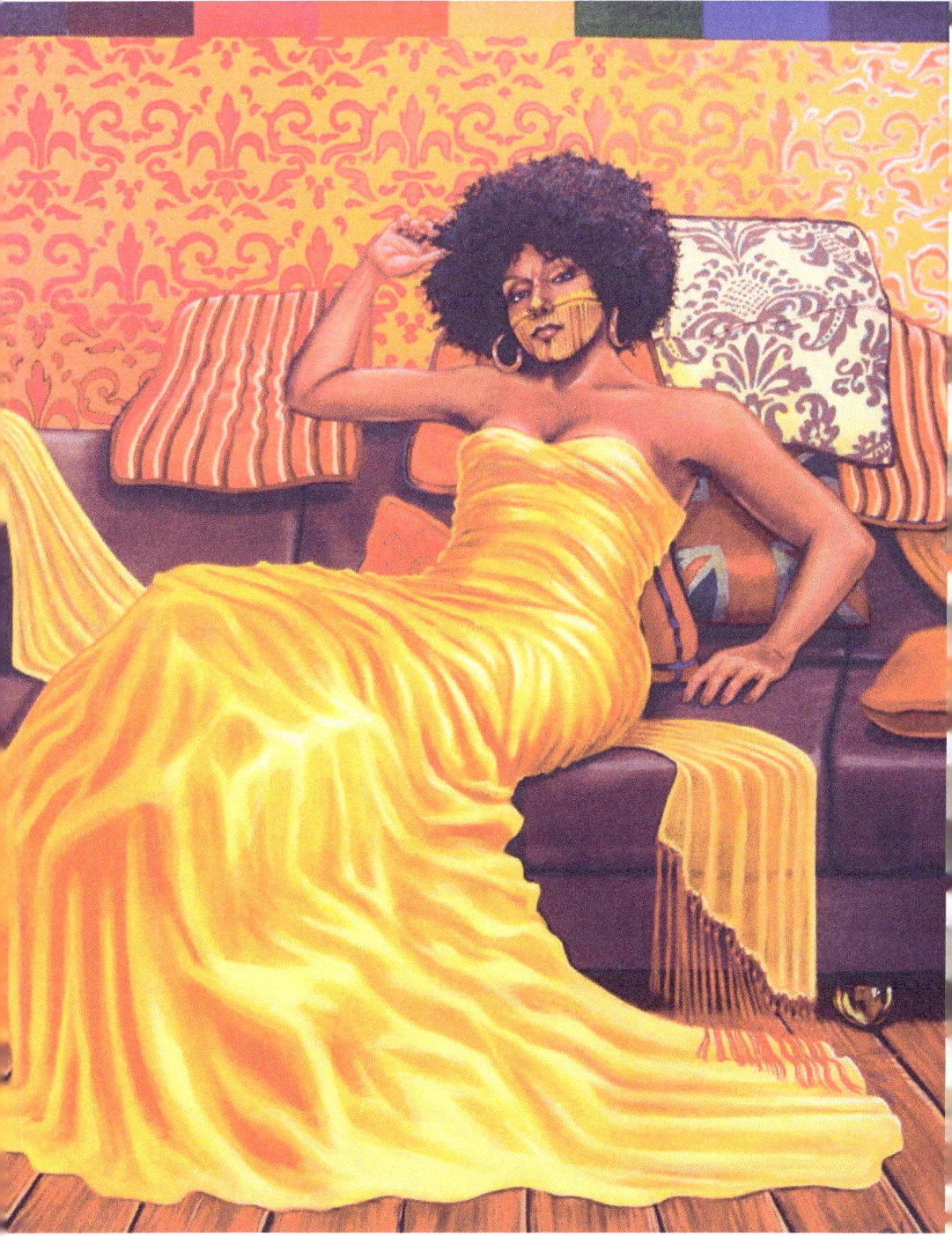

While Taylor Swift passes as a 'queer icon' these days, Sydney artist and author Guy James Whitworth isn't convinced

Originally published in Sydney Sentinel, 19 September 2020

PREVIOUS PAGE: Guy James Whitworth—*Gold Dust Woman*

Now don't get me wrong, I love me a bit of TayTay, but you know, unfortunately, a lot of what she does symbolises a big chunk of what we don't need in the world right now.

Back in the late 80s, I moved to London and joined a queer direct-action group called OutRage!, co-founded by the very awesome Peter Tatchell (if you don't know who he is, please give him a Google)

I'll be honest, when I joined OutRage!, I was really looking to meet hot, cool activists.

One demonstration I was at was a same-sex kiss-in outside Lambeth Palace, which was the official London residence of the (incredibly homophobic) Archbishop of Canterbury (don't waste your time Googling him).

Unfortunately, typically for me, I was too shy to ask anyone to kiss me, so I ended up holding the coats of people who were in amongst all the queer snogging and I ended up going home completely un-pashed and feeling a bit sad.

There was a fabulous queer-friendly magazine at the time called *The Face* which was sadly sued to bankruptcy by a then pop star called Jason Donavon (totally up to you if you want to Google him), who took offence at the magazine publishing a photo of him with a t-shirt that proclaimed the words 'Queer as Fuck.'

Although this was pre-Photoshop, and it was obviously a clumsily collaged image (and at the time most of Donovan's fan base were gay men) Donovan thought it of the utmost importance to defend his heterosexuality, hence the ensuing court case.

I didn't create the artwork, but I was friends with the person (and OutRage! member) who did. I kept the original collage in a folder under my mattress for months while my friend lived in fear of being arrested and/or sued for millions!

So how does any of this ancient history tie in with the divine Miss Taylor Swift, I hear you ask? Well, it really kind of ties in with where we are culturally at the minute.

Back in those heady 'OutRageous!' days of demonstrations and 80s music, we had an edge, we did. Us queers, we were constantly pushing the pink envelope and testing the boundaries of what was accepted by mainstream culture.

We were reckless and revolting. We could definitely see an uprising of acceptance on the horizon. The revolution was imminent.

Pop music was filled with shocking androgyny and queer love. 'Relax' by Frankie Goes to Hollywood was banned but still made it to #1! Edgy, unorthodox queerdom was everywhere. Grace Jones reigned supreme. All the lesbians I knew wanted to be Skin from Skunk Anansie (*please*, I beg you, Google her!) and all the boys I knew confusingly wanted to be Annie Lennox (you'd better know who she is without the help of Google!).

Okay, so, how does this connect to TayTay and her rebellious latest album? Well, put simply in one word: safety.

We have become too safe.

I'm aware that I'm saying this as a global pandemic rages around us, the Black Lives Matter (BLM) movement is (rightly) in full force, and around the world economies are crashing. But I stand by that word.

We (certainly white) queers have become safe. Too safe.

I currently have an exhibition open here in Sydney and I was originally going to call it *Safety in Numbness* (but went with *Enough of Your Nonsense* instead).

From where I stand, the BLM movement is spectacular and long overdue. It is powerful and it is right. No white, self-respecting, queer person cannot get wholeheartedly involved.

As we now all hopefully do, I fully understand the need for diversity and inclusivity and eagerly stand alongside my colleagues and friends of colour. Because if we aren't fighting for equality in all its forms, then we aren't really fighting for anything worthwhile.

I hope that to people of colour, the BLM movement is seen to be on the same track as the queer rights campaign of the 80s and 90s, where success, change and positive outcomes through activism can be seen as inevitable and real.

But you see, that's again why I have an issue with Ms Swift. Well, actually not her, but with a world that proclaims her to be spectacular—while really, she's also just a bit too, well … safe. Although I've gotta say the issue I have with her is one I also have with Ed Sheeran, Justin Bieber and Ariana Grande, to name just a few.

Don't get me wrong, I have played her *Folklore* album, and I like it, but if you want to hear the album TayTay could have made, please listen to Tracey Chapman's self-titled debut album from 1988.

The chilled vibe is the same, the melodies are similar, however the meaning and message are so much more passionately and authentically delivered.

Quite honestly, you need to sit and listen to the very first song 'Talkin' 'bout a Revolution' as if your queer life depends on it, because, actually, it really still might.

To me all good art should be political.

Yes, Swift is a vocal LGBTQI ally, but we still need activists pushing forward more than we do allies bringing up the rear.

In our modern world, where Trump revokes laws allowing trans people to be themselves, Russia is still persecuting and jailing LGBTQ people and in other countries, countless atrocities are being perpetrated against us queers, we can't rest easy yet.

The battle is still raging around us, and that's without counting the walking wounded where, on the cusp of intersectionality, queer, trans and black lives are especially at risk.

Unfortunately, while songs about 'cardigans' are soft, fluffy and safe, we really still need to be listening to queer black women singing about revolution.

Sorry TayTay, as much as I can appreciate your personal struggles (I watched your Netfilx special, you do seem nice), nobody ever chanted a song about a favourite cardigan whilst heading into battle.

Guy James Whitworth is a Sydney-based artist, author and provocateur. His exhibition Enough of Your Nonsense ran at M2 Gallery, Surry Hills, August-September. His book, *Signs of a Struggle* (Clouds of Magellan Press), is available online and at good gay bookshops everywhere, and he is a regular contributor to *Bent Street*. www.guyjameswhitworth.com

POLICING, PROTEST, AND THE PANDEMIC
Alison Thorne

LGBTIQA+ liberationists speak out against police abuse

2020 has been one hell of year—environmental catastrophe, COVID, a capitalist system in crisis, naked police abuse and *resistance!* LGBTIQA+ people have a massive stake in uniting with other communities to stem the erosion of democratic rights and hold police accountable.

Decades of struggle against police abuse. The contemporary queer community was forged through resisting police attacks on the right to socialise and organise.

• August 1966, San Francisco—cops target gender diverse, young and queer patrons at Comptons Diner. They arrest those who defy gender norms by cross-dressing, sparking months of protest.

• June 1969, New York—the Stonewall riots, led by trans women of colour, butch lesbians and a diversity of queer working class patrons of the Stonewall Inn, explode in rage against decades of homophobic and transphobic abuse. Inspired by the civil rights, women's lib and anti-war movements, they find role models for rebellion.

• June 1978, Sydney—police attack the first Mardi Gras and arrest 53 people. This ignites the Drop the Charges movement and months of sustained protest with many more arrests. Activists rally around the chant 'stop police attacks on gays, workers, women and Blacks,' a rallying cry to unite all police targets.

• August 1994, Melbourne—police raid Tasty, a queer night club. They hurl homophobic abuse and strip-search all 463 patrons on the pretext of a drug raid, which found nothing. A class action wins payments for false imprisonment and assault.

• May 2019, Melbourne—police raid the residence above Hares & Hyenas bookstore and event space. Nik Dimopoulos runs outside. Cops violently set upon him, fracture his shoulder and cause permanent damage.

In response to mass outrage, Victoria Police were forced to apologise to Dimopoulos and owners, Crusader Hillis and Rowland Thomson. They promised 'a thorough investigation' by Independent Broad-based Anti-corruption Commission (IBAC) and Police Standards Command.

History keeps repeating

Melbourne-based activist and writer, Emma Russell, is the author of *Queer Histories and the Politics of Policing*? in which she critiques police apologies and participation in events, such as Pride March, as public relations exercises, noting that 'policing is far from a neutral or benign force.' Russell explains, 'The normalisation of police presence at LGBT Pride events advances the process of commodification, assimilation, and exclusion that gay liberationists and queer activists have long fought against.'

Police apologies are hollow gestures, when those who perpetuate the abuse are routinely exonerated. Earnest pledges to find answers, coupled with calls to stay calm and let the system do its job are a routine response designed to let off steam and defuse protest.

Every time a First Nations person dies in custody, grieving families and others taking to the streets are promised the system will provide justice. Every time, it fails. In August, the family of Tanya Day was 'devastated and angry' when told that no criminal charges would be laid against police over her death. The Yorta Yorta grandmother was arrested in 2017 in Castlemaine for public drunkenness, while *sleeping* on a train to Melbourne.

The Hares & Hyenas team were also angry when IBAC released its report in April, finding that police had acted lawfully. IBAC declared the response was *not disproportionate*—this despite witnesses describing Dimopoulos screaming in pain, hunched in the gutter, cuffed tightly with rigid plastic restraints and surrounded by cops in riot gear, holding semi automatic weapons. Two month later, Dimopoulos announced he is suing the state government to demand compensation for his physical and mental injuries.

Just why were the police barging into the residence above Hares & Hyenas, an iconic queer community hub? The cops claim a case of 'mistaken identity'. It seems Dimopoulos was 'relaxing in a residence while brown'. This echoes the experience of so many Black, Indigenous and People of Colour (BIPOC), who routinely complain of random police interactions for 'driving while Black' or shopping, sleeping, waiting to collect take-away, travelling on public transport, walking, or a range of other everyday activities. Dimopoulos was racially profiled by police looking for a Lebanese man.

Racial profiling is rife. Korey Penny, a highly skilled Aboriginal worker, is one of six people in the country who can operate the multi-million-dollar tunnel boring machine used on the Melbourne Metro Tunnel project. In

September, the Noongar construction worker was travelling to work on his bike, carrying the required permit. Penny was racially vilified and brutally attacked by Victoria Police, then taken by ambulance to hospital with serious injuries. Like Dimopoulos, this was a case of mistaken identity. Penny is a member of the Australian Workers Union. The union's Victorian Secretary told *The Age*, 'His only crime was to be riding a pushbike to work. Would he have been treated the same way if he had been white and wearing a suit and tie? Obviously not'.

I spoke with Samia Goudie, a queer Bundjalung woman, who told me, 'When we are stopped by the police, we have to respond to the inevitable comment that we *must* have done something wrong! For those of us who are Black, gay, or refugee, we face this oppression every day, it lives on our bodies. Being queer, Aboriginal, and a woman is a triple whammy.'

She spoke about police indifference when those from oppressed communities are the targets of crime: 'I lived in Sydney for years when gay men were disappearing off cliffs, and there was little police interest in finding out how they died.'

Reflecting on 2020, she says the fight to stop racial profiling and over-incarceration and to hold police accountable is long and continuing. 'I was struck that it took the police murder of George Floyd, a Black man in the U.S., to focus mainstream attention on what's happening here. The epidemic of deaths in custody has continued for decades. So have the scandals of kids tortured in Don Dale Youth Detention Centre or an Aboriginal child charged for receiving stolen property after a friend gave them a Freddo Frog. And we have the death of David Dungay, whose last words were the same as those of George Floyd, *I can't breathe.* The wave of Black Lives Matter (BLM) protests galvanised First Nations who latched onto the moment *demanding* to be heard! Young people are playing a particularly inspiring role.'

Lesbian activist Michelle Reeves is a member of the Indigenous Social Justice Association, a group campaigning to stop Aboriginal deaths in custody. She says, 'BLM has been instrumental in raising awareness around the impacts of over-policing on the BIPOC community in Australia, and has grown to include the Black Trans Lives Matter movement, representing the heightened risks of violence faced by the trans community.

Reeves is passionate about the need to build alliances, noting that 'across marginalised communities we hear similar stories arising from increased policing'.

Health crisis increases police powers

The rise of the pandemic in 2020 has exacerbated these issues with police granted sweeping new powers. This makes the situation much worse for

BIPOC, queer youth, homeless people, those living with a mental illness and other community members who are routinely criminalised, such as sex workers.

Reeves explains the impact on the LGBTIQA+ community, which 'faces high suicide rates, family violence, homelessness and reduced access to healthcare services. None of these issues can be solved by a police response, yet a police response is what we're likely to receive in a crisis. Increased police powers give police a greater ability to patrol our communities. Emergency laws impact vulnerable youth who are at increased risk of family rejection due to homophobia and transphobia.'

Increased police powers are devastating for First Nations. Reeves says, 'High police interaction rates translate to higher rates of arrest and risks to both the person in custody and their community. The 1997 royal commission into Aboriginal deaths in custody recommended that jail be used as a last resort, yet here we are in 2020 seeing increased police powers in every state. These increase police interaction with the public and do not address the health emergency we have at hand.'

Goudie highlights that it is essential to stop powers becoming entrenched. She references the 2007 Northern Territory Intervention as an example of how so-called emergency powers can persist once in place. Introduced under the guise of concerns about child abuse, the Intervention suspended the Racial Discrimination Act and imposed heavy regulation on Aboriginal people's lives, with no consultation. These measures *still* exist today. 'We're seeing the same thing happening with COVID—the health issues are real but are being used to give more power to police, which means more racism, more homophobia and more violence weighing heavily on over-policed communities.'

Goudie, who has worked in health for much of her life, believes 'the mix of COVID and police is fraught. Measures put in place for health reasons can quickly slip into ongoing repression.' But she has no time for conspiracy theorists or anti-maskers: 'The number of people who make opposition to masks *the* focus for freedom has shocked me. This seems to be their first taste of their personal freedom being impacted! They should try being queer and Aboriginal.' She argues there is a need to have a good political anchor and to fight for democratic rights, noting that we don't have enshrined constitutional rights to free speech like they do in the U.S. If we had these guarantees here, this would be a tool to use in the fight against a creeping police state.'

Governments are using the pandemic as cover to allow more widespread use of surveillance technology, including automated number plate recognition, drones and systematic monitoring of social media. Protests organised in a COVID-safe manner, strictly adhering to health guidelines, are being suppressed—organisers being charged with incitement and slapped with hefty fines. In September, Victoria Police told the Refugee Action Collective that if they hold a media conference, they will be fined. 'It is outrageous that Victorian police have become the arbiters of who can hold media conferences, of who can speak and who cannot,' declares spokesperson, David Glanz.

Organising to win!

For the queer community, there are crucial lessons from the early days of the HIV/AIDS community. Faced with a health crisis, the community quickly recognised the political risks and got organised with clear demands. Analysing the situation, discussing solutions and formulating demands is urgently required.

Radical Women (RW) hosted an online event in June to do just this. The event, titled *Turn Rage Against Police Abuse into Rainbow Resistance*, honoured the Stonewall Rebellion. Thanks to the impact of gay liberation, murdered queers of colour are finally amongst those remembered as many march in t-shirts proclaiming *Black Trans Women's Lives Matter.* But it wasn't always like this. Queer visibility, recognition and respect in the movements had to be fought for—and in some quarters it still does. Something RW does with gusto!

Amelia Kirk-Harkin, contemporary artist, apprentice upholsterer and a member of the Construction, Forestry, Mining, Maritime and Energy Union, presented on behalf of Radical Women about the nature of the police. She explained that the role of police is to uphold the status quo. Working class people in their multi-hued, multi-gendered, rainbow diversity are all targeted by a system that protects capitalist profits, racism and patriarchy.

Kirk-Harkin discussed how public outrage and organising against police brutality rose to a new level in 2020. She had marched with the Radical Women and Freedom Socialist Party joint contingent in Melbourne's huge, disciplined, distanced, masked and very effective Black and Indigenous Lives Matter protest on 6 June. Drawing on this experience, she discussed the need to transform the expressions of rage that the global movement represents into a sustained movement for structural change, taking on the ruling class whose interests the cops protect.

Like Radical Women, many other opponents of police abuse want to bring this system down. Emma Russell also believes that to eradicate the abuse will require systemic change. She makes the case that, 'in 2020, the growth in visibility of radical movements challenging the foundational violence of policing makes clear that police reform has never and will never bring us closer to social justice. In the relatively short history of policing in Australia, it has always been weaponised to advance the intertwined projects of settler colonialism and capitalism. Police reform has played a key role in the maintenance of police legitimacy and power. Indeed, Victoria Police, as we now know it, was conceived as a reform to the disparate and brutal forces that were mobilised in the first decades of the colony of Port Phillip.'

But while working for the day when we have a system that delivers social justice for all, what can be done now?

There are important measures that would make a real difference for Nik Dimopoulos, Korey Penny and deaths in custody families, such as Tanya Day's children. We need to put an immediate end to the practice of police investigating police. Establish police review boards, elected from and controlled by the community, with powers to investigate, discipline, prosecute and sack police.

Demand the slashing of police budgets, and disarm the police! The five-year service contract for automated number plate recognition alone costs $17.3 million! Funding must be redirected to provide inclusive social services, job programs, free education and training, public housing, including for queer youth, and a free, quality public health system for all!

Support is growing amongst grassroots unionists to demand Victorian Trades Hall Council (VTHC) revoke the affiliation of The Police Association (TPA).

Michelle Reeves is a member of the Community and Public Sector Union (CPSU). She believes the union movement has an important role to play in the fight to curb police violence. 'It's so important to work within your union to build knowledge and material support for these struggles. With the groundswell of support for calls to remove police from VTHC, there's never been a better time to discuss the dangers of policing as a health emergency with your union branch and use our collective power as workers to create a better world.'

Members of Warriors of the Aboriginal Resistance, Meriki Onus, Tarneen Onus-Williams and Dr Crystal McKinnon, are unionists with the Australian Services Union and National Tertiary Education Union. They initiated an open letter to VTHC, calling on it to 'to stand against the police presence in the public housing towers and to permanently end the affiliation of TPA, including taking steps to ensure they are prevented from ever re-affiliating.' The letter attracted almost 2,000 signatures.

This campaign is resonating strongly with radical, BIPOC and LGBTIQA+ grassroots unionists. Help amplify this demand by contacting your union and urging support. Police out of the union movement! Cops are *not* workers: they serve the capitalist state against those it exploits and oppresses.

These demands can be won! Debbie Brennan, Melbourne Organiser for Radical Women agues, 'Calls to defund, disarm and put police under community scrutiny and discipline already have gained a lot of traction in the U.S., where policing has a long and brutal history—like here. George Floyd's murder was a flashpoint, which has galvanised and solidarised people across borders. Governments are responding by expanding police powers under the cover of COVID safety. A united front of resistance by all of us targeted is not just possible, it's necessary. This would be powerful.'

Brennan adds, 'The police are the armed force of an increasingly repressive state *and* protectors of an organised far right. By fighting to bring cops to heel, we would be pushing back against this double danger.'

On the day IBAC failed those hoping the cops would be held accountable, Police Minister Lisa Neville responded by 'thanking all police members for the work that they do.' *Their* job is to protect the interests of the class that rules—one that also relies on homophobia, transphobia, sexism and racism to pit us against each other. *Our* job is to disrupt the cozy status quo and build a movement, which holds police to account.

There are many ways to be part of building this movement—wherever you are in the country, I would love to hear from you and talk more about how you can contribute.

Alison Thorne

Alison Thorne is a member of Radical Women, a workplace delegate with the Community and Public Sector Union and a campaigner to stop deaths in custody, working with the Indigenous Social Justice Association—Melbourne. She is the managing editor of the Freedom Socialist Organiser. In 1983, she motivated the lesbian and gay community to recognise HIV as a political crisis as well as a health challenge, calling for united and collective organising. Contact her at alison.thorne@ozemail.com.au

Further reading

Freedom Socialist Party statement—Why increased police powers are not COVID Safe and How to resist: https://socialism.com/fso-article/why-increased-police-powers-are-not-covid-safe-and-how-to-resist/

Radical Women Statement—Black women's lives matter: https://www.radicalwomen.org/Black-Womens-Lives-Matter.shtml

Indigenous Social Justice Association campaign—Support the call for police out of Victorian Trades Hall: http://www.isjamelbourne.com

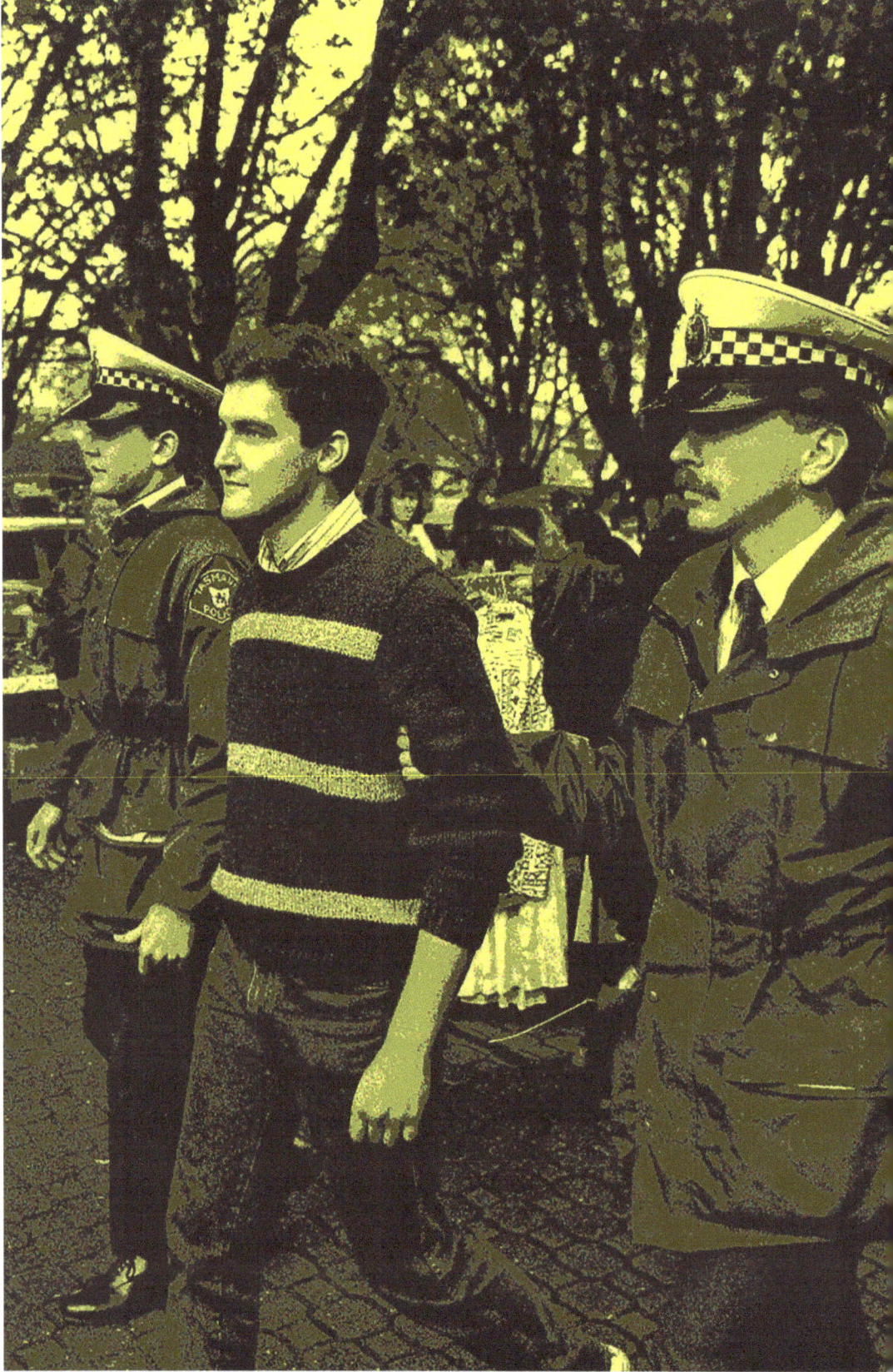

ANOTHER WORD FOR HOPE
Rodney Croome

In December 2019 the University of Tasmania conferred an honorary doctorate on Rodney Croome in recognition of his achievements. This is Rodney's address following the conferral.

Your Excellency, Chancellor, Vice-Chancellor members of the University, graduates and diplomates, esteemed guests …

Thank you to the University of Tasmania for this great and humbling honour, all the more so because of my long association with the University since I was an undergraduate.

My partner Rafael, my mother Bev, and some of my dearest friends, are here today to share this moment with me. To you, along with all those who can't be here, including my late father, I say 'thank you', 'thank you' for your love, your support, your respect, your patience and your faith in me.

I also want to pay tribute to those teachers at High School in Devonport and here at University who showed me all change begins with knowing what might be possible, and that such knowledge comes from interpreting and applying the lessons of those who have gone before us.

In 1987, as a shy University of Tasmania history student, I came out as gay man into an island society that was deeply antagonistic to LGBTIQ equality.

In Tasmania, sex between men was a crime punishable by 21 years in gaol.

Tasmania was the only state that stigmatised transgender people as criminals by outlawing cross-dressing.

There was a blanket silence about LGBTIQ people that had lasted since colonial times when homosexuality and gender transgression was intimately associated with the hated stain of convictism.

At the first gay community meeting I attended I was warned there might be police outside waiting to write down the car registration numbers of those leaving the meeting to add to their 'pink list' of 'known homosexuals'.

When we set up a small stall at Salamanca Market asking for signatures on a gay law reform petition, the stall was closed down and we were all arrested.

When gay law reform was first proposed in Parliament, angry, hateful protest rallies were conducted across the state.

While other Tasmanians believed they lived in a democracy, LGBTIQ Tasmanians lived in a police state.

It was a police state most Tasmanians were then happy to maintain. Polls showed almost 70% support for criminalising homosexuality, well above the national average.

Now, let's move forward to today.

Tasmania has the most progressive LGBTIQ human rights laws, not only in Australia but in the entire world.

Our *Anti-Discrimination Act* provides stronger protections for LGBTIQ people than its counterparts elsewhere.

Our relationship laws recognise a broader range of personal relationships than in other places.

Our gender laws provide stronger recognition and protection for transgender and gender diverse people than the equivalent laws of almost any other country.

Our state parliament led the nation on marriage equality.

Our police now have the policies so inclusive they are a global model.

We have led the other states when it comes to apologising for the past and healing old wounds.

These changes in laws and policies have been matched by changes in hearts and minds with Tasmania returning a vote in the marriage postal survey that was above the national average and second only to Victoria among the states.

In a generation, as the Vice Chancellor has noted already, Tasmania has gone from worst to best.

We have every reason to call ourselves the Rainbow Island.

The history of this spectacular transformation is long and sometimes painful.

It was only possible because many people worked together to pool their talents and encourage each other, people from across the political, religious and cultural spectrum who put fundamental values of equality and inclusion above their traditional differences.

It was only possible because we took risks that more cautious people warned us against,

…because we told truths that were hard for some people to hear

…because we protested the old laws, and the attitudes behind those laws, bravely, forthrightly but always respectfully, and

…because we refused to accept compromises that might have made the climb less steep.

Most of all it was only possible because we told our personal stories about what it meant to be treated like second-class citizens.

We had faith that if we reached out to our fellow Tasmanians they would heed us.

Based on that faith we travelled across the island and spoke about our lives to whomever would listen.

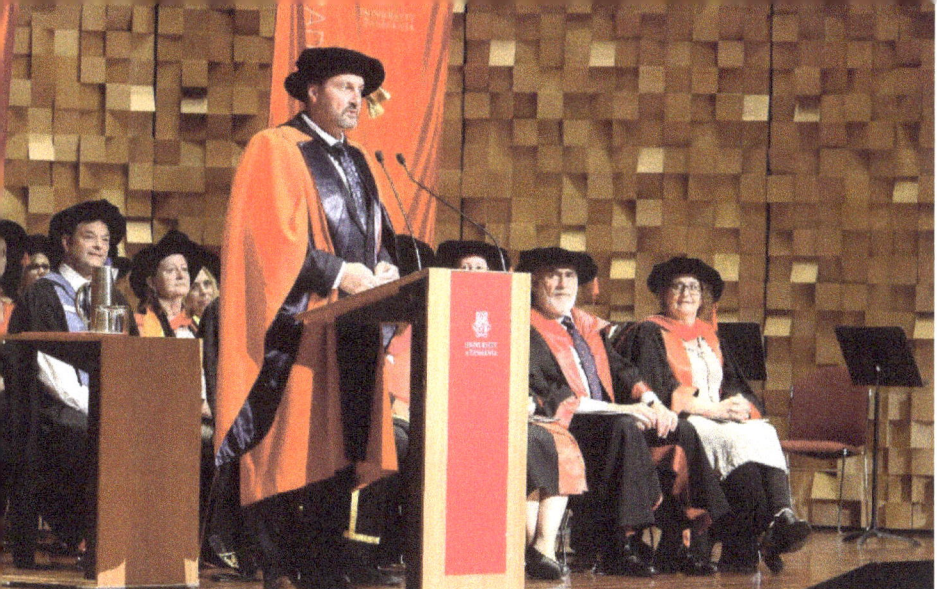

We opened our hearts to others and explained what it meant, not only to be discriminated against and stigmatised, but to be told you don't belong in the place that has shaped who you are.

We refused to react in kind to the fear and anger so vocally striding the stage of Tasmanian public life. We looked beyond the prejudices of those around us and instead saw in our fellow Tasmanians people who, deep down, wanted to do the right thing. We educated, and never berated.

If I am proud of anything more than how far we have come, it is that our faith in our fellow citizens was well-founded.

Among the lessons taught by Tasmania's transformation, there is one particularly pertinent to us today. Many of us feel pessimism or despair about the great problems of our age. We fear there is nothing we can do about spiralling climate change, escalating inequality and creeping authoritarianism.

When you feel discouraged and powerless, recall how this tiny corner of the planet defied every expectation to pull itself up by its rainbow bootstraps and re-invent itself.

Take heart that, if an island that once tore itself apart over LGBTIQ equality can become a beacon of inclusion to the entire world, there is nothing inevitable about the problems we face, profound change is possible, and each of you can be part of that change.

Have faith in other people and in the future. Always remember there is another word for hope, and that word is Tasmania.

Rodney Croome AM is an LGBTI rights activist and academic. He worked on the campaign to decriminalise homosexuality in Tasmania, and was a founder of Australian Marriage Equality. He has worked on LGBTI discrimination and parenting law reform, and on LGBTI issues in education, health and policing.

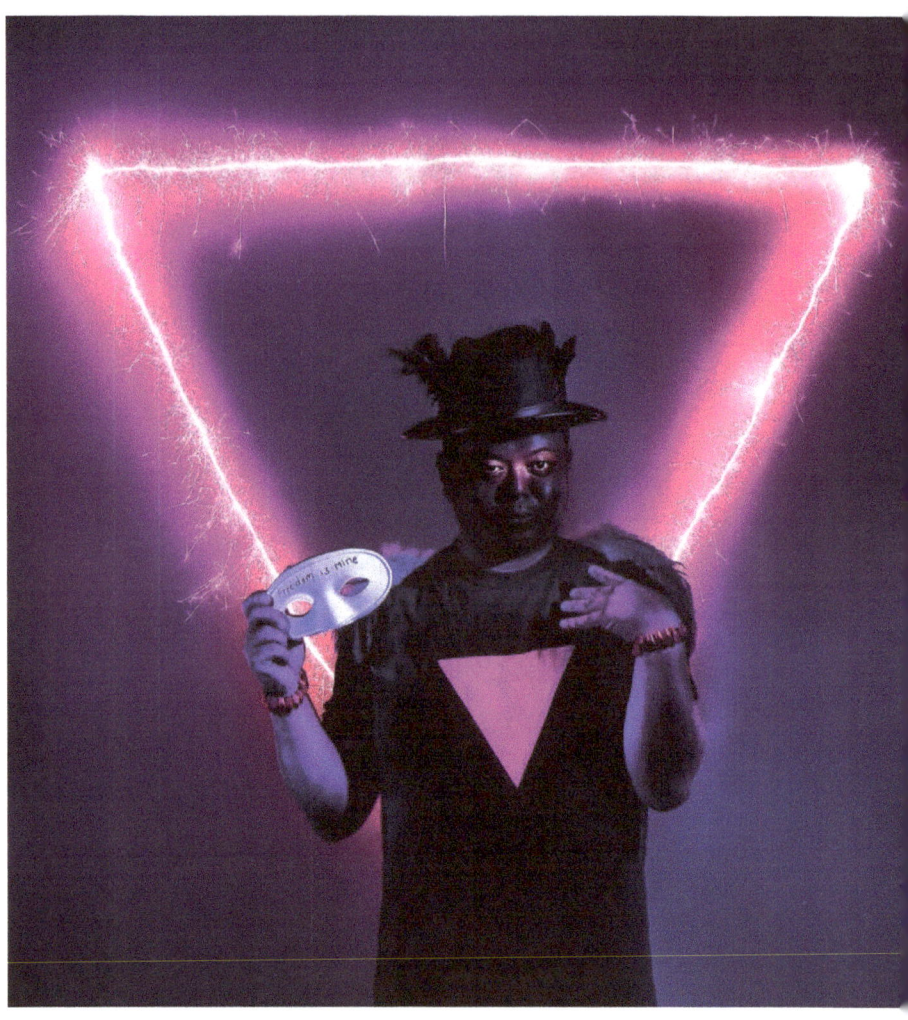

Image: Peter Casamento

MANY COLOURED SKY
Ian Seal

Ian Seal details the work of Many Coloured Sky and a recent photographic exhibition involving queer asylum seekers

Many Coloured Sky, the Queer Development Agency, partners in the development of a range of projects and activities that are driven by the

WHEN I WAS LIVING ON THE STREET, A WOMAN USED TO BRING ME CLOTHES AND FOOD. I TOLD HER SHE DIDN'T HAVE TO HELP ME, BUT SHE SAID SHE WANTED TO. I FELT LIKE SHE WAS MY MOTHER. I WANTED TO BE HONEST WITH HER AND TELL HER I HAVE A GAY HEART. BUT ONE DAY SHE WARNED ME AGAINST LGBT PEOPLE – 'THEY ARE SICK' SHE SAID. IT BROKE MY HEART BECAUSE I TRUSTED HER AND WANTED TO SHARE MY TRUTH WITH HER, BUT SHE WOULDN'T ACCEPT ME. I'M TIRED OF PEOPLE JUDGING ME WHEREVER I GO. I'M TIRED. IT'S EXHAUSTING. I WANT TO LIVE FREE. I WANT TO FLY FREE

hopes, dreams, strengths and ideas of the LGBTQI+ communities and individuals we work with—peer to peer, Queer to Queer. We provide capacity building and technical support and funding, engage key stakeholders, develop programs and strategies focused on building sustainable change and advocate for LGBTQI+ rights everywhere.

In Kenya we have a partnership with the LGBTQI+ refugee-led Refugee Coalition of East Africa, an umbrella organisation for many smaller queer refugee groups in Kenya. We provide them with funding, technical support and capacity building. We have a project supporting young queers in Uganda who have been forced to flee their homes, schools and communities, a very large project based in the Philippines and focused on LGBTQI+ young people across SE Asia, and we support a number of LGBTQI+ groups in

Indonesia. We're currently developing a new project in partnership with a group for gay and bisexual young men in PNG.

In Victoria, Many Coloured Sky is supporting almost sixty queer asylum seekers from five continents who now live in Melbourne or regional centres, in partnership with Uniting Victoria Tasmania. This number was less than 30 at the start of 2020, but since the advent of COVID-19 the number has more than doubled. People seeking asylum in Australia are not eligible for Job Seeker and Job Keeper payments, and many of them work in casual and

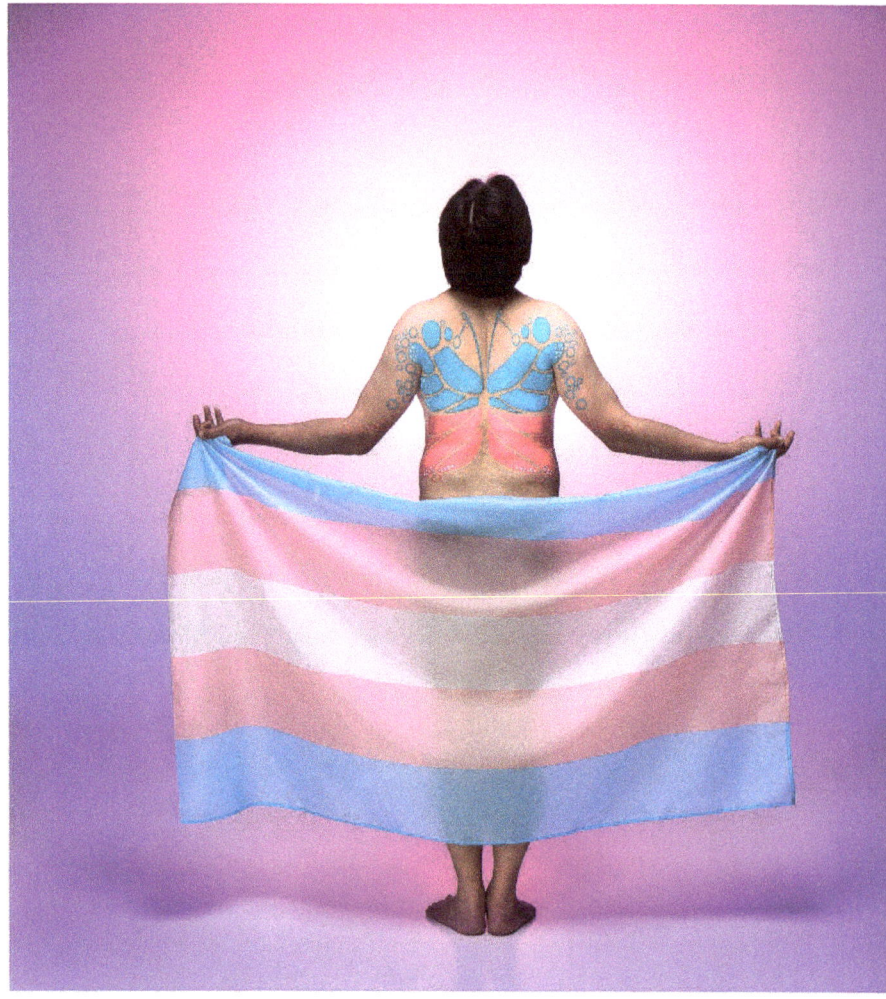

Image: Peter Casamento

marginal employment that disappeared quickly as lockdowns began. Since the onset of the pandemic we also support a small but growing group of LGBTQI+ international students, who have also been left out of government income supports. We employ a gay asylum seeker as a Peer Support and Community Development Officer, and we undertake a range of community development and capacity building strategies to support the growing peer-led group Queer Refugee and Asylum Seeker Peers, which has developed from our partnership with Uniting and is now actively working towards becoming

MY LIFE IS LIKE THAT OF A BUTTERFLY. I HAVE BEEN LIKE A CATERPILLAR— INSIDE A BODY THAT IS TEMPORARY AND NOT TRUE TO WHAT IS INSIDE. RIGHT NOW, I AM DEVELOPING AND GROWING, STILL HIDDEN IN SOME WAYS BY THE CHRYSALIS, BUT GAINING COURAGE AND CONFIDENCE. I AM STRONG. DESPITE ADVERSITY, I WILL CONTINUE TO FLOURISH. I WILL BE TRUE TO MYSELF. I WILL SPREAD MY WINGS LIKE A GLORIOUS BUTTERFLY WITH THE CONFIDENCE AND FREEDOM TO BE ME.

an independent organisation. Since COVID, all of our programs have become much more challenging. While continuing to focus on long-term strategy and capacity building where we can, we are now providing emergency support to most of our partner communities around the world, covering food, medication and other needs to the extent that we can, including for the group here in Melbourne. We are a small, registered charity relying mostly on donations from individuals, which are fully tax deductible.

Early this year (just prior to COVID) we launched a portrait exhibition of queer asylum seekers to raise awareness of their multiple challenges. The exhibition allowed participants to share some of their experiences while also protecting their identities. We plan to continue growing, sharing and touring the exhibition in a range of spaces as the pandemic and our finances allow. Please check out our website www.manycolouredsky.org or contact us for further information via mail@manycolouredsky.org. LGBTQI+ refugees, asylum seekers and international students in Victoria can also contact us via peersupport@manycolouredsky.org. Queer Refugee and Asylum Seeker Peers operates only in Victoria but if you live elsewhere we can try to assist you in finding local or online support.

Ian Seal is the Executive Director of THREE for All Foundation, of which Many Coloured Sky is the Queer Development arm. Ian identifies as queer and has worked in community and international development forever, especially in LGBTQI+ community development.

Clouds of Magellan Press is proud to donate the proceeds from the sale of this edition of Bent Street *to Many Coloured Sky, in support of LQBTIQA+ asylum seekers and refugees in Australia and overseas.*

Other groups involved in refugee asylum seeker issues include:

Refugee Action Collective, Victoria
https://www.facebook.com/racvic | https://www.instagram.com/rac_victoria/
PO Box 578 Carlton South, Vic 3053

No Pride in Detention (Sydney)
https://www.facebook.com/noprideindetention/

Refugee Action Coalition, Sydney
https://www.facebook.com/RACsydney/
PO 433, Newtown NSW, 2042.

Refugee Action Collective, Queensland
Email: rac.qld.contacts@gmail.com
Mail: PO Box 8086, Woolloongabba, Qld 4102

Rainbow Refugees
https://chuffed.org/project/humans-in-need-rainbow-refugees

AS IF ...
Edwina Shaw

An excerpt from Edwina's memoir-in-progress 49 is a Dangerous Age.

'I'm just going to kiss you on the cheek,' Alex said, leaning over in the dark of the car as I dropped her off at the bus stop.

Then she opened the door and jumped out with a wave.

All that night, beside my sleeping husband, I lay awake, tossing and turning. What had she meant... just? Where else would she kiss me. On my lips? On the mouth? I couldn't sleep for thinking of all the different places she could kiss me.

Alex was a fellow writer I'd met at a festival. We'd discovered we were at the same university, that we knew many people in common. She told me she was gay, and I shrugged—so what? I told her that despite being married to a man for almost twenty years, I'd spent most of my life hanging out in the gay community. No worries.

But after that just it made all the difference. That flame, so elusive, had started up in my belly. Not a spark, not a small blue flicker– but a bushfire that was going to burn everything down.

The second time Alex and I went out, we went to a community writers' centre Christmas party. The moment she knocked on my door that night, I felt it—a tug like the world's most powerful magnet, drawing me to her. Inescapable. Through the evening, as we stood in the crowd listening to interminable speeches, though I tried not to, I found myself leaning towards her. Edging as close as I could to her. The smell of her skin was intoxicating. I fed her rich sticky brownie from my fingers and let them linger on her lips.

This tall beautiful dark-eyed woman had put some kind of spell on me. After the party we walked by the river and sat on the grassy bank watching the city lights reflecting on the water. We talked about the earth and the heart and the human condition. We laughed, and when she laughed the world looked brighter. When she laughed in the moonlight she looked like Julia Roberts. A smile that wide.

And she said things. Things my husband had never said. 'I've been looking for you for such a long time.' And, 'You're so beautiful, so very beautiful.' And, 'I'd love to make you scream.'

She also said, 'I'm not a good person.' But I didn't believe her.

That night when we sat down by the river, she told me her relationship with her girlfriend was over, that they hadn't really been together for five years. She was going to leave her, as soon as she got a job.

Alex said she was looking for a soul mate. She thought I was the one.

I didn't know what to say.

On the way to drop her off at the bus stop again—she didn't drive and lived far away in the outer suburbs—I gathered courage. 'I like you too. I really like you.' I didn't tell her that it hurt to say goodbye, that I had to be near her. Be with her. We'd only been out a couple of times. All I knew was I wanted her to touch me, to hold my hand, to lean closer so I could feel the warmth of her. I wanted her to kiss me. More than anything. But she didn't.

At the bus station, she hugged me. I didn't even get a peck on the cheek. After all she'd said.

I couldn't sleep.

What the fuck was going on? I was married with two children almost grown. I had a husband who still loved me, I thought. It was hard to tell.

For many years I'd felt as if I was struggling to keep my marriage alive alone. All of the conversations I had with my husband about our relationship consisted of me talking, mainly to myself. I'd ask a question, but he'd only respond with a facial expression—a raised eyebrow, a half-smile or a frown or a grimace. I'd interpret it however I could. I have an active imagination, I'm a writer after all; I could interpret those expressions in a myriad of ways. Some expressions gave me hope. Others filled me with grief. It was the grimace in bed that killed our marriage, the night I'd given us one last chance. He hadn't known it was our last chance, then. But it was.

By that stage, I'd known something life-changing was happening with Alex. I hadn't told her about my feelings yet, only that I enjoyed her company, that I loved spending time with her and hanging out. Nothing had happened between us sexually, though kissing her, fucking her, was all I could think about. But I was married, and I wasn't going to cheat on my husband if he still loved me. If there was any hope of reviving our relationship.

After that second outing with Alex, it was my wedding anniversary— twenty years. To celebrate, I went to dinner with my husband but trying to prise conversation from him was like pulling weeds from a bone-dry clay bed. So different from the effervescent conversations I had with Alex that I never wanted to end. Then, that night in bed, he grimaced.

That grimace was the final clod of earth on the coffin of our love. I only really realised then that our romantic and intimate connection had been dead and buried a long time. For many years I'd tried to revive the corpse but had never succeeded. All that time I'd fought and cried and begged, but all I ever got back was a shrug or a half-smile.

Earlier that year, about six months before Alex turned up, I'd gone back to school-teaching: an effort to appease my husband's anger at my lack of financial success as a writer. Unfortunately, I was landed with a class of wild young refugee kids who broke my heart and made me roar at them like an angry goddess. They pushed me to the very edge. I had come home from a day of this teaching horror story and was writing in my journal, exhausted, completely emotionally drained after the failure of my latest novel manuscript to sell, pulverized by my students. I cried.

My husband came over to where I was writing and crying over my journal. 'I've been meaning to say you should stop writing,' he said.

Suddenly I felt as awful as I did as a suicidal teenager. Writing was the only thing holding me together, yet my partner couldn't understand that— after all our years together, he didn't seem to know me at all. That may have been when I stopped bending over backwards trying to keep our marriage alive. Consciously, all I knew was that I couldn't go on like that.

After that second time out with Alex, I started writing her emails, telling her how much I enjoyed her company, finding things to share I thought she'd like. I started sharing my works in progress with her. She sent back pieces she'd written. I loved her writing and for me that was important. She was a dream I hadn't even known I'd had come true—a best friend and lover all in one sexy package. I felt like I was falling in love for the first time, though I'd fallen in love with my husband and thought I'd loved my previous lovers too.

But with Alex it felt different: proper, grown up love. I knew love was supposed to be like this—this meeting of minds and hearts, not just bodies.

We started seeing each other very day. I couldn't get enough of her, couldn't get close enough. We made excuses to our partners and made plans to see each other again and again and again. We still hadn't kissed. A few weeks of this and I was beside myself. I couldn't eat. Every night I lay awake beside my husband, my mind filled with Alex.

One afternoon I found myself sitting with her in my backyard, telling her in a low voice, so my children wouldn't overhear me, 'I think I'm falling for you… I can't help it.'

Whatever it is that binds two hearts was at work, some otherworldly magic had brought me a person my soul drank in like nectar. I felt as if Alex understood exactly who I was without me having to explain it, we seemed to resonate at the same frequency. Whatever that magnet is that draws lovers together, it was a hundred-fold with her. If love with my husband when I was a young traveller in the 90s was a ripple, this was a wave. A tidal wave.

Suddenly everything seemed to make sense. I was a dyke! I knew it. But still, even after sleeping with girls in my teens and twenties, it felt strange to be so sexually attracted to another woman. It didn't matter. Whoever Alex was, I would have fallen in love with her. But she was a woman, a beautiful woman, and I couldn't wait to spend the rest of my life with her, kissing her, fucking her, sleeping in her arms.

Trouble was, she was leaving. She'd told me as we sat by the river that night that she was travelling with her girlfriend over to Europe to study for six months; it hadn't seemed important then. As our love grew it became a horrible obstacle. Alex said she couldn't get out of it, flights were booked, studies were enrolled in, accommodation was already paid for. They were leaving in only a few weeks. She had to go. It didn't seem fair; we'd only just found each other. It made us even more desperate for time together. But still we hadn't done anything more sexual than sit outside my local shopping centre holding hands, her long fingers gently stroking my inner wrist. I was going mad.

We didn't have anywhere to go. I couldn't take her to my place, not when all I wanted to do was kiss her. It wasn't right.

'We shouldn't kiss,' she said. 'It will only make the missing worse.'

I didn't care. I only knew I needed to sleep, and I couldn't, because every night I lay awake thinking about her lips, her mouth on my breasts. Her tongue between my legs. 'I'd like to make you scream,' she'd said that night by the river. I wanted her to do just that.

Alex was struggling behind her wide smile. I knew she'd had a troubled life, but I believed our love could heal anything.

One day, I took her on a picnic to a mountain rainforest park not far from the city. It was cloudy and a little rainy, so after a walk we had the place to ourselves. We stretched out on a blanket and ate chocolate. We lay facing each other, and then moved closer. So close we were sharing the same pillow. We leaned our foreheads together and then, finally, finally, she kissed me. We lay on that rug until the sun set, pulling it under the cover of a giant fig tree when it started to rain, kissing, entwining like one great amorphous kissing creature. Our 'one kiss' we called it, because it never stopped. Except when I had to drive her back down the mountain to the bus stop.

The next day we went for another drive and found another secluded place where we could be alone—a small-town graveyard that backed onto a quiet lake. We kissed more. And more. For that whole day we kissed. Eight hours of kissing.

That was the day I told her.

'Have I told you I love you yet?' I asked.

'I think you just did.'

I didn't know if I had actually spoken out loud, because the words had been running constantly in my head for so long, I thought she could probably see them written across my forehead.

The kissing didn't cure me though. I still couldn't sleep. I felt as if I would never be able to rest properly again until I was in a bed with her, breathing the same breath. I felt certain I was going to spend the rest of my life in her arms. That in those beautiful long limbs I would find a new home and a truly exceptional relationship that was both best friend and lover. It felt as if our love was meant to be, that the stars had finally aligned. I couldn't fight it.

I had to sleep with her.

'We shouldn't,' she said. 'It will only make it worse when I leave.'

'I don't care, I don't care, I don't care.' I slid my hands down the back of her pants. 'You can't go without it happening. I'll go mad!'

That Christmas was surreal. In between secret passionate rendezvous with my lesbian lover I was shopping for family Christmas presents, preparing food and performing all the usual Christmas festivities with my extended family. All the while nursing the delicious secret. A friend was going away and needed someone to look after her pets. She offered me her place as a love nest for the last few days before Alex took off for Europe.

I invited Alex over to my friend's place.

Finally, we were alone.

'Take off your clothes and get into bed,' she said. And we were on. She told me to 'surrender to the moment' with a wicked grin and did things to me that no one had ever done before.

I called out her name over and over.

As we slept together, I would have followed her anywhere, all over the world. Wherever she went I wanted to be with her, beside her, inside her. I wanted to marry her, make her my wife. I was ready to leave everything for her. My job, my husband, even my children. I would follow her to Europe, and we would live happily ever after.

When we paused in our marathon of lovemaking, exhausted and flooded with pleasure, she gazed into my eyes and said, 'I love you deeply. I love you truly. I love you always.'

As if she meant it with all her heart.

I believed her.

Edwina Shaw is the author of *A Guide Through Grief—First Aid for your Heart and Soul, Thrill Seekers, In the Dark of Night* and over 40 short pieces that have appeared in literary journals and anthologies including *Best Australian Stories*. She is the contributing editor of *Bjelke Blues* and co-editor of *Our Inside Voices*. She holds a Masters in Creative Writing and has been teaching creative writing at UQ and in the community for over 10 years.

www.edwinashaw.com

THE PANDEMIC HAD
SHIFTED HOW WE
THOUGHT ABOUT
HOW OR WHAT OUR
WEDDING MIGHT
LOOK LIKE AND
INDEED EVEN ITS
CENTRALITY TO US
AND OUR FRIENDS IN
A WORLD THAT HAD
TURNED GHASTLY
OVERNIGHT

PERIWINKLE BLUE
Erin Riley

The wedding's off, but something else is on …

When you google image search 'shades of blue' tables filled with all the blues appear across the screen. There is navy blue, cobalt, steel, spruce, electric, Persian, oxford, ultramarine. There is berry blue, indigo and Egyptian blue. Sky blue. Azure, Airforce and bleu de France.

I was googling all the blues because there was a blue that sat, deftly, on the tip of my tongue. A blue I had forgotten. It was the colour of blue that covered the outside of the tiniest most delightful terrace house my partner Merryn and I had just bought together. I was trying to write the letter we had long avoided writing. A note to tell our friends that we would not be getting married as we'd planned in November. The pandemic had halted that situation, for now. We knew it was impossible to have the kind of party we had dreamed about with our friends who were locked inside—their only holiday to a shop within five kilometres. The pandemic had shifted how we thought about how or what our wedding might look like and indeed even its centrality to us and our friends in a world that had turned ghastly overnight. Each weekend we'd promise to send out our note and each Sunday would roll by without us having written anything. It was as if every weekend we pushed back against reality, staving off sadness, hoping our denial might fuel an alternate reality.

What is the colour of our new house? I asked Merryn after work. I did all the googling and it was not an easy find, but Merryn knew.

Periwinkle blue. Though it is often disguised as lavender.

That's it. I put it in our note. Told our favourite people that we'd not be getting married in Summer but that we had poured our love and commitment to each other into a tiny periwinkle blue terrace in Erskineville.

There is a lot of privilege in both of these things—the getting married and buying a home. Many, myself included, appreciate that in a world that remains so unequal and unjust, these are not often at the top of queer people's lists of life-dreams. Many have hesitations and complicated feelings about participating in the theatrics of homo-normativity—particularly the desire to enter into an institution that long slammed the door in the faces of queer people.

As queers—despite the privilege we have, as white people from families who have been supportive of our queer lives, educated and with stable work—both of these things for a long time felt out of reach. So far out of reach they weren't even aspirations. For years, I perceived queers wanting to get married as blind to the dangers of capitalism. I was ok for the institution to be entered into and used to support continent-scattered lovers gain citizenry, yet I still opposed it—out of dogged principle.

Marriage is mostly culturally appreciated as monogamous and an institution that promotes traditional-types of relationships. For radical queers, queers entering into these dusty old dynamics were seen as diluting their own radical histories and solidifying a technology of social control. Getting gay married is seen by its critics as way of queers assimilating, of shoring up a rubbish institution—of buying into media hype that somehow marriage is the gateway to a meaningful life.

And here I am, still thinking it's rubbish and needs dismantling. With my complicated feelings about my own complicity. I don't believe my getting married neglects the violence of the institution, nor do I think my not getting married undercuts or dismisses wholly the struggles of queer and trans justice more generally. There is an argument that says queer marriage just puts a shine on a system that has always been harmful and that queers entering harmful systems won't change social or cultural outcomes for people who live on the margins—that marriage's deeper sexist, colonial, racist structures remain. .

We live in a deeply imperfect world. I held onto radical queer ideas because this was what I thought I needed to do. I hold them still, but with a less vice-like grip. I hold them with a sense of hope that things can sit together and that I am imperfect. A living and messy contradiction.

It is an individual desire, in a world that remains still so virulently homophobic and transphobic, to want to have something that culture and society has long denied to you—even if it's mythology. Even though I thought I didn't want it, I think, for many queer people, we internalise some of this—and deny ourselves the things (or even the idea of things—for maybe that's all it is?) that might give us joy. Things we can re-make, re-story and re-purpose.

Sure, marriage doesn't do much for unpicking the structural inequalities that infect queer and trans lives, but still I want to stand up in my finest outfit, with my budding moustache and tell my favourite people how much my partner means to me, how they have made my life profoundly joyful and commit to this life together—as a team. So much of my existence has been about other people's comfort. It has been about blending in and not making too much noise.

It is just simpler to me now.

I am making a home and this is what it looks like.

After the auction we farewelled Merryn's dad Stewart. Stewart, a paediatric oncologist, was on call for the afternoon. Merryn, their mum, Jill, and I walked in a sort of hazy elated daze up the street to have a coffee. I called my parents. I put them on loudspeaker—*we bought a house!* They were thrilled for us—yelping and congratulating burst though crackly reception. I called my aunt who had helped us out with a very generous loan and left a message on her answering machine.

We drove Jill back home over the harbour bridge—our nervous systems flooded with adrenaline. *What the actual fuck* said our eyes. We continued to look at each other in disbelief. Someone had died in a tragic head on collision on the harbour bridge just two days earlier. It felt almost unfair to be so happy—to think of the losses of others. That someone's dreams and hopes had been dashed, lives instantly thrown into grief while our future simultaneously felt profoundly bright.

Driving home again, over the bridge to our rented unit.

What do we do now? We just bought a house!

What do you even do? No appetite yet—out hearts were in our mouths. Until Merryn took mine out and suggested we go home and fuck.

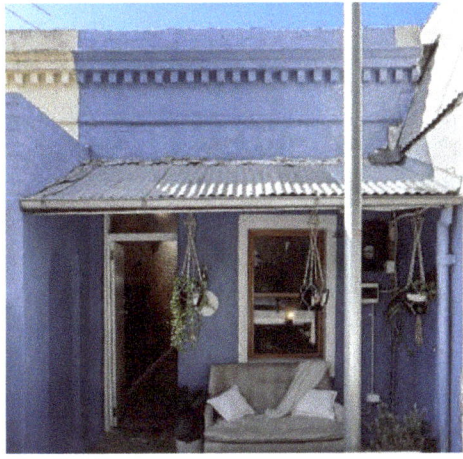

There's something nice about fucking when you know that it's been put on the list of plans for the day. You just know the fucking is going to happen. I appreciate these conversations when they happen, like on auction day—at least half an hour from home and in a very matter of fact way. Like talking about what's needed at the shops, or going to the gym. Later, soon enough, the plan is we are going to fuck each other. It's really hot. No fucking about, so to speak. I think this is a good thing for me sometimes, because it avoids the anxious moments you might have with a partner where you're not sure if they want to have sex or just keep making out for a while. Those are spontaneous moments which are hot in a different way, in their unpredictability—but there is something wild to me about the nod of the head that happens when we plan like that.

I nod at Merryn in the car in Harriet Street Cremorne Point and quietly imagined the fucking that would happen later. The fun part about making fucking a task of the afternoon and there being many conversations in between, mostly about whether to reseal the wall after settlement or if we should get Terry the electrician, who over-shares but is sweet and kind, to fix the dodgy wiring, is that the reminder to get on with the task is also one that can be done in a similarly pragmatic fashion.

Are you ready to go into the bedroom?

We were drinking tea on the couch while continually repeating to each other *we bought a house* because it still felt as if body snatchers had acted on our behalf at the auction and this was not our actual life.

I'll just wash up these cups.

And so, I went into our bedroom overlooking the pool and stripped down to my undies and my singlet while Merryn took a piss.

I like for layers to come off when we fuck—but I wanted to make it easier for Merryn. I enjoy these rituals, they feel strangely adult, disconnected and transactional but also intentional and in no way less hot. This is important—let's make time. This is important—let me piss first. And so Merryn finds me, their faggot prince in white ribbed cotton, lazy and waiting. We fuck as the sun shines through our cream curtains. Just as we planned.

Once a week, we walk a small dog that belongs to some busy psychiatrists. It is a job that brings both of us a lot of joy. The small dog's name is Fizzy and she is mostly ignored at home—her family working, schooling, forgetting her milling around their feet. And so, she comes with us in the car—and we take her to all the parks we know. Sometimes we'll take her to the beach—though she is not a fan of water. She is a beautiful sight, our Fizzy, who is part sausage dog, part kelpie. Many passers-by look at her quizzically, some getting it right, others merely stating the obvious—*oh a big sausage dog!*

Fizzy is not one for balls, she just wants friends to run around with. She walks off the lead and doesn't run away and she turns back for reassurance when she runs a little too far—as if to get permission to keep playing. Fizzy's favourite person is Merryn—a thing we both share. When we pick her up and unlock the back fence, she writhes around in unadulterated ecstasy, jumping up and down, racing around in circles, trying to kiss our faces which are too far away for her. Barks of happiness come from deep inside her lumpy body and she is almost unable to contain her own joy. I haven't had my heart broken by a dog until I witnessed Fizzy catching a glimpse of her favourite human.

It was a Saturday when we bought the tiny periwinkle blue terrace. We had saved Fizzy for the afternoon—knowing she would be the salve our souls needed if we did not have the winning bid at the auction—which we thought might be our reality. She would be the perfect bookend to our day— no matter what happened.

Because we had spent so long celebratory fucking we had finally developed an appetite, and so, on the way to collect our weekly dog, we stopped off and got felafel rolls from our favourite Lebanese pizza joint. I put on my green raincoat with the warm fleecy insides and the enormous pockets. Winter was almost at its end—though the air was still crisp at 4pm. Merryn drove the car and I spent half the ride texting our favourite people our house news. Our faces flushed, oxytocin overloaded, we continued to look at each other, smiling at our good fortune. Still shocked by this new reality. *We bought a house.* We balanced felafel rolls, a crunchy oily mess full of garlic sauce, pickles, tomato and kalamata olives and fresh deep-fried green crispy felafel, on our knees, oil seeping through the wrapping between desperate mouthfuls.

We pulled into the driveway of Fizzy's house to the sounds of her familiar yelps. We drove her to Sydney Park—the dog wonderland which once upon a time was an enormous city rubbish tip but is now one of the most beautiful city parks around. Our new periwinkle blue terrace is only a few streets walk from Sydney Park. We have decided that we would like to see our new home, outside the madness of an auction and so once Fizzy has chased a few uninterested dogs around, we take ourselves to just stand outside our home and just look at it. We find some friends on the way—who we convince to come with us. *We bought a house today!* we say. There is it with its SOLD sticker and its wonky front door, with the triangular gap at the top big enough for a piece of pizza to slide right through. They are impressed and we stand across the road in the small park opposite and imagine the life we will have inside there soon.

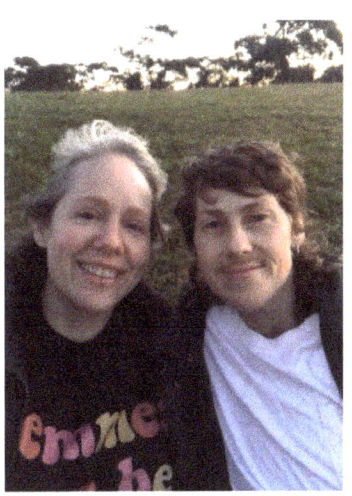

We stroll back through the streets of our new suburb back to the old tip. We let Fizzy off the lead and she runs and plays and comes back for reassurance and encouragement. Merryn gives this to Fizzy and she scuttles off again. We sit quietly on the edge of the park overlooking the city. Taking in one of the biggest days we have lived—a day where our commitment to doing life together has taken on new meaning— we hold each other gratefully as the sun sets and the air gets icy. We will be able to walk here soon—maybe with a dog of our own. Our future dog's name is Egg and we speak often about how much Egg will love it here in Sydney Park. Merryn says that it would be a crime against the dog community if we rescued a dog that did not like parks or other dogs. I agree. The sun begins to sets and we take a selfie with the green grassy hill behind us as we watch the light fade over the city—beaming into the camera.

After we had dropped Fizzy back home to the psychiatrists, we stopped by my mum and dad. They had spent the day with my sister and her family—dad was wiped out from endless block-building with Lilah, my two-year-old niece. Dad had bought a bottle of prosecco on the way home. Dad's love language is gift giving and he's really thoughtful that way. Holding onto small bits of information—what you like, what you need—he shows his care in the only way he really knows how. Once, when I worked at Civic Video Newtown, in my first stint living out of home and struggling to pay rent, I looked up at the next customer and it was dad, hands full of groceries.

So, we popped the champas, to celebrate the periwinkle blue terrace on the one-way street opposite the park that we still cannot comprehend is ours. We toasted this big life achievement and re-told our auction story. The audacity of my undercutting the vendor bid, Stewart and Jill with their duck bill face masks on either side of us whispering words of wisdom—reminding us to keep our cool. How before the auction we'd asked the agent whether the owners might be willing to add the fire pit into the contract and they did and now we have a house and a firepit.

I'm an easy drunk now. Though I still drink at the same pace I did when I wasn't as easy. We downed two glasses of bubbles and got to that sweet spot where the anxiety of family relating is dulled and things are just a little easier. I don't know how we got onto the topic of hands, but we did. Mum's sister, my aunt Dianne, who died a few years ago, had the most beautiful hands, mum reckons. She'd have them manicured and painted every week and on her deathbed in the palliative care unit in Greenwich Hospital—they were still painted bright red and beautiful. Mum recounted a story about a hand model from the 50s who did nothing in life but constantly wear gloves. She did nothing else in case she ruined them. No swimming, no washing dishes, no rock-climbing. What a wasted life.

I was instantly reminded of Nicole Kidman's strange clapping at the 2017 Oscars. Except she is not clapping really. She is slapping her palms together with her fingers outstretched, curving outwards as if her fingers were trying to escape their life attached to Nicole's hands. She is clapping as if she has flippers instead of hands. Clapping like a seal—her hands inverted parentheses protecting her 119 carats of diamonds, apparently. Like any good meme, when plucked from the crevices of memory, it provides the most gratifying laugh. My parents had not seen this video and I had completely forgotten it existed. We pulled it up on YouTube and watched it many times over and fell about laughing.

We drove home. I didn't post a photo on the internet about how we had just bought a home. It felt too showy for the current moment. We will tell people in time, we thought, but not on Instagram. Though I do post the photo of the two of us on the hill.

In the photograph, if you are looking at it, Merryn is on the left and I am on the right. We smile into the camera. Merryn's hair is wispy and tied back, though strands of it curl upwards and catch the last sunlight. Merryn's hair is mostly silver now, grey strands interrupted by snowy rivers and I never tell them this enough, but I am so into it, that salt and pepper. Dimples pierce both of Merryn's cheeks and pull at the edges of a toothy smile. I am smiling too—my face crinkled at the mouth and at the eyes. My wrinkles are ripples in a pool, retreating into my cheeks. My mullet, untrimmed since March, falls in barrel curls at my shoulders and the top sits flat and neat, as if a side part has asked the rest to walk in the other direction.

There is a lot of performativity in a selfie, though this photo lacks the orchestration usually reserved for the main page—which needs multiple takes for the perfect imperfect shot of a moment. In polyvagal theory, a bodily understanding of the role the nervous system plays in shaping understandings of safety, there is a concept called 'neuroception'. It is the ways in which we, unconsciously, respond to cues of safety from within our bodies. It is a seeking out for who is safe, approachable. It is our eyes that do this work— and it is in the wrinkles of the eyes where this seeking out begins. It communicates not only that we feel safe, but that we are safe for other people. In diving into polyvagal theory, I have learnt more about the face. And it is with this new obsession that I look at this photograph of us on the hill in Sydney Park.

There is a genuine smile and there is a social smile. I know that the genuine smile is also known as the Duchenne smile, after the 19th Century French physician Guillaume Duchenne who spent years studying facial expressions. In his smile—the eyes close, the cheeks move and the eyes crinkle at their edges. The muscles that move the cheeks are called the zygomatic major and those that wrinkle the eyes, the orbicularis oculi. Ours are well alive in this photo, they are dancing. We are sending cues far and wide that we are safe and we are home.

Erin Riley is a 36 y/o non-binary social worker who lives in Sydney. They have worked in aged care for most of the last decade but now work as a palliative care social worker in the (in)justice system at Long Bay Prison. Erin enjoys reading, making breakfast, routines that rarely change, riding their spin bike in the garage and endless cups of tea. Erin read 30 books in 2020 and has appreciated the time away from full time work to continue working on becoming a better writer.

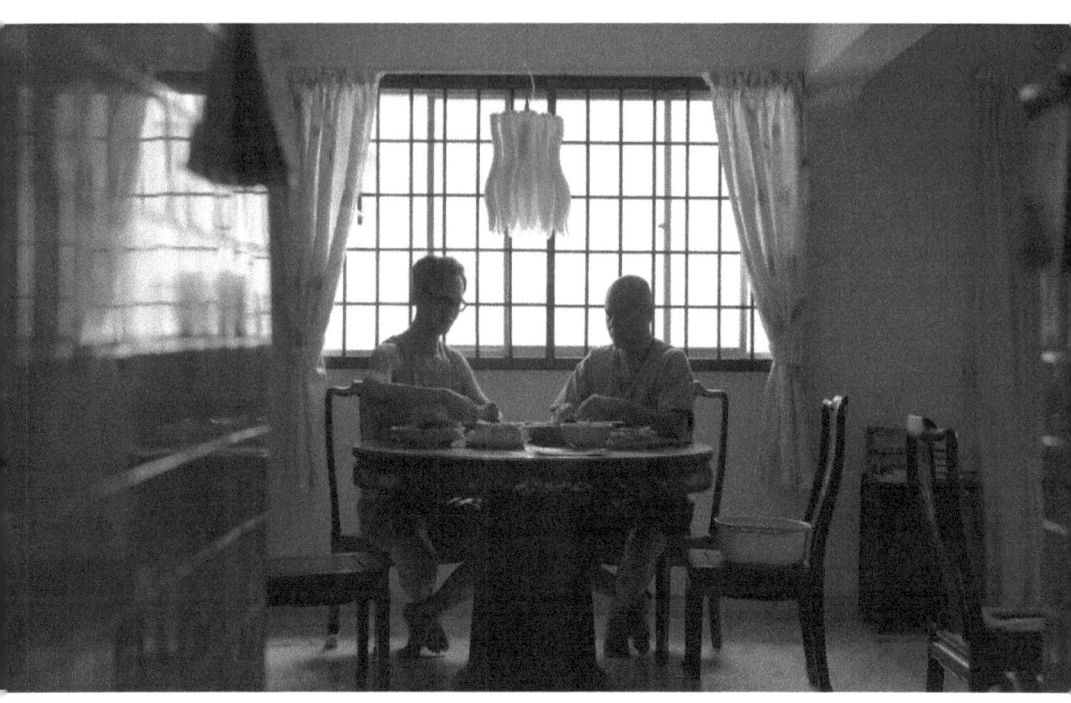

Still from *A Thousand Words Unspoken*. Derek Ho

UNSPOKEN
Derek Ho

Derek Ho writes about his newly released documentary.

Recently, I asked myself a question: How do I apologise for outing my brother when there are no memories of it? This difficult question required a complex answer. The result was the film, *A Thousand Words Unspoken*.

Thirty years ago, I outed my brother to our traditional Chinese parents in Singapore. My brother Jeremiah was twenty years old. I was thirteen and struggling with my own sexuality. It was, and still is to this day, illegal to be gay in Singapore due to the archaic penal code 377A the country inherited during its days as a British colony criminalising homosexuality.

I moved to Australia as an international student when I was twenty-one, carrying the dreams of one day becoming a film maker. I had also arrived during the heights of anti-Asian sentiments in the late 90s.

I literally became a minority overnight. As a gay Asian man who has struggled with discrimination from society at large and from within the gay community, due to my sexual orientation and race, it had led me to an experience that was deeply conflicted with self-acceptance. It took me a long time to find contentment and peace within.

While I have embraced my identity as a rainbow atheist in Australia, Jeremiah struggled with his life as a gay man in Singapore and spiralled out of control. It was during his darkest hours that he found hope in Christianity.

I often wondered about the downward spiral of my brother's life as a gay man and his recent denouncement of his sexual identity, and how much of that has got to do with his traumatic coming out experience that was caused by me. I know deep down whatever happened in the past can never be reversed. Making *A Thousand Words Unspoken* was the first step towards letting go of the guilt and forgiving myself while working towards reconciliation and acceptance with my family, especially my brother.

My documentary is a portrait of love and trauma, where two brothers find themselves navigating the space between trust, faith and healing. I am telling this very personal story for healing and closure. I also hope those who have doubted their value and existence can find strength from my story.

A Thousand Words Unspoken was first broadcast on 19 July 2020 by ABC Compass. The film has also been selected to screen at the Melbourne Documentary Film Festival and Shanghai Queer Film Festival. A review of A Thousand Words Unspoken by Rajesh Krishnamuti can be found on bentstreet.net.

GOODBYE TO ALL THAT?
Gina Ward

For me, 2020 was a year in which being queer took a back seat. While the pandemic has gone on changing the way I think about being old, white and a woman in a neoliberal world, it hasn't yet made me rethink what it means to be lesbian.

Don't get me wrong, I can see that lockdown's having a specific effect on queers, to the extent that 'Impact of COVID-19 on the LGBT community' has its own Wikipedia entry. There are as many young people wondering whether they might be queer in 2020 as in any other year but fewer ways for them to investigate or experiment. And the pandemic is making things even worse for anyone whose queerness has caused or exacerbated their poverty, isolation, homelessness or ill health, physical or mental.

On the other hand, it didn't take a pandemic to convince me that it's never easy to be a member of a marginalised group. When I say I haven't had to rethink what it means to be queer, I mean the pandemic hasn't forced or helped me to reassess my sense of what queerness *is*—although now I'm getting started on this optional reassessment, I can't help noticing that something about my sense of my identity has changed since the last time I looked.

One of the big changes is that I've increasingly been feeling as though I'm being asked to identify as LGBT or some even more inclusive acronym—LGBTQQIAAP+, for example. I'm definitely a lesbian and I'm happy to call myself gay or queer but I couldn't claim to be an ally, asexual, bisexual, intersex, questioning, pansexual or trans.

So where does this leave me? And where does it leave everyone else? Does anybody actually tick all the boxes in LGBTQQIAAP+? That's not just a rhetorical question: in the 1970s, when people used to use 'pregnant Jewish lesbian' as a synonym for 'ridiculously impossible', I had a friend who was black, Jewish, lesbian and a mother. But was the term LGBTQQIAAP+ ever intended to apply to one particular person?

I could, of course, sidestep these questions by deciding that the term LGBetc describes a way of organising, not a way of being. Organisations, from trade unions to multinational corporations, are often known by their initials, rather than by their key words, and loyalty to your social grouping is a classic form of identity: people have fought and died for acronyms like the IWW or the WSPU.

Then again, the International Workers of the World and the Women's Social and Political Union were actual organisations, whose members could meet and debate, set policy and then change it. I'm not sure where I'd go if I wanted to debate (for instance) the idea that the word 'queer' is a form of hate speech that should be transcribed as 'the q-slur'. My automatic answer would be 'social media' but that doesn't seem to be working too well as a forum for debating trans matters, so—in short, I'm not convinced that LGBTQQIAAP+ is supposed to be the name of an organisation, either.

Maybe I should take a cue from Wikipedia and think of LGBT as a community. At first sight, that looks as if it would cure most of my cognitive dissonance. While I can't say I identify personally as LGBTQQIAAP+, my girlfriend and I have friends who match all of those categories, including the plus sign, which I see as covering the friends who identify as sexual outlaws in ways that aren't on the current lists. (Furries, marriage resisters, polyamorists.) But our friends aren't a community. I'm Australian and Vix is British, so most of them have never met. The only thing that binds them all together is that they're our friends and although 'friends of Dorothy' was a famous slang term for queers when I was at uni, I don't think 'friends of Gina and Vix' is likely to catch on.

And the wider world seems just as random. In the regional city where I live, I've heard about an LGBT group at the university and seen a youth group advertised at the local library: the internet says there's also a local lesbian group and a gay men's group on Facebook. I like living in Wollongong, because we see gay couples in the street several times a year, something that only ever happened once in the eight years when we lived in supposedly-hipster Bristol. But I reckon it would be a stretch to describe any of this as 'community'.

Although my interpretation of 'community' may be too narrow. When I go back to my Wikipedia clue and examine it more closely, I notice that it's talking about '*the* community', as if the sense of community that's being invoked is more abstract and less embodied than I've been assuming. So maybe terms like LGBTQQIAAP+ are aspirational. I've been thinking of the acronyms as descriptions of places where a wide range of social groupings already live, work and socialise together in some form of community but maybe I should be reading each acronym as a performative attempt to create a particular alliance.

But where does the desire for these alliances come from? I can only guess at the answer, because I don't share the desire. The alliances that have interested me over the years tend to have names like 'Lesbians and Gays Support the Miners' or 'Queer Climate Group'. I can see the value of forming coalitions to work for big general social changes but I'm less convinced that there's something to be gained from a coalition of sexual minorities, whose interests aren't necessarily aligned. It's a lesson I learnt in the now-forgotten sex wars of the 1980s between anti-pornography feminists and sex positive feminists, long before the current terf wars.

My first guess is that the people who keep adding letters to the acronym are trying to make it truly inclusive. If so, it's an attempt that's bound to fail, partly because the most comprehensive list always leaves something out and partly because this particular list is clearly based on exclusion, as well as inclusion. Sado-masochism and bondage were integral to the argument of the sex positive feminists of the eighties but there's no BDSM in LGBTQQIAAP+. And in the counterculture of the seventies, a lot of people listened to the ideas being put forward by the North American Man/Boy Love Association: I can't see that happening now.

So my second guess is that the acronym is a list of all the causes that are currently approved of by, um, the people making the list. That would explain why it gets my back up. As a lesbian in her seventies, who believes every word she's heard from Carole Cadwalladr, Jarod Lanier, Jacob Silverman and Shoshana Zuboff and therefore steers clear of social media, I wouldn't even know where to look for the people who come up with the acronyms and I definitely don't know how to go about modifying or contributing to their list of approved causes.

Having your identity defined for you is never much fun. I like the identity that I'm being offered in 2020 far more than the identity I was offered as a trainee lesbian in the 1960s but I'd still prefer to choose my own alliances. So 2020 may be the year in which I finally give up on any attempt to identify with the term LGBT, let alone LGBTQQIAAP+, and decide that I'm just a lesbian.

Language is one of the main sites of activism at present, so it's not surprising that terminology is an important part of my changing sense of queer identity. But activism has to include some action as well and, although there's been plenty of locally-based queer activism all through the twenty-first century, its defining action would have to be the global campaign for same-sex marriage.

It's taken me a while to work out what I think about the acronym but I've always known what I think of marriage. I never fantasised about weddings when I was a kid—white isn't my colour and I find rituals stressful—so it was easy for me to internalise the feminist analysis of marriage as a key factor in the oppression of women. Most of the heterosexual couples I know aren't married: I was surprised to find out that so many queer couples want to be.

With a background like this, I'm definitely not the right person to give an overview of the same-sex marriage debate, so I won't try to reconstruct or deconstruct the arguments for and against, the way I've done with the acronyms. Instead, I want to take a step back, in order to put both issues in the same perspective and see what they have in common.

The first thing I notice from this angle is that in both cases I had the same instinctive response. My basic principle so far has been that (as the internet used to say) I don't want to harsh anyone's squee. If it makes some queers happy to get married or define themselves by acronyms, I'm happy for them. If the acronyms go viral and the same-sex marriage campaigns are successful, then that's a win for someone who isn't a right wing populist—and don't we all need to see wins like that at present?

But the second thing I notice is that I've instinctively been tamping down my own reactions, in order to protect the happiness of people I've never met. The truth is, from the angle I'm standing at, same-sex marriage and the acronyms look more like an own goal than a win. That's a perfectly reasonable opinion, just as reasonable as making same-sex marriage your priority or defining your identity with an acronym. So why have I been trying so hard to avoid thinking about these issues? Why have I effectively been censoring my own thoughts?

This time the questions I'm asking *are* rhetorical, although I have two separate answers, one personal and the other political. In personal terms, I'm in the denial stage of grief, putting off the moment when I have to admit that the gay movement I once loved has disappeared into the past. On one level, the Gay Liberation Movement was always a civil rights movement but on another level it was a great place to meet other outsiders. I remember sitting in a gay bar, looking round and thinking, 'These are my people', because I knew that everyone had taken some sort of risk to be there; because I knew that we had all resisted some of the things we'd been told about ourselves. For a while there, I thought queerness was inherently resistive. It took me a long time to realise that once the gay movement had achieved a certain degree of civil rights and social acceptance, queers wouldn't be outsiders any more. For me, the current focus on same-sex marriage and inclusive terminology indicate that we've reached that tipping point, in which case—given that my secret identity is 'outsider', not 'girl who has sex with girls'—it's time for me to move on.

But where can outsiders go, in an increasingly monetised and branded world? Maybe the answer's already contained in the question. Fifty years ago, saying you were queer would have caused more of a flutter than saying you were a socialist but those positions seem to have been reversed. At the end of September, for instance, the UK Department for Education forbade schools to use resources from 'organisations which have expressed a desire to end capitalism', on the basis that anti-capitalism is 'an extreme political stance'. The problem here is that while I've been going about my everyday business, I haven't come across any socialist groups that sound as though they're looking for recruits like me. But there's always something to hope for. A few weeks ago I was unexpectedly inspired by Michael Sandel's new book *The Tyranny of*

Merit, where he argues that politicians like Tony Blair, Bill Clinton and the Hawke-Keating government justified taking on the neoliberal economic policies of Margaret Thatcher and Ronald Reagan by promising to establish a meritocracy in which minority groups would be given an equal chance to succeed.

If Sandel's right, then at least some of the gains for queers have come at the cost of implicitly endorsing a slightly more liberal version of neoliberalism—a depressing thought in the short term but one that in the long term reopens some possibilities for queer activists. Instead of working to expand the list of minority groups with a designated seat at the table, we could think about making alliances that could potentially overturn the table. 'Lesbians and Gays Support the Gig Economy Workers' would play even better than 'Lesbians and Gays Support the Miners': on the basis of having seen *Pride*, I'd be prepared to bet that there are more openly queer gig economy workers than there were openly gay miners...

So here I am, slouching towards the end of 2020, still wondering whether queer activism is heading off to a place where I can't follow it or whether there's still room in the acronym for people like me. The only thing I can say for sure is that I was wrong when I began by announcing that this was a year in which I hadn't thought much about being queer. My subconscious has clearly spent 2020 coming up with a whole lot of questions.

Although the definitive answers will probably have to wait till 2021.

Gina Ward lives in Wollongong and as a committed pessimist, she's still in lockdown, which is giving her a lot of time to think.

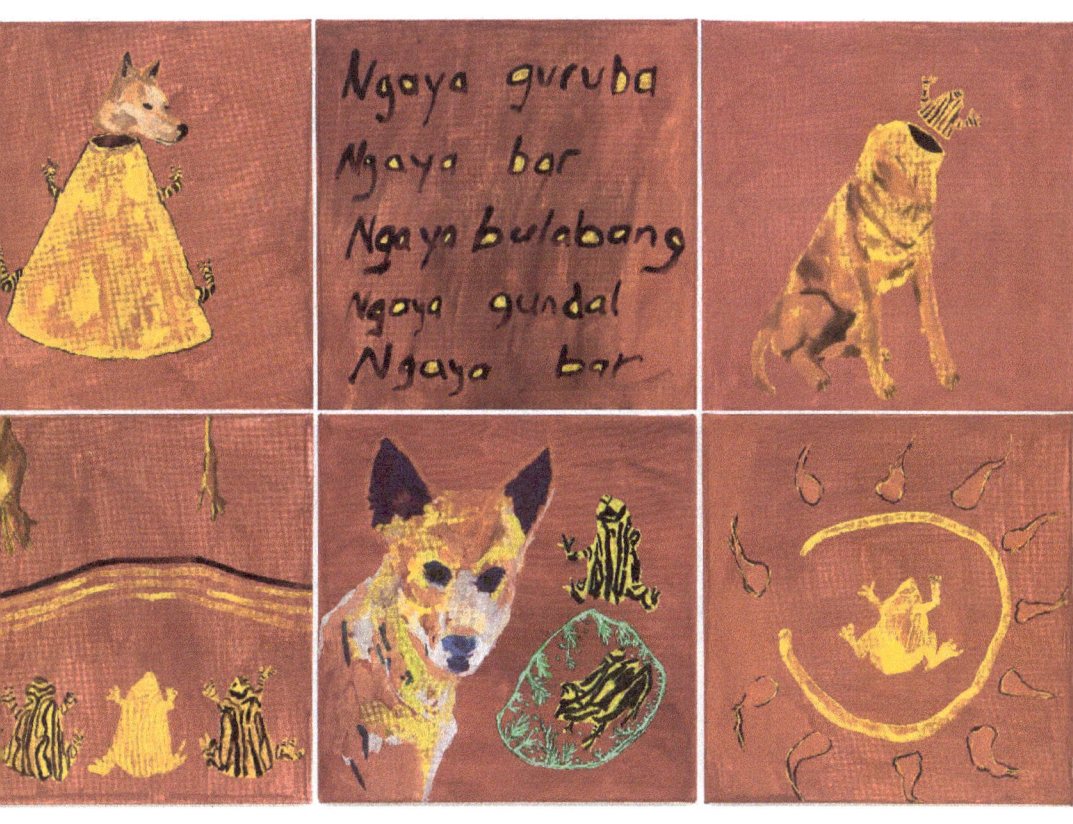

Peter Waples-Crowe—*Kin 2020,* 6 panels, each 30 x 30 cm, gouache and acrylic on canvas

A meditation on containment, Country and COVID-19

Peter Waples-Crowe is an indigenous queer artist, involved in art production and health education. He lives in Melbourne. @pwcrowe insta @peterwaplescrowe

ENDING HIV
Don't Believe The Hype
James May

As a long-term survivor of HIV/AIDS, I'm frustrated with the current discourse around HIV in this country. There is a perception that we have this issue solved, and that living with HIV is 'no big deal', thanks to advances in medication. There is pressure from within the LGBTIQ community to uphold this image, even though living with HIV is more complex than popping a pill each day. Also, while HIV transmissions have reduced in Australia, there is a long way to go before we can declare the 'end of HIV', and this campaign must include the entire LGBTIQ community.

As someone living with HIV, I feel excluded from this campaign.

To illustrate this, ACON recently unveiled a major policy paper, *Imagining HIV In 2030* [1], at a panel discussion in August 2019. This begs the question—how are people living with HIV (PLHIV) supposed to imagine a future without the virus if our peers in the HIV sector can't?

As a long-term survivor of HIV/AIDS, I feel let down by AIDS organisations that were established to represent us, but seem happy for us to swallow pills for the rest of our lives. Many people endure uncomfortable side-effects from these drugs. In *Imagining HIV In 2030* [2], the authors note that limitations of current treatments include 'toxicities associated with lifelong care, the need for daily pill-taking and associated psychological burden and costs'.

The report also observes that, 'PLHIV have an increased risk of serious non-communicable diseases, including cardiovascular, liver and kidney disease, malignancies and bone disorders.'

Clearly, the 'Ending HIV' mantra of AIDS organisations does not apply to those of us living with HIV who face a life of daily medication and the risk of co-morbidities from both this, and the virus itself.

While HIV transmissions have reduced in this country, *The ACON Annual Report 2018/19* [3] confirms there were 278 new HIV notifications in NSW alone in 2018. Of particular concern is that between January and June 2019, there were 75 new HIV notifications of overseas-born MSM (men who have sex with men), a 23% increase compared with the same period over the previous five years.

Imagining HIV in 2030 concedes that 'the 'virtual elimination' of new HIV transmissions may not occur as early as we had hoped.' While the number of transmissions is declining overall, this is not the case among the indigenous community or migrants to this country where infection rates continue to rise.

HIV/AIDS is still a very real threat, particularly to those living on the margins of our society. The HIV sector has not reached these communities with their health promotion efforts, and there is a long way to go before they can declare the 'end of HIV'.

After living with HIV for twenty years, I've also watched the HIV sector roll out various health promotion initiatives, but none has perplexed me more than the 'Ending HIV' [4] campaign.

This campaign is misleading on a number of levels.

Not only does it make hollow claims about ending HIV (the campaign aims to reduce HIV transmissions in the state of NSW by 80% by 2020), it does nothing to 'end HIV' for those of us who have the virus. There are around thirty thousand people [5] living with HIV in this country. Once again we've been ignored by policy-makers in the HIV sector.

As someone living with HIV, I'm also not encouraged by the Undetectable=Untransmittable (U=U) campaign [6] endorsed by the HIV sector. This campaign still puts the onus on people living with HIV to swallow pills for the rest of our lives, rather than the onus being on medical researchers and drug companies to find a cure.

People living with HIV have already endured years of moral scrutiny and control of our bodies—not unlike that experienced by those who test positive, or risk testing positive in the COVID-19 pandemic.

According to *Imagining HIV in 2030*, the U=U campaign has also failed to reduce stigma against people living with HIV. 'Discrimination on the basis of HIV status continues to occur within the gay community, including in the context of hook-ups where HIV negative men choose not to have sex with HIV positive partners, even if they are undetectable.'

In fact, it is now more common than ever for men on dating apps like Scruff to promote themselves by stating, 'I am taking PrEP' and 'HIV Status Negative' in their profiles.

So I don't think 'Everything Has Changed' and 'We Can End HIV' with these drugs. People living with HIV are still reliant on pills and facing social disadvantage, prejudice and discrimination. Meanwhile, we're assaulted with 'Ending HIV' slogans on social media and elsewhere, knowing we'll be stuck with HIV for the rest of our lives.

According to *Imagining HIV in 2030*, HIV-related discrimination remained high in NSW in 2018. 'An online survey conducted in 2016 as part of the Stigma Indicators Monitoring Project found that 74% of PLHIV reported stigma related to their HIV status. Over half reported negative experiences or different treatment by health workers.'

A number of indicators also point to socio-economic disadvantage among PLHIV. *Imagining HIV In 2030* found that, of the PLHIV who completed the *HIV Futures 8 Survey* [7], half were 'living on household incomes substantially lower than the average Australian income'. Further studies [8] reveal that 30.8% of Australian PLHIV reported their annual income to be less than $30,000 in 2019, which puts them at the edge of poverty. Despite this, we're meant to pretend that 'living with HIV is easy' and that taking medication for the rest of our lives is 'no big deal.' We're meant to post a happy-go-lucky pic on Grindr with '+ Undetectable' stamped on our foreheads.

As someone living with HIV, I find the label 'undetectable' insulting. I don't want it stamped on my profile like some kind of badge, and I don't want to explain it to people for the rest of my life. I want to get rid of this virus and the pills and stigma that go with it.

Excluding people who are living with HIV from the Ending HIV campaign is deeply hurtful. We will continue to bear the brunt of inequality, prejudice and discrimination while we remain HIV Positive. The fight to 'end HIV' should extend to everyone in the LGBTIQ community, including those of us who have the virus.

References

[1] https://www.aconhealth.org.au/imagining-hiv-in-2030

[2] https://www.acon.org.au/wp-content/uploads/2019/08/Imagining-HIV-in-2030-Discussion-Paper-Spreads.pdf

[3] https://www.acon.org.au/wp-content/uploads/2019/11/Annual-Report-2018-2019_FA_WEB_spreads.pdf

[4] https://endinghiv.org.au/ending-hiv/

[5] https://www.afao.org.au/about-hiv/hiv-statistics/

[6] https://livingpositivevictoria.org.au/share-news-undetectable-untrasmittable/

[7] https://www.latrobe.edu.au/__data/assets/pdf_file/0004/874309/HIV-Futures-Financial-Security.pdf

[8] https://www.starobserver.com.au/news/increasing-calls-for-hiv-homelessness-reform/196839

James May has written for Positive Living, HIV Australia and Living Positive Victoria. His writing on LGBTIQA+ themes has also appeared in *The Guardian*, *Sydney Morning Herald*, *Overland* and *The Big Issue*.

LIMITLESS BOUNDARIES
Ayman Barbaresco

Ayman Barbaresco, who passed away in June this year from ongoing medical complications, was a passionate advocate for people living with special needs. He was a long-standing volunteer for many organisations, including Switchboard, Thorne Harbour Health, Drummond Street Services and Queer Space. For many years, Ayman worked with Switchboard as a volunteer on the phones, before joining the organisation's board and becoming a member of Switchboard's community engagement committee. Friend, writer and *Bent Street* contributor Daniel Witthaus wrote in June, 'I had the honour of holding Ayman's hand during the last few weeks, and I did my best to let him know that an entire community would've gladly taken my place.'

The following article by Ayman was included in *Living and Loving in Diversity* (chief editor Maria Pallotta-Chiarolli, published by AGMC (Australian LGBTIQ Multicultural Council) with Wakefield Press).

'When life gives you lemons, you just want to squeeze them and make lemonade!' Well in my life, I have been given many lemons and am still squeezing them.

You see, I was born with a neurological disorder called Neurofibromatosis Type 1 (NF1) and this was the start of a life that has always, still is and will always involve many doctor appointments, MRI scans, blood tests and the list goes on.

I was born on Tuesday 14 February 1989 at 2.01pm (yes I am a Valentine's baby) in Sydney, Australia, to an Italian mother and Middle Eastern Father. I am the youngest of two. My brother is three-and-a-half years older than me. For the first two years of my life, we lived in Burwood, Sydney, and then moved to the north coast of NSW to the beachside town of Coffs Harbour. I went to a public primary school and three high schools, one public, one co-educational private and then a senior college for years 11 and 12.

For me, growing up in a regional town had mixed emotions. I mean, I couldn't choose where I lived but I had many mixed experiences and that wasn't just during my schooling years. The biggest thing that impacted me was my identity. Growing up, especially having a disability and being sick as a child, was confronting. I was always picked on at school because I was different. I was the odd sheep amongst the crowd.

Part of my condition in having NF1, you are diagnosed with numerous tumours. My first brain tumour was diagnosed on my third birthday. This tumour sat on my brain stem and was inoperable and I had less than 20 per cent chance of survival. My doctors and specialists trialled a new regime of drugs. I was given extreme doses of chemotherapy and radiotherapy and it eradicated the tumour. As I write this story I am 23 years in remission and am damn well proud of where I have come from and where I have been.

Growing up, my father was never really around. This made it very difficult for my mum who was trying to look after me, deal with my treatments and brain tumour as well as raise my older brother. Thankfully we had the beautiful and amazing support of my maternal grandparents who were there every step of the way and provided that much-needed support. For treatment, my mum and I would travel to Sydney with Ansett Airlines (yes that shows my age) every six weeks for an average of eight weeks. This process went on for almost two years. Even after I was given the all-clear, mum and I would still spend many months travelling to Sydney for follow-up appointments, scans and tests.

Despite being sick and not really having a childhood, there were still many happy memories of my time in and out of hospital. I remember flying with Ansett in the 1990s and being lucky enough to be taken up to the cockpit and see the pilots fly the plane. This is a privilege that kids who are growing up today don't get to experience and I feel pretty special.

Another great part was staying at Ronald McDonald House in Camperdown, NSW (now Westmead). This amazing organisation provides a home-away-from-home for seriously ill children and their families who are more than 100km away from their family unit. The atmosphere created within this house is truly remarkable and special. The bond that families have within these houses is special and because of the amazing support I received as a kid, this is one organisation that will always be in my heart. As I write this story, they are also one of the organisations that I volunteer for.

To date, I still live with many ongoing medical complications. I was diagnosed with scoliosis at the age of 12, diagnosed with my second brain tumour in 2012, and my third in 2016, and I know that my medical journey hasn't ended. The roller coaster is still running. I am a little uncertain of where it will take me but I keep living my life, I keep being myself and having fun.

If my medical condition and everything I was going through wasn't enough, my sexuality came into play in 2001 when I was 12 years old. I realised that I was gay. I liked guys. A lot of people ask me how I came to terms with my sexuality and for me, it was nothing. It was just another part of me. I mean, I have overcome childhood cancer and dealing with scoliosis, so my attitude was 'so what if I am gay'.

Throughout my work in the LGBTI community, I have heard many coming out stories. I have three different coming out stories. My first one was in 2001. I remember it was a Saturday afternoon when I walked up the stairs of the family home. My mum was in the lounge room and I said to her, 'Mum, I've got something to tell you. I'm gay.' And Mum says, 'I always knew' and gave me the biggest hug.

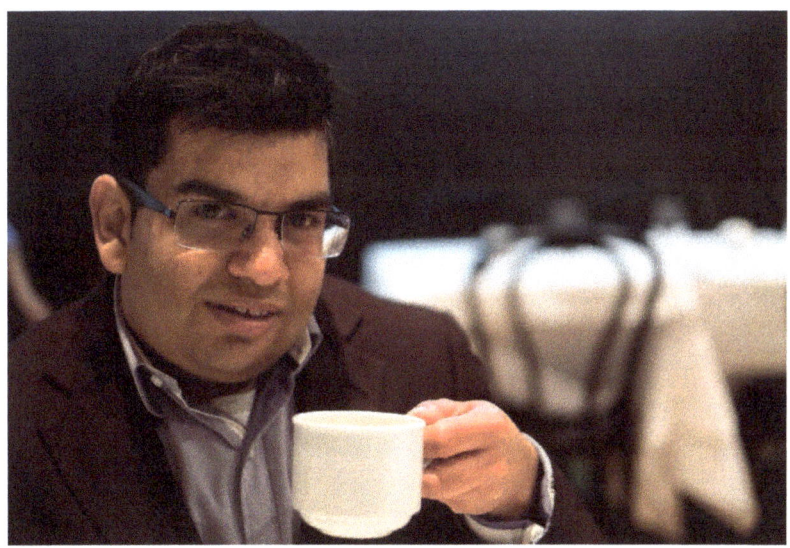

My second one was to my best friend in high school. I was in year eight at a Catholic co-educational school. Not long after, I was bed-ridden due to my scoliosis, so I was stuck at home watching TV and not doing a lot. After that three-month bed stint, I returned to school where I had been outed by my best friend. He told everyone in my year and people at my old high school also found out.

My third coming out story is to my dad. I came out to him in 2004 when I was 15. See, my mum and dad divorced in 1996. When I came out to him, he told me, 'No, you're normal, you're going to have a wife and kids.' That was quite confronting for me. I thought my dad would've accepted me for who I am but in looking at it and knowing what I know now, because he is from a Muslim background, it was quite confronting and challenging. In saying this, just the other week (June 2017) he phoned me said, 'I don't care that you're gay, I just want you to be happy.' He has accepted me 13 years later and that's quite nice to have some form of closure.

For me, growing up in a regional town and being gay was quite difficult. I had very little support and there was nothing around when I was growing up. We had a couple of services and groups that met, but after a while, it was the same people doing the same thing and got quite boring. There were very little support services online and I had a counsellor who was ok but not the best.

Young people these days are so much luckier than when I was coming out with all of the support services they have access to. There are online chat platforms and discussion groups, in Melbourne there are organisations like Minus 18, JOY 94.9, Headspace, Switchboard and the Victorian AIDS Council just to name a few. I had none of that. Yes, there's still the gay hate, which is horrible to see. And I still hear stories of kids being thrown out of home for being gay. I mean, who cares who you love? Whether you're gay, bi, trans, straight or you're asexual. So long as you love someone for who they are in the heart and not for what's between the legs, that's what matters. I think given enough time we will get there. I think whatever your sexuality is, your gender, whether you have a disability, you're from the deaf community, you're yellow, black, brown, whether you're male, female, or somewhere in between, the main thing I want people to do is to be themselves, have fun and enjoy the ride. Because you never know where life will take you.

And there's still this whole misconception that people with a disability don't or can't have sex. So where do you go with that? I've been single my whole life, I've never had a boyfriend and I find that challenging, especially being gay with a disability, because there's this dominant perception in the gay community that you have to look a certain way, you have to act a certain way. Why is it that as a minority we victimise and reject a minority within a minority? You can't be 147 centimetres of energy like I am, you have to be six foot tall, dark and handsome with a gym-toned body. You have to be this Prince Charming. But what's wrong with someone who has a little character? I have a goddam awesome personality and a contagious sense of humour. Did I mention that I have an infectious smile? Who cares if they have a few kilos and they don't look like Prince Charming? I may not be who you expect (or want) me to be but spend just five minutes with me and you will find that I am just like that guy you swiped right. I am just like that guy you woofed at. My disability will not leave me. It will be by my side, as I lie beside you. I can't become someone else who will meet the 'gay hook up' checklist requirements that we all have in the back of our heads, because my disability won't let me. Nine times out of ten, I've had to pay for sex and that takes a lot of guts to acknowledge. The thing that I would love the most is intimacy. It's not necessarily about the sex but it's more about the cuddling and the intimate connection that I would love. My bed gets very cold during the long Melbourne winter.

In the 28 years I've been on the planet, I look at it as I'm healthy, I'm happy, I'm living a life that I never thought I would live, ever. I'm breathing, I feed myself, I clothe myself, I don't rely on anything or anyone to keep me alive. I'm so damn lucky! I'm a big believer that because I've gone through so much shit in my life, there must be a reason. There must be some underlying thing that's keeping me here. Life is what you make of it.

The main thing that I want you to know is that you should always be yourself, have fun and enjoy the ride, because you never know where the path will take you.

Article reprinted from *Living and Loving in Diversity: an anthology of Australian multicultural queer adventures.* The book is an anthology of personal stories on queer multicultural multifaith Australia, with more than sixty voices from across the spectrum of sexualities and genders, families and relationships. All royalties go to AGMC to continue its work.

BELOW: Firdhan Aria Wijaya—*Seeking our voices in heteronormative society*

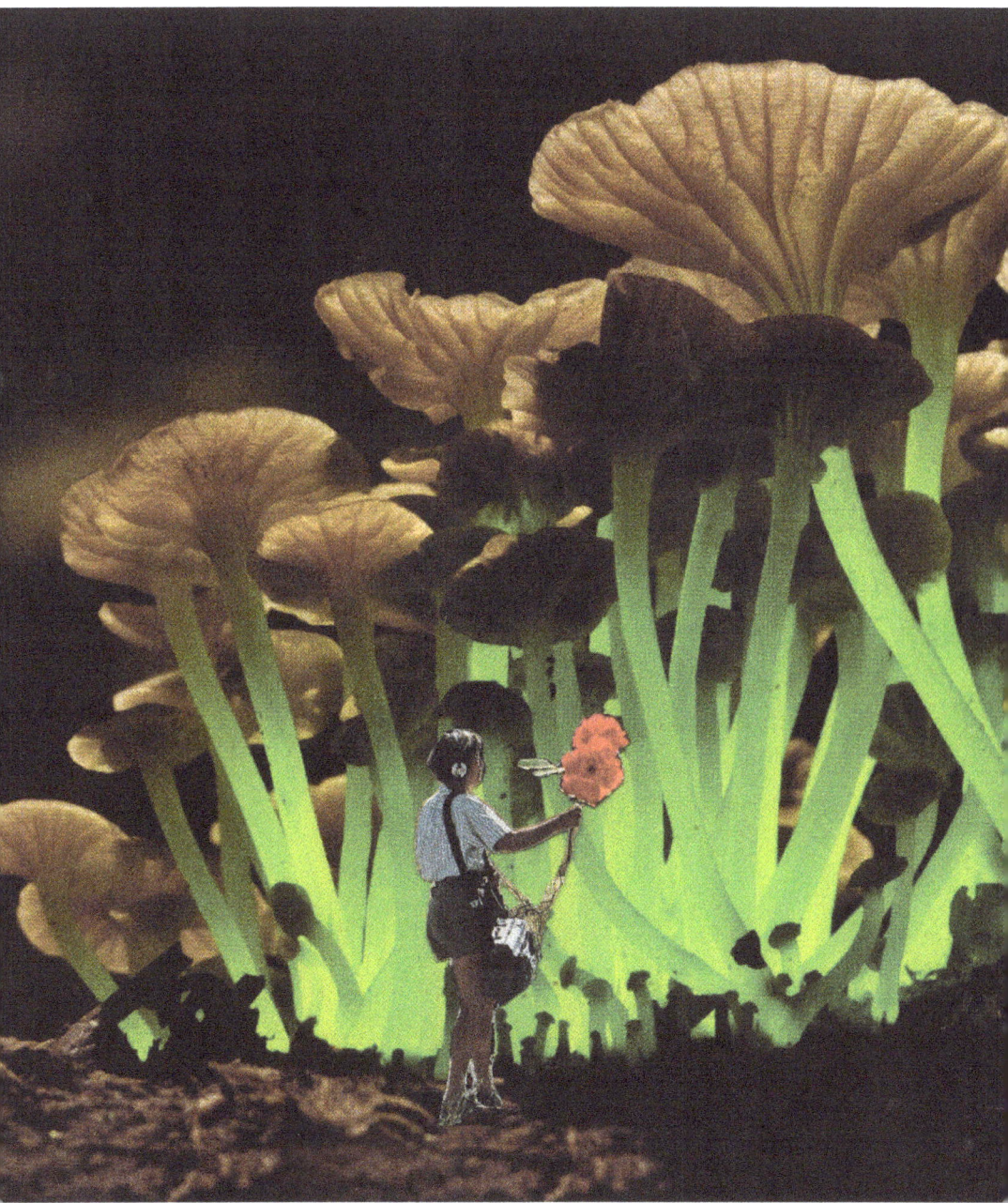

I SAID TO HER IN REFERENCE TO MY TRANSITION FROM FEMALE TO MALE, 'NOBODY WARNS YOU, YOU MIGHT LOSE YOUR FAMILY.' AT LEAST NOBODY WARNED ME. BUT THEN, YOU CAN'T REALLY LOSE WHAT YOU NEVER REALLY HAD.

MY MILKSHAKE
Blair Archbold

I

This is a true story. Every word.

II

In 2016 I went so far as to go to the Andes Mountains in Chile to find a cure for my chronic back pain. I struggled through a training in shamanism that lasted twenty-eight days. But I ended up finding what I had been searching for all along in 2019-2020 at a pain clinic in Melbourne within walking distance from my house.

My time in Chile definitely helped me though and it continues to help me. That much I know.

III

It was one day during February of this year, after the fires but before lock down when I lay down on my bed and I said a prayer to the four directions, a prayer I've said many times before. But this time something different happened. I asked for guidance, and then I fell asleep and I had a dream.

It was quick, just an image, a flash and then the sensation of wind rushing straight into my left ear as I woke up.

I felt like I was in a Western. I was standing outside and there stood three figures all facing me, cast in silhouette by the rays of the sun. I had a clear sense that something important had just been spoken. A decree. I could feel the significance hanging in the air.

Suddenly above the heads of the figures in silhouette rose ravens and crows that burst into the sky. One of the figures raised his hand and flicked his finger towards me. In the same instant a form the same colour as the birds took shape and flew directly at me.

Jolting awake with a gasp, I was convinced something had just flown straight into my ear. I'd felt the wind rush in and the sensation of flapping wings. Panicked, I swiped at my ear but there was nothing there.

To project outward spiritual aspects of the self to achieve a task is a common practice of sorcerers and shamans. Ravens and crows are thought by some to symbolise death, birth, magic and mysticism. In Norse mythology

Odin has two ravens as helping spirits. Known as Hugin and Munin, they are concrete expressions of the thoughts of Odin.

A few days later I found Richard Grannon's work on YouTube.

IV

The following paragraph comes from a book that I found difficult to read because of how disturbingly accurate it is. By Christine Lawson, it is called, *Understanding the Borderline Mother.*

> Developmental psychologists now know that before the age of 3, children are incapable of understanding deception because they are unable to discern the difference between what they believe and what their mother believes. They also do not understand incongruence, that mother might feel one emotion while expressing another or that hostility can be masked by a smile. And yet their survival depends on the ability to understand this individual who controls their universe.[1]

V

I ended up at the pain clinic from October 2019–July 2020 because I'd had chronic pain for sixteen years. My treatment included hydrotherapy, tai chi, gym rehabilitation, psychological support, occupational therapy, as well as consultations with a dietician and social worker. I honestly was really impressed and got a lot out of it.

One of the really important aspects of my experience at the clinic was my sessions with Erika, a health psychologist. I said to her in reference to my transition from female to male, 'Nobody warns you, you might lose your family.'

At least nobody warned me. But then, you can't really lose what you never really had.

I also said, 'Sometimes I feel I'm missing important building blocks to know who I am.'

Part of what was hard about transitioning in a way I didn't expect was how my mum used to call me by my new name and used male pronouns (when she remembered) but really, the painful truth was that what she really wanted was for me to remain where I was and always had been—under her thumb. Parentified. Zombiefied. Enslaved. Cooking dinner, washing dishes, folding up washing while my brothers sat there and did nothing. She wanted me to remain her punching bag, her counsellor, her confidant. How desperately she wanted to keep me under her control. I was her hostage.

It's called fusion-merger co-dependency. Abuse has occurred that has meant the lines have become blurred between subject and object. Grannon contends, this all-encompassing and inescapable trauma affects your relationship with reality itself.[2] You are entrained against your will, without consent, to fuse and merge at the emotional level with your abuser. This is why when people have asked me over the years, what was it that my mum did to me; I had no words for it. How do you find the words to describe this?

VI

Erika said to me during our final conversation, 'Your mum used guilt and shame to control you. She groomed you to have weak boundaries so she could get what she wanted.'

And what did she want?

My milkshake, as Richard Grannon would say.

For us to remain always, as Sam Vaknin so poetically puts it, one organism with two heads.

Vaknin describes it as 'ambient incest'. When a parent doesn't allow their child to separate and individuate.

VII

My mum told me during one of the rare moments I found the courage to challenge her, 'How dare you!? I have always loved you unconditionally!!' Her face vibrating with rage.

It is a co-dependent response to split the abuser into two people. When they're being nice that's the real them. When they're nasty and mean, that's not them. And when they're nasty and mean, whose fault is it? *Mine. It's my fault.* That is the programming. That is the entrainment.

Grannon describes this co-dependent response as a skill (an unhealthy one) that is non-consensually entrained. It is learned and practiced over time. He says, it is essentially spiritual and psychological suicide.

VIII

So it was earlier this year while I was half way through my time at the pain clinic when I discovered the work of Richard Grannon. His videos and courses were a godsend. I was in desperate need and his work helped when nothing else did. His understanding and approach to treating Complex PTSD is unmatched in my experience. (I have experienced CPTSD for longer than the back pain). With powerful metaphors to describe things that most people aren't even aware of, his work is in the area of helping people recover from and protect themselves from narcissistic abuse.

One of his metaphors is to compare this kind of abuse to an act of evisceration by a zombie witch doctor. The 'zombie witch doctor', he says, will (metaphorically) cut you open, gut you and put their toxic stuff inside you.

A narcissistically abusive parent may do this to their child.

My mother did this to me while calling it 'love'.

Drawing on the work of Pete Walker[3], Grannon says CPTSD symptoms consist of emotional flashbacks, a toxic Inner Critic, a neurotic urge toward co-dependency, what he calls People Pleaser Syndrome, emotophobia (a fear of emotions in self and others), and pronounced fawning.

And I have to say; I think he is spot on.

A crucial part of healing from narcissistic abuse, according to Grannon, is to learn to stand up to narcissistic types, and I have found when I have applied Grannon's strategies for dealing with narcissistically abusive people; it really has been like practicing a psychological or spiritual martial art.

IX

It was his mnemonic device for reducing emotional flashbacks that I started doing first. I'd had a horrible day with the CPTSD. I'd been having flashback after flashback, or as Richard Grannon calls them, stacked emotional flashbacks.

I went on YouTube, typed in the words 'emotional flashbacks' and found his videos. He has a number of channels and the channel Fortress Mental Health Protection System is where I went first. It is a series of videos that make up a free course for treating CPTSD.

Just like that my life began to change.

Even though he says to do the mnemonic device five times a day for thirty days, I did it at least thirty times a day for the first few days. At least.

Because I had to.

Until gradually by 'Day Thirty' I didn't really need it anymore.

Which was exactly what he said would happen.

I talked about it with the staff that worked with me at the pain clinic. They were impressed and wrote down his name. Erika even watched some of his videos. I suggested adding his stuff to their clinic program and Erika asked but was told there wasn't enough funding. She said, 'Make YouTube videos about your experience, Blair.' So I did. I have. It has been spookily good for me.

X

In one of his courses[4] Grannon says, 'Nothing and no one can keep you from being the person you were born to be'. It is a bold and powerful statement.

To me, it is a crime against nature for a parent to keep their child from being the person they were born to be.

A crime against nature.

My mum tried to keep me from being who I was born to be.

She tried.

She failed.

Here I am.

People say blood is thicker than water.

What they don't tell you is, you can walk away.

And sometimes, you must.

XI

The Q'ero people are said to be the last remaining of the Inca. They live in the Central Andes of Peru at 4000–5000 metres, where the sky meets the earth.

It is said the shamans of the Q'ero are the keepers of ancient knowledge and that they still practice the healing ways of the Inca.

The shamanic training I did in Chile was based on their traditions.

They remind us that we are as sacred as everything else in this world.

In the West we have inherited the myth that we have been banished from the Garden of Eden.

The Q'ero don't believe this. They believe we were never banished. They believe we belong in the Garden. They believe we never left.

XII

In one of Grannon's courses[5] he asks the question, 'What would be an appropriate response to what has been done to you?'

At first when I thought about that I had no answer. Then I realised the appropriate response for me is to tell the truth about my experience.

XIII

Εϖερ σινχε I ωασ α λιττλε κιδ I϶ϖε λοϖεδ μψ μυμ ανδ I τριεδ μψ βε στ το ηελπ ηερ.□ I διδϽτ ρεαλισε σηε ωασ σομεονε νοτ το βε τρυστ εδ.□ I κνεω τηατ σηε ωασ υνωελλ βυτ I διδϽτ ρεαλισε σηε ωασ α ζ

ομβιε ωιτχη δοχτορ.□□I διδνѣτ ρεαλισε τηατ σηε ωουλδ εϖισχερατε
με.□ I διδνѣτ ρεαλισε εϖεν ασ ιτ ηαππενεδ τηατ σηε ωουλδ□χυτ με
οπεν, γυτ με ανδ πυτ ηερ τοξιχ στυφφ ινσιδε με – ιν τηε σπαχε ωηερ
ε I ωασ μεαντ το βε λεαρνινγ αβουτ μψ οων νεεδσ.□ Ιτ ωασ ινϖασι
ϖε.□ Ιτ ωασ αβυσιϖε.□ Ιτ αλμοστ δεστροψεδ□μψ σπιριτ.□ Σηε σηου
λδ βε ασηαμεδ□οφ ηερσελφ.□ I ωαντ τηε τραυματισεδ λιττλε κιδ ιν
με το κνοω τηατ ωε γοτ αωαψ φρομ ηερ.□ Ανδ νο ματτερ ωηατ ηαππ
ενσ ωε χαν ηανδλε ιτ βεχαυσε νοτηινγ□ωιλλ εϖερ βε ασ βαδ ασ ηα
ϖινγ το συρϖιϖε ηερ. I ωαντ τηε λιττλε κιδ ιν με το κνοω ιτ ωασνѣτ
ουρ φαυλτ, ωε διδ□nothing□ωρονγ, ανδ νοτηινγ ανδ νο ονε ηασ τηε
ριγητ το κεεπ υσ φρομ βεινγ ωηο ωε ωερε βορν το βε.□ Τηισ ισνѣτ τη
ε ενδ, τηισ ισ τηε βεγιννινγ.

The above paragraph is something I wrote in an email to Erika when I was
about to have my final appointment with her. The only thing is, I don't know
how I did it. I wrote it in English. Yet this is how it came through to her.
Maybe it was a glitch in the formatting. Maybe it was a glitch in the matrix.
All I know is, only one word is in English and that word is 'nothing'.

My sessions were coming to an end so I wrote a paragraph about my life,
and I asked Erika to read it out for me during my final appointment. Paul
Gilbert who has done work on compassion-focused therapy has developed
this technique. The idea is that by Erika reading out my words describing my
life as if it was her life, I would be able to experience feelings of compassion
for myself.

Eager to give it a go and after checking with Erika that she was happy to
do it (she was) I wrote her an email and sent it off to her when we were due
to have our final phone chat in only a few hours. And then with about forty-
five minutes left I checked to make sure she'd received it and I saw she'd
replied saying it was in Russian. (It's not Russian). Could I send it through
again in a different format? *But I wrote it in English. It was in English in my email.*

Wondering how I'd managed it, I copied and pasted the original
paragraph from out of my email into a Word Doc and sure enough, it came
up as the unknown script. With time running out before my appointment I
quickly rewrote it from scratch in a new email and hoped this time it would
work.

Here it is:

Ever since I was a little kid I've loved my mum and I tried my best to
help her. I didn't realise she was someone not to be trusted. I knew that
she was unwell but I didn't realise she was a zombie witch doctor. I didn't
realise that she would eviscerate me. I didn't realise even as it happened
that she would cut me open, gut me, and put her toxic stuff inside me - in

the space where I was meant to be learning about my own needs. It was invasive. It was abusive. It almost destroyed my will to live. She should be ashamed of herself. I want the traumatised little kid in me to know it wasn't our fault, we did *nothing* wrong, and nothing and no one has the right to keep us from being who we were born to be. This isn't the end. This is the beginning.

References

[1] Christine Lawson, (2000). *Understanding the Borderline Mother*, pxi-xii.
[2] Richard Grannon. *Summoning the Self* [online course]. Available at www.spartanlifecoach.com.
[3] Pete Walker. (2013). *Complex PTSD: From Surviving to Thriving: A Guide and Map for Recovering from Childhood Trauma.*
[4] Richard Grannon. *Heal the Super Ego.* [online course]. Available at www.spartnlifecoach.com.
[5] Richard, Grannon. *Overcoming Narcissistic Abuse* [online course]. Available at www.spartanlifecoach.com.

Blair Archbold has contributed writing and voiceover work as an inspiring trans community leader, including as a co-host on *3CR's Out of the Pan: Sally Goldner and Blair Archbold.*

CREATIVE ZEN
Yannick Thoraval

Found my old mp3 player the other day. I was restoring order in my life by emptying one of several 'junk' cupboards in my house and there it was, at the bottom of a shoe box, under a Ziploc bag of bulldog clips and a knot of power chords for devices I once cherished: a tape recorder, a Nokia mobile phone and a 'portable' video camera the size of a half-loaf of bread. There it was, like buried treasure, my pre-smart-phone, 2004 Creative Zen Micro, purchased the same year I moved from Vancouver to Melbourne.

Apple's release of the iPod Mini that year had bred a swarm of competing micro hard drive music players. I chose the Zen. If Apple's sleek design for the iPod envisioned a future of clean-lined minimalism, then the Creative Zen was its aesthetic counterpart of chunky, Soviet pragmatism. Stout and blocky, the Creative Zen anticipated a more violent future for itself, a life of bumps and scrapes, of falling off bar tops and spilling out of bags onto busy city sidewalks.

My Zen was ugly and weighed a pocket full of nickels, but I loved that mp3 player. Its boxy design accepted me for who I was, rather than coax me towards achieving a higher version of myself. I could live *with* it, didn't feel the need to live *up* to it. Zen was a music player. Its creator, Singapore-based Creative Technologies, made no further promises.

I'd had many portable music devices before it: a Walkman, several Disc men, but this was different. 1,500 songs in one place! Wow! I could now leave the house confident I'd have enough musical variety to harmonize with whatever emotional peaks and troughs the day threw up.

I spent weeks pouring my CD collection into my Zen. People I met topped the device up with songs they wanted to share with me. I wasn't just building a music library, I was keeping a personal record, a catalogue of my tastes and social interactions.

Over the next few years, the music in my Zen became the soundtrack of my young adult life as a new migrant to Australia. Imperceptibly, those songs also grafted themselves onto the mis-en-scene of those memories.

Now here they were, waiting to be re-heard, re-seen. If it still worked, my Creative Zen was a tangible link between myself then and now. It wasn't just an mp3 Player anymore. It was a time machine.

I plugged it in. My eyes widened as the familiar blue glow behind the 1.8 inch touchless video screen came to life. The artists names scrolled across the display: Tosca; Radiohead; Blind Willie McTell. Their songs continued in the random order they'd been set to when I last put my Zen down.

The old songs took me on a journey, a wizard's Pensieve, reanimating dormant memories, filling the lacunae of remembered experience.

Hilltop Hoods and I am on Swanston Street, heading to the Melbourne Town Hall where I work as a caterer; Modest Mouse and I look out the tree-lined window of the office I share with three other postgraduate students in the John Medley Building at the University of Melbourne; Blur and I melt back into the liquid androgyny of my early twenties; Gotan Project and I'm out for dinner with a German international student I'd hoped would become my friend; The Shins and I'm drinking beer with a former colleague I promised to keep in touch with but who, like so many others, receded into my personal mist of ambition and domestic responsibility. That's how time flies.

I needed the music to be reminded of this time, these people. I miss them. And the idea of them. And I miss all the possibilities of what I then imagined my life could and would become.

Yannick Thoraval is a writer, teacher and freelance communications consultant. He holds a PhD in creative writing and teaches professional writing at RMIT University in Melbourne.

DREAMING BIG
Baburam Poudel

I am Baburam Poudel. Born in the mountains of western Nepal nearly fifty years ago in a village called Nawalparashi, my upbringing was culturally rich and economically poor. To be poor in a third-world country is to be very poor indeed.

Fortunately, my mother believed in education. She also welcomed my presence cooking, cleaning, dancing and singing with her friends. She loved me. Protected me. Respected me. My parents did not force me into an arranged marriage.

My mother worked very hard. She was generous. She was kind. She always looked to the future for her children. Even before I was raped by a family member, she told me, 'Keep away from him. He's bad, that one.'

By the time I was 12 years old, I knew I was attracted to boys more than girls, even though most of my friends were girls. Same-sex attraction was not heard of in my village of fifty houses, nor was it heard of in the next largest town two hours' walk away where I attended high school, tending my small farm to pay for tuition and food for me and my brother.

This was 1985. In this remote, rural patriarchal society, Nepalese women had few rights. Young gay men had none. Amid the rigid traditional belief that only male and female exists, homophobia was rife. There was no formal sex education in the country. Birth control had only just been introduced. The AIDS epidemic was spreading through Asia. The news regularly reported police bashings of gay men. My religion rejected 'people like me', believing if you could not or would not make babies, you were worthless. I did not want to shame my parents. My own internalised homophobia and fear of abuse kept me in hiding.

Staying silent meant staying safe.

Silence also forced me to live an isolated life. My world brimmed with pretence, anxiety and depression. Despite my strong, brave soul, I wanted to die.

I finished high school in 1991, studied Science at university, but had to drop out because I could not pay the fees. I pursued a career in hospitality, becoming qualified and experienced in all aspects from reception to cleaning to food preparation and cooking. I left Nepal when I was 22 to seek my fortune in the United Arab Emirates, but was deceived by the employment agent in Mumbai, India. He took most of my money and all of my chance to get to Abu Dhabi.

For seven years I lived in the slums of Mumbai. Not all slums are created equal. The first one was disorganised and dirty. The residents used the alleys as toilets. Dogs attacked you for your food. There were no mosquito nets.

I became gravely ill with malaria, typhoid and pneumonia. Fortunately I had made friends. One of these friends took me to hospital. According to the emergency doctor, I had just hours to live.

Recovering slowly, I worked three jobs in one day, seven days per week, sleeping just four hours at night before starting all over again. These were my worst days. I was lost and alone. At times, suicide seemed possible and preferable.

Living in a windowless room the size of a large cupboard with a blue tarp for protection from the monsoon, one day my six roommates were out and I found myself alone. From my locked suitcase, I removed a magazine.

Furtively, I read an article about the stigma of being gay. About how society's attitudes needed to catch up to the reality of how people live their lives. About how gay men suffered daily discrimination, which led to depression and suicidal thoughts.

For the first time in my life, I understood that I was not the only one. That there may be answers to the thousands of questions clouding my head. That I might live my truth.

Until then I had searched for answers through religions. I was born Hindu, and pursued insight through Christianity, Islam, Buddhism, Sikhism, Hari Krishna and Sai Baba. They taught me that I was impure, inauthentic and non-productive.

The magazine article had been written by an Australian named Geoffrey Heaviside. I made contact with him. We became friends. When Geoffrey came to India to set up support and advocacy for gay men, I worked as his translator. Through the Brimbank Community Initiative, Geoffrey helped hundreds and hundreds of people find their safety, negotiate the system, and live full lives.

Through utilising self-help and local community-based organisations, Geoffrey empowered the poor to access food, education, housing and employment. He provided financial, legal and medical support to gay people who had been abused. He advocated on health issues associated with gender minorities. He worked with the UNHCR. When the time came, he established support networks through social media and developed online tools to support people through suicidal ideation.

Over the years, we talked about Geoffrey sponsoring me to move to Australia. In 2007, I did move to Australia. I found work in kitchens and worked my way up to the position of chef, but did not make friends easily. I was quiet, shy, and unused to expressing myself. My English was improving but nowhere near fluent. I didn't know my way around. How would I ever meet anyone, let alone someone to love, who would love me in return?

The gay scene seemed loud, almost aggressive. I tried nightclubs, online dating, meeting people through mutual friends. Aside from a couple of fun nights, I felt financially, physically and emotionally used, scared, even more isolated. I wanted a special person to share my life with. To trust, respect and understand. Together.

My dad passed away in November 2014. My mum passed away in January 2016. My best friend, mentor and housemate, Geoffrey Heaviside, passed away in January 2020. Now I walk alone.

I know these most important people want me to live my happiest life. To do this, they have given me an assignment: do not fear, do not be silent, do not hide yourself. Live a full life.

For too long I have feared pure rejection.

I fear not getting a job, losing a job, barriers to promotion. I worry—every day—about how I will earn enough money to live. I am unable to access community benefits and health services due to discrimination, for example with the stigma of HIV AIDS. I feel unwelcome in the mainstream community. I fear losing the few friends I have. I worry that my family will reject me. I am a target for financial exploitation, physical harassment, and sexual abuse. I fear that my self-esteem will never recover. For people of colour, discrimination doubles.

This is why it has taken me forty-seven years to muster the courage to show my true feelings. Though a few close friends, family and colleagues know I am gay, today I come out to the rest of the world.

The human experience is unique to every individual. My gender identity, sexual attraction and relationship to my body are mine alone.

From today, I will not live behind. I will life my full life and, through, Brimbank, I will empower people like me to do the same.

Baburam Poudel is a gay man who has lived in Nepal and India, and moved to Australia in 2007 with the support of the Brimbank Community Initiative. Poudel works to expand opportunities for other people facing various struggles through Brimbank's outreach and networks.

Geoffrey Heaviside (28/9/1943-29/1/2020) was a supporter and advocate for LGBTIQ, HIV, and Other Minorities, and was actively involved with PFLAG, Metropolitan Community Church, Positive Living and the Victorian Aids Council. In 1998 Geoffrey established the Brimbank Community Initiative Inc. From 2005 Geoffrey set up support for LGBTIQ and HIV-positive international students in Victoria through the Brimbank International Student Support Services

ESSAYS

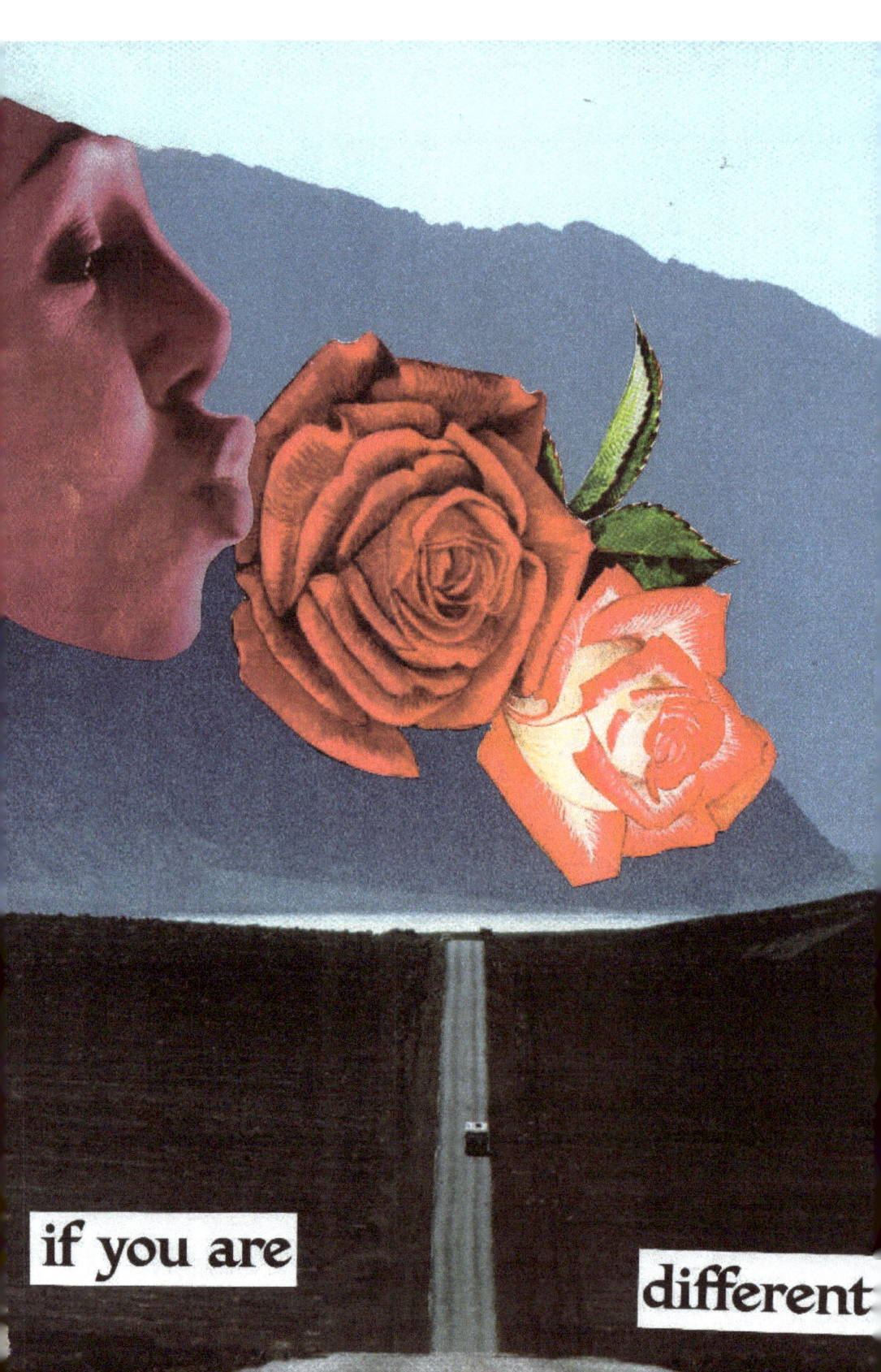

if you are

different

TORN APART:
The Liminal Life of Queer Studies in Indonesia

Hendri Yulius Wijaya

OPPOSITE: Firdhan Aria Wijaya—*If you are different*

In August 2020, I was invited to give an online talk about my first academic book. The event was organised by an Indonesian queer grassroots community, *Panggung Minoritas* (Minority Spotlight). Located in the city of Bandung of the West Java Province, this community group organises monthly discussions, movie screenings, and book clubs for queer communities and their allies. From the Q & A session, I still vividly remember a question from a participant, critically asking me why I published my work in English with an academic publisher if my intention was to introduce queer studies and Indonesian queer politics to a broader local audience. Putting it differently, when there are many Indonesians who don't speak English as their first language and do not have easy access to queer academic books, isn't my attempt ironically perpetuating academic elitism? Such a question stunned me, forcing me to reflect for a few days, and subsequently, to write this short piece. What if queer studies does not only have a class problem, as the U.S. queer theorist Matt Brim has proclaimed in his book *Poor Queer Studies* (2020), but also a parochialism problem when it comes to its international engagements? Here, I would argue that this insularity of queer studies in academia, which unfortunately is still dominated by U.S. queer scholarships and English-language coloniality, has marginalised many forms of knowledge, including ones that do not produce and publish knowledge in (perfect) English and top tier journals. At the same time, it is also important to understand that local queer scholarships have also suffered their own problems, apart from the above hegemony. From the place where I have been writing, Indonesia, queer studies has also been continually marginalised due to an ever-expanding homophobia. For instance, mainstream publishers are afraid of publishing queer-themed books, and some universities must be 'careful' in teaching that subject due to the increased fear of potential controversies.[1] Here, I decide to use the term 'liminal' to signal the ways that Indonesian queer studies lives in the interstices between academic imperial-capitalism and local homophobic politics. In other words, I am constantly 'torn apart'.

---

[1] For more discussions on the developments of queer studies in Indonesia, see Wijaya (2020b), 'Pedagogy of the Homeless: Poor Queer Studies in Indonesia'

Acknowledging Alienation

Let me begin by providing a little background about my work. My book *Intimate Assemblages: The Politics of Queer Identities and Sexualities in Indonesia* (Palgrave Macmillan 2020) is based on my thesis as the requirement to complete a research master's degree in Gender and Cultural Studies at Sydney University. In brief, it is about the historical shifts of queer identities and politics in Indonesia, and how contemporary homophobia shapes the subjectivity and politics of queer Indonesians. I wrote this thesis at a time of unprecedented anti-LGBT paranoia back in my home country, shortly after my work with the United Nations Development Program's (UNDP) 'Being LGBTI in Indonesia' was shut down by the government in mid-2016. With a full-scholarship in hand, I flew to Sydney to start studying and writing about queer studies in a more structured manner. During the unprecedented crackdown on Indonesian LGBT community in 2015-2016, I wrote a copious amount of articles for both international and national media to counter homophobic public discourses associating 'LGBT people' with 'abnormality, contagious behaviour, immorality, and even mental illness' (Wijaya 2020a). Throughout this period, media reports on the danger posed by the LGBT community were proliferating, followed with a raid of the alleged gay sauna and the caning of two gay men in Aceh, among others. Those publications, while helping in organising and cultivating my future thesis, did not always address the sense of alienation I constantly felt coming from the discipline that I should have embraced as my road to a better understanding of myself and the community I belong to.

The American Blueprint

Deeply influenced by French post-structuralism, U.S. queer theoretical frameworks have become a hegemonic force, making it inseparable from what Jasbir K. Puar calls, 'an imperial knowledge production' (2018, 226). Appearing unmarked as if it is transcendental and hence suitable for multiple geographical and cultural domains, queer studies are often unmarked as 'American studies' (ibid.), in which historical, socio-cultural, and political analysis of queer America becomes prescriptive, a blueprint for non-American scholars to follow. Ultimately, academic infrastructures, from the publishing industry, ranking systems, to access to intellectual resources, have also exacerbated the unequal power relations within the discipline itself (Brim 2020). It is indeed easy to predict that non-white scholars whose English is not their first language, along with limited access to American queer theory books, are more likely to struggle to engage in this hierarchical academic game. People do not come from the same level of playing field, and structural inequalities do exist. This is where the irony lies: a field that prides itself on critical inquiry fails to be critical of any power relations unfolding from itself. Especially, when it is now deeply entrenched in academic institutions and thus must deal with its politics.

Intimacy between queer studies and myself, has always been fraught with 'potential failure to stabilise [the] closeness' (Berlant 1998, 282). Too many challenges slowly but surely alienated me from what queer studies was talking about. Growing up in a small city, Bandar Lampung, where the English language was a luxury and access to TV cable was almost non-existent that time, I was indeed not familiar with the May 68 protests, the Greek pederasty, Al Pacino starred film *Cruising*, the Stonewall Riot, the 9/11 racial politics, or the life and works of Jean Genet, among others. With the high price of queer theory books published by university presses and academic publishers, so many times I myself wondered: 'Who can afford these books in Indonesia? Who can also read and meaningfully engage with these books if English language still becomes the main barrier? How can we connect our histories with these Western historical trajectories?'.

Having witnessed and experienced how all these barriers affect non-white scholars, I have argued in *Social Text Online*:

> To be theoretically engaged and listened to, one must publish. To get published, one must be not only fluent in English but also proficient in queer theory literature, mostly written in English and published by the academic presses or trade publishers with a high price (at least, in relation to Indonesians' living standards). Without adequate English language skills and understanding of the genealogy of 'Western' queer scholarship, it is improbable for local scholars to engage in a meaningful way (Wijaya 2020b).

No wonder, then, during my study (and even, still in my ongoing work) I must have 'double consciousness'. It helps non-white people to navigate two 'social worlds'. But, considering the homophobic alienation I feel from my home country, sometimes 'double consciousness' does not always work that simply. Often, when I diverted my mind across to Indonesia, the feeling of rejection and exclusion upsurged, becoming inescapable.

Southern 'Stealth-mode' & Scant Access

The other world that I live in, that is, my home country, consistently denies the existence of queer people. While it is essential to critique the discourse that quickly places Western countries as 'more civilised' for their tolerance toward homosexuality, we cannot erase the fact that homophobia does exist and persist in many countries in the Global South (and also, in the West). Since the unprecedented attack on LGBT people in 2016, it has become more challenging to teach queer-related stuff in universities, as some academics told me about their fear of potential controversies that might erupt if some homophobic raise this activity in the public sphere. However, it does not mean that they stopped teaching in its entirety. Some integrate queer-stuff into their existing courses, for example, in gender, cultural studies, or literary studies, but using stealth mode (Wijaya 2020b). Again, Indonesian queer studies exists in liminal space, between existent and non-existent—an absent presence.

Recently, I received a message from an Indonesian professor, asking me if she could use my writings to show queer theory in an Indonesian/Asian contexts. The fact that there are local academics teaching queer-stuff, however limited it is, does not solve the issue of scant access to Western queer academic texts, and importantly, the meagre amount of local queer texts. Publishing queer stuff in Indonesia is not easy at all. For instance, the publication of my Indonesian book on porn and queer studies, '*C*Bul: Perbincangan Serius Tentang Seksualitas Kontemporer*' (P*ERV: Conversations on Contemporary Sexualities)[2] was cancelled by the publisher itself because the editor worried the contents would spark controversies. Strangely, this suddenly happened around two weeks prior to the publication date.

Of course, the domino effects continue: a shortage of Indonesian queer scholars in the international academic circuits. It is thus not only the marginalisation of queer issues in the public sphere strongly affecting the life of queer studies in academic and public settings. Instead, central to all these problems is the language barrier and minimal intellectual resources that many Indonesian scholars must grapple with in order to engage with the global academy's politics. Unfortunately, in practice, the term 'global' still preserves the U.S. at its epicentre—in some cases, books published by the U.S. based academic presses are considered more prestigious compared to other books with non-English languages.

---

[2] After the mainstream publisher cancelled the publication, in 2018, this book was eventually published by an independent publisher, *Marjin Kiri*. For me personally, this event has shown the politics of the publishing industry in Indonesia. The fact that mainstream publishers are reluctant to publish queer-themed books (particularly, non-fiction) should not obscure how independent publishers seem to be increasingly more willing to publish queer books.

Conclusion: Alternative Academies & Access

Back to the question that the participant addressed to me, I am reminded of the central purposes of writing *Intimate Assemblages*. It is the manifestation of my hope to see more scholarly works on queer studies coming from queer Indonesians themselves, and to demonstrate how queer Indonesians can continue to challenge both the academic-imperialism and the looming homophobia. I completed and published the full manuscript two years after I finished my study and return to Jakarta. Writing a book whilst working full-time for business sustainability was not easy, especially as someone located outside of the academy with limited scholarship infrastructures. I saved some portion of my income to purchase academic books, so that I could continue engaging my work with what was happening in academia. Important to highlight here is that publishing is not merely an intellectual endeavor, but also, equally, a materially implicated landscape.

Whenever I reflect on this experience, I am convinced that despite all the hurdles, it is still possible for queer studies to emerge and live outside of the formal academic settings. And that is what many grassroots queer activists and scholars have been doing in Indonesia: continuously teaching and spreading queer knowledges with whatever resources are available in hand, including even a set of photocopied materials.

References

Berlant, Lauren (1998). 'Intimacy: A Special Issue'. *Critical Inquiry*, 24(2), pp.281-288.

Brim, Matt. (2020). *Poor Queer Studies: Confronting Elitism in the University*. Durham: Duke University Press.

Puar, Jasbir K. (2017). *Terrorist Assemblages: Homonationalism in Queer Times (Tenth Anniversary Expanded Edition)*. Durham: Duke University Press.

Wijaya, Hendri Yulius (2020a). *Intimate Assemblages: The Politics of Queer Identities and Sexualities in Indonesia*. Singapore: Palgrave Macmillan.

Wijaya, Hendri Yulius (2020b). Pedagogy of the Homeless: Poor Queer Studies in Indonesia, *Social Text Online*. Accessed 21.9.20. Accessed at: https://socialtextjournal.org/pedagogy-of-the-homeless-poor-queer-studies-in-indonesia/

Hendri Yulius Wijaya is an Indonesian author. His most recent books are *Intimate Assemblages: The Politics of Queer Identities and Sexualities in Indonesia* (Palgrave Macmillan, 2020), and *C*BUL: Perbincangan Serius tentang Seksualitas Kontemporer* (Marjin Kiri, 2019), an Indonesian book on porn studies. Wijaya is currently a book reviewer for *DNA Magazine*, and also preparing his first poetry collection, *Stonewall Tak Mampir di Atlantis* (Stonewall does not stop by Atlantis), published by EA Books in October 2020.

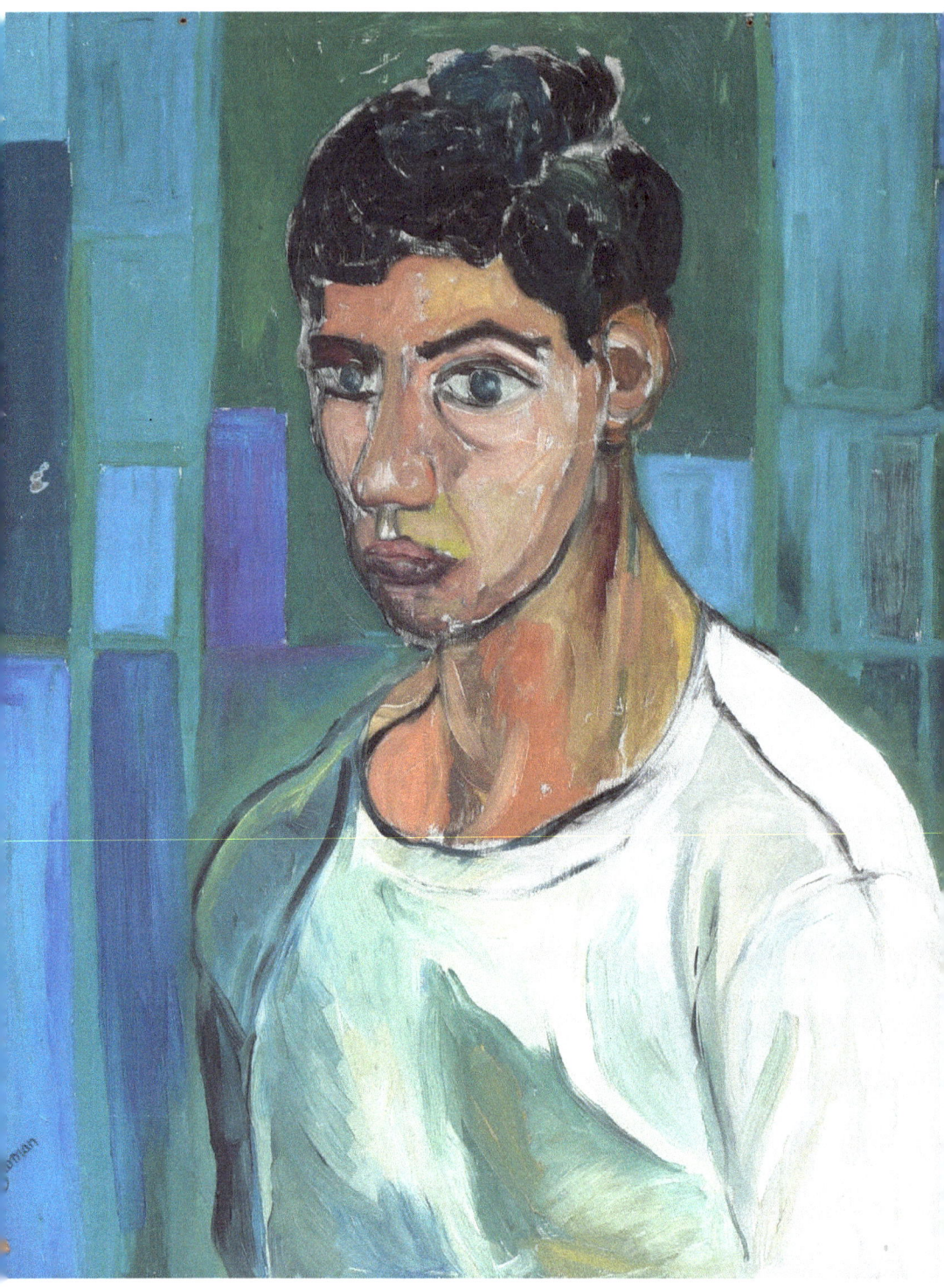

DEREK JARMAN'S QUEER RESILIENCE
Marcus O'Donnell

A major retrospective in Dublin, which is set to travel over the next three years, has finally brought together the many aspects of British queer icon Derek Jarman's career. Marcus O'Donnell talks with the exhibition's curator, Seán Kissane

Prospect Cottage, a black tar-stained fisherman's shack with bright yellow window frames and door, on a shingle beach in one of the bleakest parts of England, has become an enduring symbol of an artist's lifelong attempt to craft poetry out of the everyday. On one wall this is literally writ large: a fading sculptured scrawl traces John Donne's beautiful poem, *The Sun Rising.*

Busy old fool, unruly sun,
Why dost thou thus,
Through windows, and through curtains, call on us ?
Must to thy motions lovers' seasons run ?
Saucy pedantic wretch, go chide
Late school-boys and sour prentices,
Go tell court-huntsmen that the king will ride,
Call country ants to harvest offices;
Love, all alike, no season knows nor clime,
Nor hours, days, months, which are the rags of time.
In that the world's contracted thus ;
Thine age asks ease, and since thy duties be
To warm the world, that's done in warming us.
Shine here to us, and thou art everywhere ;
This bed thy centre is, these walls thy sphere.

British queer filmmaker, painter, writer, theatre designer and queer activist, Derek Jarman bought the cottage in 1987, six months after he tested HIV positive, and for the last eight years of his life this was the calm centre of his chaotic world.

Prospect Cottage is a miracle three times over. First, the emergence of Jarman's verdant garden from this desert landscape is completely unexpected and one of the major artworks of his final years. An artist's stubborn tribute to impossibility. Second, the miracle of love and grief in the years after Jarman's

Derek Jarman—*Self Portrait*, 1959, oil on board, 65 x 76 cm, Private Collection, Photo IMMA

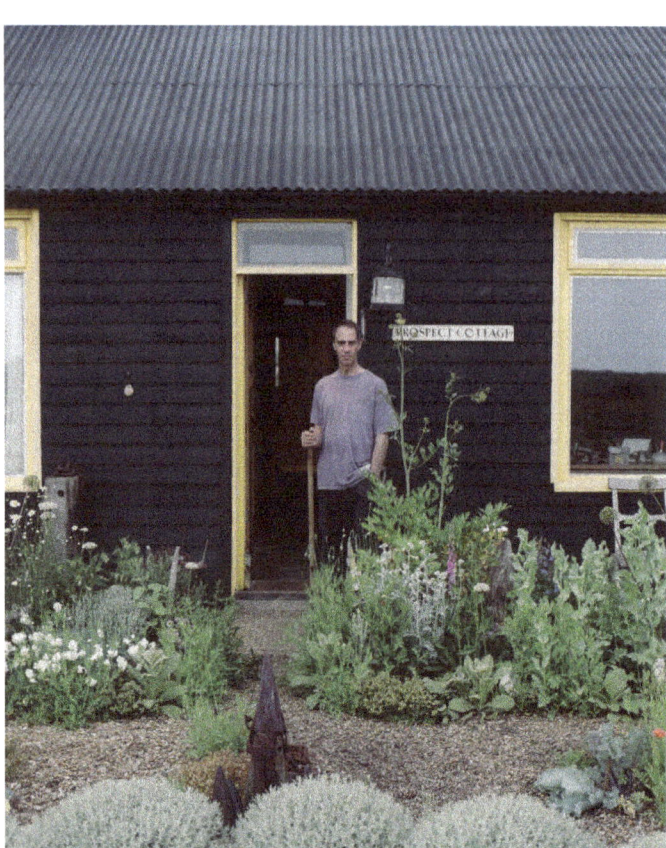
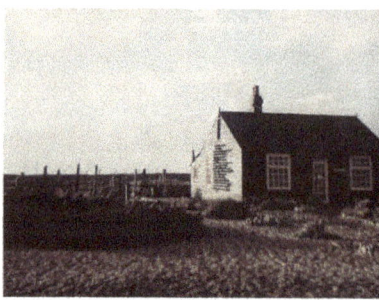
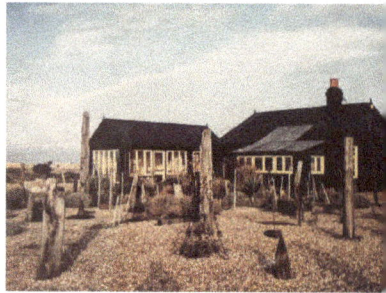

Derek Jarman—*Prospect Cottage*. Main image, Howard Sooley. Other images *Prospect Cottage New Year's Day 1999*, Gordon Thompson

death as his partner Keith Collins devoted himself to the landscape and to Jarman's legacy.

And early this year, with the cottage in danger of being sold following Collin's sudden death in 2018, we saw a third miracle when Jarman's celebrity friends, led by actor Tilda Swinton, crowd-sourced 3.5-million pounds in a matter of months to ensure the cottage will be preserved as an artist retreat.

Jarman's garden has always been one of his most popular creations, the beautiful picture book, *Derek Jarman's Garden*, published just after the artist's death in 1994, is one of Thames and Hudson's best-selling books. It has been translated into multiple languages and has a strange crossover appeal where his queer fans and grandma gardeners meet. It is not just the celebrity fundraising campaign that has brought Jarman and his garden back into the public spotlight, 30 years after his death he is now the focus of two new exhibitions. The Irish

Museum of Modern Art, Dublin has finally brought together the many aspects of Jarman's career in a stunning retrospective exhibition and catalogue and London's Garden Museum staged a smaller exhibition focused on Jarman as a gardener.

Both exhibitions garnered international media coverage with the gardening show, in particular, capturing the imagination of a number of writers under lockdown. Writing in the *New York Times* in April, Mary Katharine Tramontana, asked: 'During this coronavirus pandemic, it is perhaps worth exploring what can be learned from Jarman's act of nurturing plants during his own health emergency. Can the simple, tactile pleasure of pottering in the dirt or watching seedlings sprout comfort us at a time of loss and bewilderment?'

Talking to Tramontana, Stephen Deuchar, one of the team behind the Prospect Cottage fundraising campaign, noted how unusual Dungeness is. Not only is it a rough shingle, or pebble, landscape but in the background rises a sprawling nuclear power station, and a miniature steam train stages another mechanical interruption as it cuts across the headland.

'It's as if there's a contest between the optimism and audacity of plants, and the relentlessness of the shingle,' Deuchar said. 'There's something moving about a small plant that springs up, forging its way to the surface through the stones. It's what makes his garden—his last great work of art—so mesmerizing.'

Howard Sooley, one of the friends who cared for Jarman in the final years of his life, often spent weekends chauffeuring Jarman from London to Dungeness and became a key collaborator on the garden. A photographer, it is Sooley's images that have brought the garden to the world. He told Tramonata what a powerful impact the garden had on Jarman:

'Gardening carries you to a fundamental place of living, rather than doing,' Sooley said. 'When he was quite ill, he'd just grow the second we got onto Dungeness, gardening all day like he was breathing air.'

Seán Kissane, the curator who brought the Dublin Jarman retrospective, *PROTEST!*, to life admits that the breadth and depth of Jarman's achievement surprised him. It also became his biggest challenge. Because the eclectic artist roved across so many art forms over a busy 35-year career, Kissane says curating Jarman was like herding cats.

It began with a casual conversation with Amanda Wilkinson at a social event soon after her Gallery had taken over the Jarman estate. Kissane had no idea where it would lead, but out of curiosity he set up a time with Wilkinson to look through the work next time he was in London.

'I arranged to go to her warehouse and there was a team of four guys and they started to unpack all these huge paintings,' he tells me in a Zoom

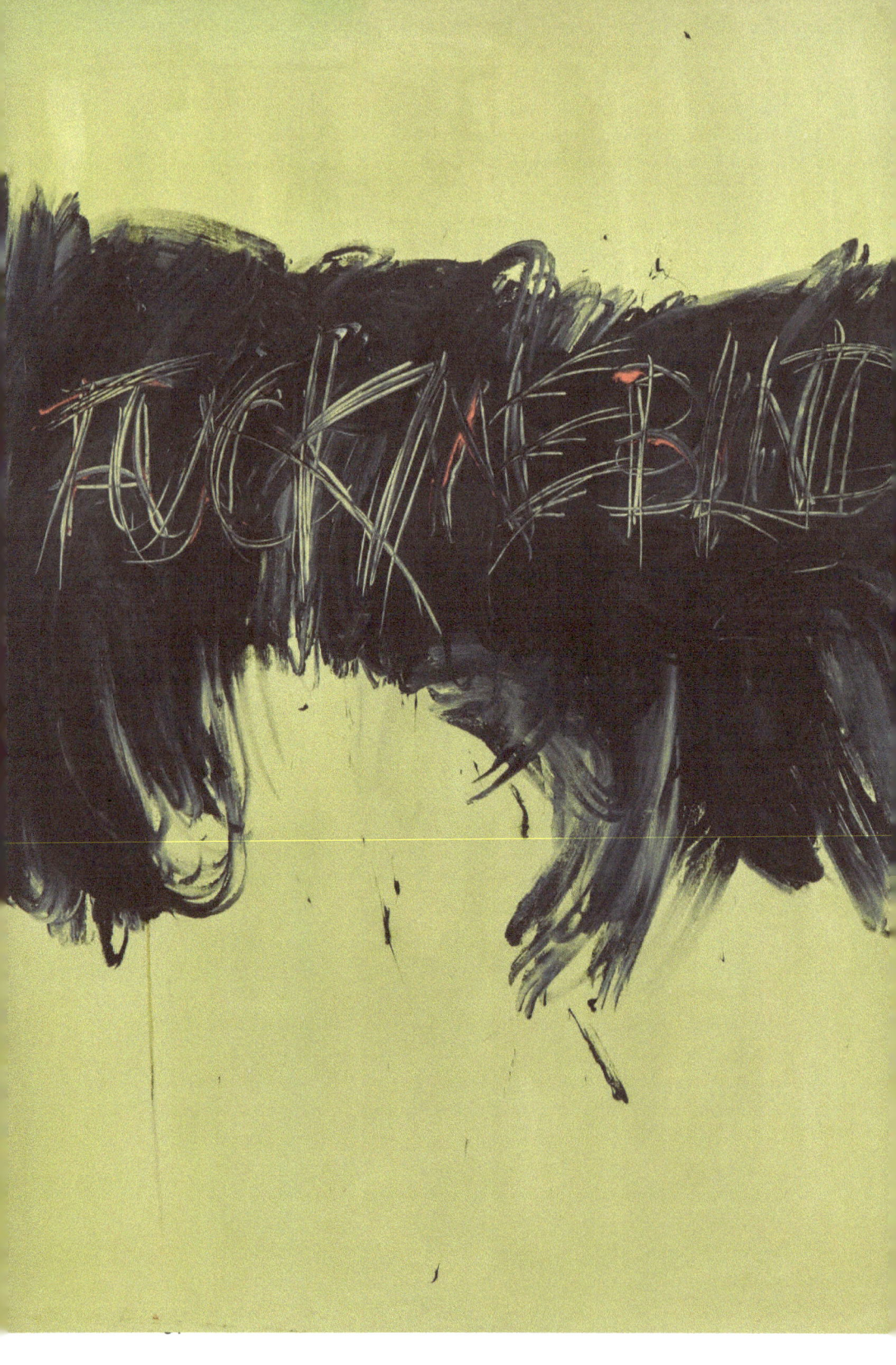

conversation from Dublin, where he is, like I am in Melbourne, in lockdown.

'So, small paintings, huge paintings, things from the 60s, things from the 90s. They were all just coming out in a complete jumble, you know, there was no rhyme or reason. It was just this is this, this is this. And I quickly realized I knew absolutely nothing about Derek Jarman.'

But from that visit the seed of the show was sown. Kissane says: 'This provoked me to see what I could do'.

In that first visit to Wilkinson's warehouse, as he looked at the series of slogan paintings Jarman made at the end of his life, rich abstract canvasses with camp slogans—'Dizzy bitch' 'Fuck me blind' 'Infection'—he sensed a key idea. He wrote down a working title for a possible exhibition: *PROTEST!*

'That was the overwhelming impression I had been left with by my visit to the warehouse. It was of rage and sadness actually, and so it really was just capital letters P-R-O-T-E-S-T exclamation mark; and then it sat there [as a working title] and as the project continued there was no reason to change it.' As he began to research Jarman's work Kissane realised that this sense of radical critique was there from the start, in even Jarman's earliest work.

'I was finding this sense of responsibility and social engagement, connection to literature, connection to philosophy and a rage against particularly English, social structures, political structures, cultural structures; and that was the overriding theme which I found through all of those *cats* that I was trying to herd.'

'My practice as a curator has very much focused on researching around the edges. I really enjoy that kind of process of uncovering things that are really obvious when they're done but haven't been done for whatever reason until now,' he tells me.

This can in a sense mean working blind.

'So up until the last week of the installation I had no idea was this show any good,' Kissane confesses with a smile. 'I was kind of too close to the work and I had no real external feedback. But then the critics came in and their reaction was similar to mine. None of them really knew the full extent of his practice.'

Even just looking through the 300-page catalogue is an adventure. It is a beautiful production bound in mock black leather with gold and red lettering, giving it the impression of one of those medieval alchemical spell books that so fascinated Jarman. It is of course richly illustrated and comes with 18 specially commissioned essays that show off Jarman's remarkable achievement. I've been a Jarman fan since first seeing and writing about his work in the mid-eighties and my library has all of Jarman's books and films mixed in with several biographies and studies, but Kissane is right, it's a

< Fuck me blind, 1993, oil on canvas, 251.4 x 179 cm, Collection Julia Muggenburg

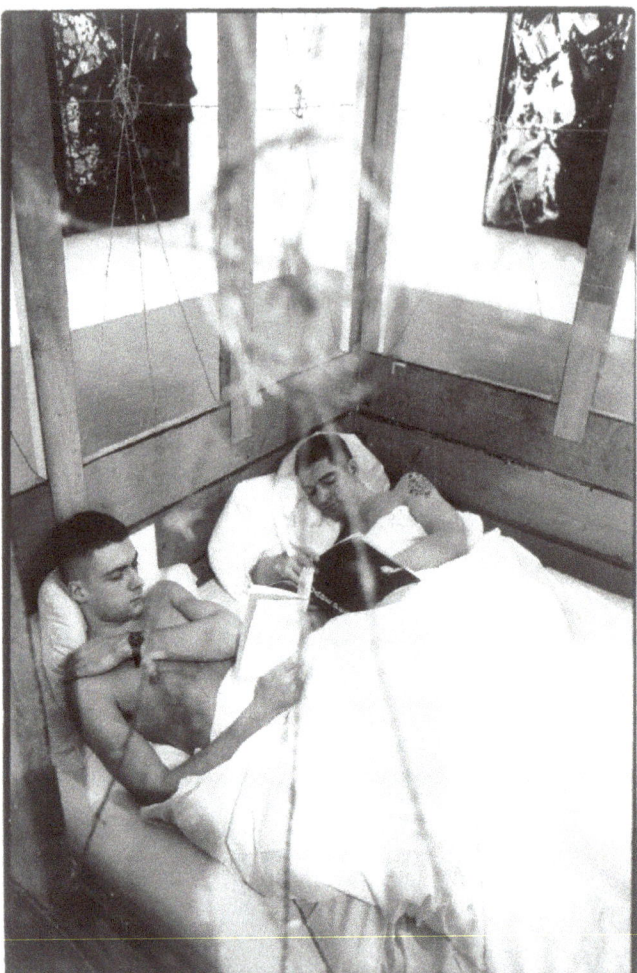

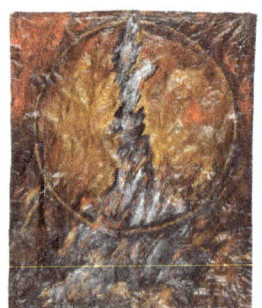

(left) National Review of Live Art performance, Third Eye Centre Glasgow, 1989, detail. (bottom right) GBH Series VI, ICA, 1983-84, Mixed media on newspaper on canvas, 289.6 x 241.3 cm, Private Collection | (top right) Derek Jarman PROTEST! IMMA installation view.

revelation to see the early paintings, up against the films, the writing, the stage design and the activism. This really is Jarman in a way most of us haven't seen him before. Not only do we get to see the full scope of his painting—something Jarman never really stopped even when he was more publicly known as a filmmaker—but there is new insight into his working methods and collaborations, his ventures into radical drag, and even a detailed exploration of his private 1200 book library.

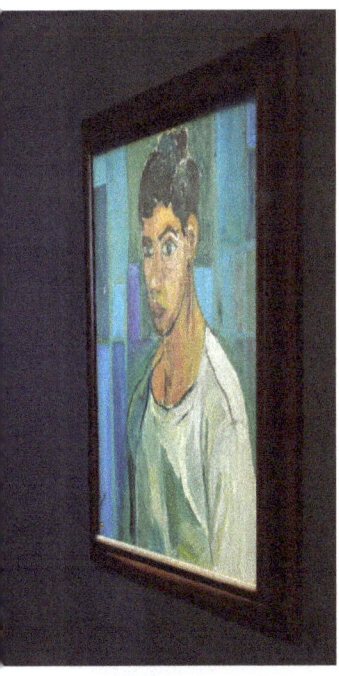

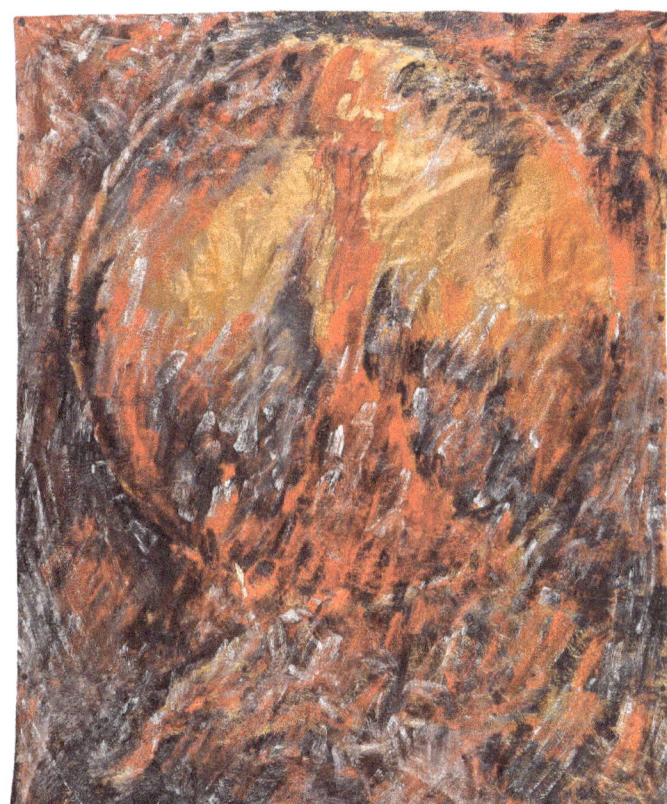

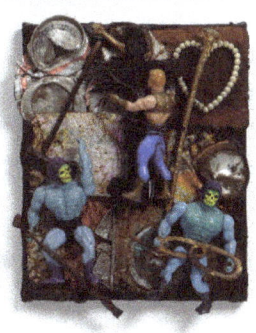

(bottom left) I.N.R.I., 1988, oil and mixed media on canvas, 33.5 x 27 x 8.5 cm, Courtesy Keith Collins Will Trust and Amanda Wilkinson Gallery, London | (top right) GBH Series VI, ICA, 1983-84, mixed media on newspaper on canvas, 289.6 x 241.3 cm, Private Collection.

In the first room of the Dublin exhibition visitors were greeted with a 1959 self portrait of a 16 year old Jarman—this Picasso-esque, but strikingly realist portrait, is juxtaposed with the adult filmmaker's last and most radical work, his film *Blue*. *Blue* presents a vibrant shimmering blue screen for 80 minutes—no discernible images and a lyrical soundtrack that ruminates on art, death and love. Made at the end of his life when HIV was playing havoc with his eyesight it is also a hymn to seeing and memory.

This juxtaposition is very deliberate as Kissane explained in a curator's talk, now available on the IMMA website:

'The approach for the whole exhibition was to try to always remember this paring when approaching his work,' Kissane says. 'Because what you are seeing is the making of an icon, the making of an image and then this work of total iconoclasm, the almost complete destruction of the image. There is also this oscillating, this shifting constantly between figuration and abstraction, stillness and movement, materialism and the mysticism, the body and the soul.'

The *PROTEST!* catalogue gives a sense of this juxtaposition, but the exhibition design took this further and allowed one type of artwork to bleed into another—creating what Kissane describes as a deliberately overwhelming experience to match the diversity and passion of Jarman's many art practices. The soundtrack of *Blue* can be heard in the room of early paintings and Shakespeare's sonnets from the *Angelic Conversation* soundtrack bleed into another room of stark black and gold paintings. This seems only appropriate for an early innovator in pop videos, a filmmaker whose work celebrates collage and a diarist who moves quickly from the blazing nightlife of London's gay disco scene to the silence of Dungeness.

Jarman called the United States 'the billboard promised land' which captures a sense of alure wrapped in a sarcastic dismissal. He thought at one point that he might live for a while in New York, and returned there often on visits, but in the end Jarman was distinctly English and his work emerges out of a deep engagement and critique of British life and history

Kissane draws an analogy to Jane Austen.

'Jane Austen described her writing as being done 'with a fine brush on a little bit (not two inches wide) of ivory'. What she means is that her entire world emerges from two drawing rooms and the minute observation of the nuances of life within that very limited structure. Jarman said England was his small frame, partly because he couldn't speak for people outside that frame but also because of the richness of experience that could be found there.'

Like Austen, Jarman drew from his everyday experience but Kissane says he 'stretched' this by combining it with a deep sense of history and sense of baroque vision which is often over the top and sometimes even kitsch.

Jubilee one of Jarman's early features begins in a country garden and we have Queen Elizabeth I with an alchemist, John Dee, who calls forth the spirit Ariel to show the monarch a vision of the future of her kingdom. This vision turns out to be a post-apocalyptic version of punk Thatcherite England. But it is also Bankside—the then rundown area of London where artists like Jarman lived in abandoned warehouses. A spread in the catalogue

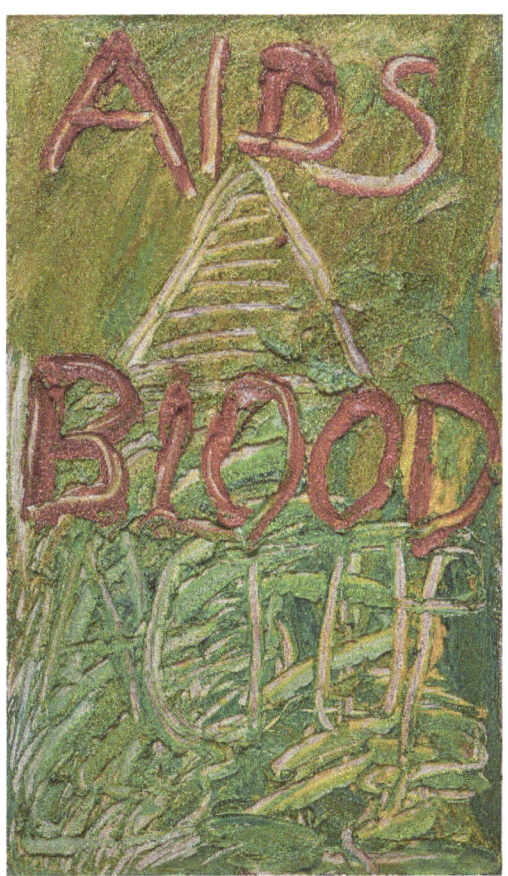

Derek Jarman, Aids Blood, 1992, Oil on canvas,
61 x 101.5 cm Courtesy Amanda Wilkinson Gallery

that mixes images from Jarman's various studios and residences with stills from *Jubilee*, gives a compelling insight into how he worked with his own tiny piece of ivory.

'So, he kind of buys into this National Trust English identity, or cliche of what Englishness is, and then collides it with this kind of Bankside reality. And I guess that's part of where the tension is,' Kissane says.

Although Jarman's life and work was deeply political, 30 years on his films are not as well-known as his garden. The beauty and power of his garden has resulted in what Kissane calls a kind of 'unintentional middle-class washing' of a radical artist ... Because so many people had this strong sense of him being a gardener ... the kind of punk and activist and troublemaker had been erased,' Kissane says. 'So, one of the reasons to emphasize the political and the protest was to brush up in a very rough way against this gentler identity because there was also a sense of needing to rebalance that.'

An exhibition about Jarman the troublemaker couldn't have come at a more appropriate time. Jarman's activism grew out of the early years of the AIDS epidemic and the homophobic policies of Thatcherite popularism. It is not hard to find parallels with 2020.

Although the exhibition has been in the making for a number of years the current political climate—the international rise of right wing popularism, the

Black Lives Matter movement, and the COVID epidemic—has added to the sense of urgency already inherent in Jarman's work.

'The Coronavirus and HIV and the way they were handled by Britain and the United States were similar,' Kissane says cautiously, 'which is right-wing politicians like Thatcher and Regan putting their heads in the sand and saying, 'Take personal responsibility. This is not our responsibility.' And so, you can draw parallels there. I still think it's a little bit soon to start drawing parallels between coronavirus and HIV/AIDS, but at the same time, government inaction has been the thing which has seen most casualties, and in the case of Trump wilful ignorance.'

We can only speculate what Jarman might be saying about Boris Johnson had he lived. He died well before the onslaught of social media but today you can imagine him having a pretty rousing twitter feed. His book *Queer Edward II* intersperses his film script with campy queer protest slogans that would get lots of shares and retweets on social media. Kissane says that part of the appeal of the exhibition to younger audiences new to Jarman were the 'gramable' moments: with plenty of selfies in front of the big slogan paintings like 'Fuck me blind'.

It's another example of the multiple ways that Jarman's work can be read and the multiple audiences it appeals to. His oeuvre embraces everything from a cerebral 'imageless' film and work which reaches back into deeply researched histories of strange English alchemists, to paintings of campy slogans and pop video clips for Pet Shop Boys.

The triumph of his posthumous garden book as one of his most enduringly popular works would have thrilled Jarman, who said towards the end of his life that perhaps he should have been a gardener rather than a filmmaker. But Kissane's deeply researched retrospective under the banner headline *PROTEST!* would have confirmed for Jarman that he had, at last, actually been understood. He might have laughed that it took some Irish distance to understand this quintessential British artist and, always fond of appropriating a biblical quote, he might very well have muttered something about prophets, honour and their hometown.

PROTEST! Edited by *Seán* Kissane & Karim Rehmani-White is published by Thames & Hudson RRP $100. The exhibition will travel to the Manchester Art Gallery in mid 2021 and to the Yale Center for British Art in 2024.

Politics, performance, and painting: exploring Jarman's work

GBH Series VI, ICA, 1983-84, mixed media on newspaper on canvas, 289.6 x 241.3 cm, Private

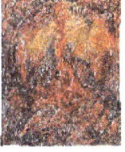 Collection.

The GBH series, that Jarman created as the headline pieces for a 1984 retrospective at London's ICA, have been acclaimed by art historian and Jarman biographer Michael Charlesworth as his greatest paintings. The layered construction of paint and newspaper creates a shimmering effect and at their recent showing in Derry, as a satellite to the IMMA show, Joanne Laws wrote of their visceral impact in her review: 'their scale, verticality and primal rage engulf... the body.' There are six in the series, all variations on a theme, the shadowy shape in the middle being more or less recognisable as a map of Britain or a mushroom cloud in each variation. Jarman said GBH could stand for 'whatever you want it to: grievous bodily harm, great British horror, gargantuan bloody H-bomb'.

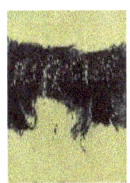 Fuck me blind, 1993, oil on canvas, 251.4 x 179 cm, Collection Julia Muggenburg. From Jarman's final exhibition, *Evil Queen*, like his previous *Queer* series it drew on both his ongoing interest in expressionist abstraction and a tabloid sensibility to humorously provoke questions about his own illness, queer rights and British politics. Jarman was very fragile at this point and was assisted by two studio assistants. One of them Karl Lydon remembers Jarman asking for a sickly, hospital yellow for the background of this image. The slogan has an Australian connection: the other assistant, Piers Clemett, had an Australian roommate who used the expression constantly and, in this instance, it doubled as a sick joke about Jarman's failing eyesight.

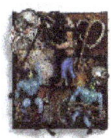 I.N.R.I., 1988, oil and mixed media on canvas, 33.5 x 27 x 8.5 cm, Courtesy Keith Collins Will Trust and Amanda Wilkinson Gallery, London.

One of a number of assemblages made at Prospect Cottage, where Jarman produced work that experimented with tar, thick black impasto and a kaleidoscopic range of found objects, often referencing as this one does, religious themes. Kissane speculates that I.N.R.I. was done in response to a famous British blasphemy case brought by campaigner Mary Whitehouse against a poem about a Roman centurion having sex with the dead Christ. Jarman has in effect recreated a camp version of this poem and can therefore be seen as a deliberately provocative blasphemy in the same year Margaret Thatcher introduced 'Clause 28' which banned local authorities from activities that 'promoted homosexuality'.

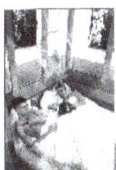 National Review of Live Art performance, Third Eye Centre Glasgow, 1989, Performance detail.

In 1989 Jarman created this show in Glasgow, where Keith Collins and Andy Marshall read and slept in a cage throughout the exhibition. On the walls were seven tarred-and-feathered mattresses hung as artworks. Around pillars and other spaces in the gallery were outrageous British tabloid headlines. My personal favourite: 'Gay Wolfman got his claws into Holly'. The theme of two boys in bed recurs in Jarman's work and may relate to a story he told a number of times of being roughly ripped out of the bed of a classmate at boarding school by the headmistress, publicly humiliated and whipped. In Glasgow he created a scene of everyday queerness, two men sleeping and reading, but entrapped by their cage and the encroaching signs of homophobia.

Marcus O'Donnell is a writer, visual artist and academic. His fiction, journalism and poetry have been published in periodicals and anthologies including, *Verandah*, *Siglo*, *Bent Street*, *New Writing*, *OutRage*, *Hard*, and *The Conversation*. He is currently an Associate Professor and Director, Cloud Learning Futures at Deakin University, in Melbourne Australia.

DIVERSITY RULES
Hannah Gillard

Paid queer diversity work. Do you need to be queer to do it?

'Female, white, able-bodied, straight and binary. It is not a dating profile for Tinder but a description of the predominant profile of Australia's workplace diversity and inclusion (D&I) practitioner' (Annese 2018). This is how Lisa Annese, the head of the Diversity Council of Australia (DCA), began a 2018 article in the *Sydney Morning Herald* about a lack of diversity amongst paid diversity workers in Australia. The statement was based on a study undertaken by The University of Sydney Business School, DCA and the Australian HR Institute (2018, p.1) of the last two body's members, and included 279 respondents. The point of Annese's article is clear: when it comes to paid diversity work, minority groups are underrepresented, and identity matters.

What Annese's piece does not focus on, but which I turned my mind to during my doctoral research on queer[3] workplace diversity, are the affordances *and* the limitations of people outside a particular community doing paid diversity work on their behalf. I contemplated this specifically in relation to paid queer diversity work. These reflections started as a result of a situation I encountered during my interviewing and observational research with workplaces in NSW. At one organisation, the sole queer diversity practitioner role was held by someone, Alex[4], who was not queer herself.

In this essay, I argue neither that one needs to be queer to do paid queer diversity work, or the reverse. Instead, I argue that *both sides* of the conversation need to be considered, to enable a nuanced consideration on what is politically gained and lost by specifying that queer diversity workers must be queer themselves.

My ability to write this piece is indebted to the friendship and genuine passion for queer diversity work that 'Alex' showed me whilst doing research with her organisation. If she was not genuinely committed to constructing more queer friendly workplaces, she would not have spent months of her already busy full time schedule, introducing me to workers to interview, enabling my access to meetings, and assisting my research project wherever possible. The queer diversity work I am performing through writing this

---

[3] I use 'queer' throughout this essay as an imperfect shorthand for those who are LGBTQI+, or, put another way- those who are not straight or cisgender.

[4] This is a pseudonym - I have anonymised participants in my research with their consent.

piece, does not sit in opposition to Alex's work, but is in line with the self-reflexive spirit and constant interest in improving queer workplace diversity efforts that Alex demonstrated with a passion.

I further preface my conversation by recognising this discussion is a luxurious hypothetical for some workers. Through speaking with employees who do queer advocacy labour in workplaces, I know that many organisations do not have paid queer diversity roles, and many workplaces expect this labour to be performed uncompensated. For instance, one worker at an organisation I did research with indicated that whilst diversity work for women was compensated on a board he was on, queer diversity work was not.

What does a queer diversity worker do?

Through my observational doctoral research within workplaces, some of the common tasks of queer diversity workers are:

- giving advice to workers about how to best support their queer clients, and interact with other queer workers
- liaising with queer community groups and organisations
- organising events for queer awareness days
- operating across diversity portfolios to work on intersecting diversity projects (for instance, one queer diversity worker I spoke to was attempting to get queer feedback on a disability strategy for the organisation)
- creating queer diversity promotional materials
- attending educational seminars about how to improve queer diversity efforts, and;
- if that workplace is a member of Pride in Diversity, creating submissions for the Australian Workplace Equality Index-[5] an accreditation system that ranks workplaces according to their level of queer friendliness, based on things like the organisation's policies, and queer diversity events they hold during the year.

Given these tasks and objectives, should a paid queer diversity worker be queer or not?

---

[5] I acknowledge the important critiques that writers like Business Queer (2019;2020) have performed of the Australian Workplace Equality Index in *Archer Magazine*.

Firstly, I do not think that identity is irrelevant to the performance of queer diversity work. Given my own experience, and findings from the PhD project of Jan Filmer (2020), some queer people do tend to alter their behaviour and what they feel comfortable discussing with people outside queer communities. I know from personal experience that the way I interact with people within and outside queer communities generally differs. The language I use, my defensiveness, my sense of comfort and the topics I talk about often change depending on whether the person is part of queer communities or not. A similar phenomenon was expressed in Filmer's PhD project. Filmer (2020) interviewed queer people to learn about the construction of queer spaces in and around Sydney, Australia. One interview participant in his project, Jeff,[6] said that the things he talked about with straight[7] friends differed from what he felt at ease talking about with queer people. Filmer states, 'when I asked him why that might be the case, he related this to the kinds of things he feels comfortable sharing with other queers, such as matters of sexual health, people's views on family and children, or issues to do with 'boys'. Further, Jeff gave the example of a straight female friend of his, who he did not really feel comfortable talking about gay matters with. Thus, it can be seen both Jeff and I changed the way we moved through the world when encountering people outside queer communities. To me, this emphasises that the identities of diversity practitioners working with and for queer communities has significance. It made me think about whether there are limits to how effective people outside queer communities could be in these roles, given their lack of lived experience with queer marginalisation, and the fact that queer people might not be as comfortable being open with them about their experiences.

Secondly, arguing you do not need to be queer to do paid queer diversity work creates a slippery slope for the idea that other types of diversity advocacy—for instance, women's and disability advocacy—do not need to be filled by people in these groups. On the contrary, there is a large amount of commentary from people in these groups about why it is important for folks in these communities to be put in prominent diversity and advocacy roles representing them (Price 2013; Waters 2014; Innis 2014). One reason for this

---

[6] The names were changed by Filmer in his project to protect the identities of interview participants.
[7] My view is that Jeff probably also meant to specify 'cisgender' here, given the way straight people form part of queer communities too— for example, being straight and trans, or straight and intersex. However, I cannot confirm this.

is that people from these groups have a history of being spoken on behalf of by people outside their own communities. An example of this would be when former Prime Minister Tony Abbott occupied the role of Minister for Women, something many feminist writers critiqued, and claimed it was more appropriate for a woman to occupy this role (Price 2013 and Waters 2014). Indeed, these commentators recognised the significance of lived experience for advocacy work. So too did former Disability Discrimination Commissioner Graeme Innis, on the grounds of how invaluable lived experience of a disability was for disability advocacy work (Innis 2014). While there is a heterogeneity of views and experiences within groups like women and those with disabilities, there are strong views that it is preferable for marginalised groups to be represented by their own. By saying it's fine for non-queer people to do paid queer diversity work, I worry this can be used as ammunition by conservatives to justify the irrelevance of identity for advocacy roles.

Thirdly, as Annese notes, there is already an issue with diversity positions in Australia being dominated by straight, cisgender people. Marking out particular roles as only being for queer people can work to address this issue. A straight, cisgender person occupying a paid queer diversity role sits awkwardly alongside the high rate of unemployment for trans workers. For instance, a 2018 study found trans unemployment was 21%—quadruple the general unemployment rate in Australia (Cheung et al. 2018, p.232). In a later study, Equality Australia listed the trans and gender diverse unemployment rate at 20%, following the rise of COVID-19 in Australia (Equality Australia 2020, p.18). Marking out paid queer diversity roles as specifically for queer people, and applying positive discrimination in hiring practices for marginalised groups within this community—for instance, for trans people (Olsen 2019)—could help address the dominance of people with straight and cisgender identities in diversity practitioner roles.

Perspective B
People outside the queer community should be able to be paid queer diversity practitioners too

Though there are compelling reasons why only queer people should be able to do paid queer diversity work, persuasive arguments exist for why this does not necessarily have to be the case. I address three of these arguments below.

Firstly, not having to deal with queer oppression personally can free up the energy of allies to perform queer diversity work, where queer workers sometimes cannot.

I found this in an interview with a queer worker (Charlie) in Alex's organisation. While Charlie acknowledged there could be benefits to queer people occupying these roles, they also said the expectation that only queer people could do paid queer diversity work could be hugely, 'taxing on that person. Because you're doing that [being queer] 24/7. So already outside of work life, you've got to be an educator, you know—to your family, to your friends, to your health professional—to everyone. Then at work, you're *also* being that educator' (italics added). Charlie stated they were glad they did not work in a paid queer diversity role full time, as the labour of educating people about queerness at work, in addition to already doing it outside of it, would be too much. Indeed, they said, 'it's tricky to be flying the flag all the time. Because you've got to be flying the flag everywhere … and I think people who aren't from a minority group don't really get that'. Thus, their point was that sometimes it could be appropriate for non-queer people to do paid queer diversity work, given it may not be as exhausting or all-encompassing as it could be for some queer workers.

Following Charlie's perspective, my second point about why there should not be a rule about non-queer people doing paid queer diversity work relates to the way it perpetuates a binary between those who are queer and not queer. This inhibits understandings of the ways heteronormativity oppresses people on both sides of the fence (Cohen 2005, p.22). Heteronormativity does not simply refer to the way in which heterosexuality becomes normalised, but the means through which heterosexuality intersects with vectors like race, class, disability and age to marginalise those within and outside queer communities. Scholar Cathy Cohen argues that queer politics needs to challenge heteronormativity, not simply heterosexuality. Informed by the late 1990's US context, she argues this needs to happen to appreciate how heteronormativity oppresses not just queer people, but also Black single mothers on welfare, for instance, who experience the brunt of classism, racism and sexism—all components of heteronormativity (Cohen 2005, p.26).[8] Cohen's piece makes me reflect on the ways that, while an organisation may appoint a queer person to a paid queer diversity role, if they are a white, gay, middle-class cisgender man (as has occurred at one of my workplaces), it is evident that their positionality does not just challenge heteronormativity, but also perpetuates it.[9] Cohen's chapter can be used to argue that one does not necessarily need to be queer to do paid diversity

---

[8] Cohen (2005, p.44) does not argue for the abolition of identity categories like queer, but rather contends that constantly querying them is an important ethical project for queer politics.

[9] My reflection on this point was not just stimulated by Cohen's piece, but also through a late night party conversation with my friend Tanja Dittfeld, who encouraged me to consider the way intersecting oppressions impact, and are perpetuated by, queer people.

work, and that constant reflection needs to occur in relation to the ways queer people are simultaneously both oppressors and oppressed.

My third argument regarding why one should not have to identify as queer to engage in paid queer diversity efforts is that it makes outing oneself mandatory. This can demand adherence to a white, Western coming out narrative that is not comfortable or applicable to all. Writers Nonno and Aroosa (2018) explore this phenomenon in their essay 'A QPoC Manifesto: fighting for invisibility in a world that loves to talk'. In this chapter, they discuss their own experiences of not disclosing their queerness publicly based on their interest in being, 'respectful members of ... [their] ... communities' (Nonno and Aroosa 2018, p.185), whilst noting this does not mean they cannot experience their queerness in a fulfilling way. Being out for them would involve a trade-off in some respects between their communities and identities they say they are not willing to make. For instance, Nonno and Aroosa state, 'no matter how awesome the queer community is, it can't replace your family of origin and the culture you grew up in' (Nonno and Aroosa 2018, p.191). Their piece raises serious ethical concerns about requiring one to be out to do paid queer diversity work, given the way that this requirement can perpetuate a hegemonic coming out narrative that dismisses the heterogenous ways in which people express their queerness culturally.

Beyond perspectives A and B

Beyond debates about who should do paid queer diversity work, it is also important to reflect on how people come to identify as queer, and the barriers to this identification. In a night-time Skype session, my queer friend from Norway, Jenny Duggan, mused about the articulatory possibilities open to straight, cisgender women (one of the most popular demographics of paid diversity workers in Annese's article). Jenny argued for a nuanced conversation about the structural barriers to people learning about queerness growing up, or even envisioning it as a possibility for them. Her point resonated with my own experience. It was not until I was privileged enough to attend university, and do a queer studies unit there, that I thought being queer might be a positive prospect for me. Queer sex was never spoken about in my high school sex ed or at home, and queer identities were rarely talked about positively, if they were spoken about at all, while I was at school. Thus, I'd never seriously entertained being queer as an option.

Since coming out as queer, I've learned more about the myriad of political forces in Australia that can operate to inhibit queer identification. The abolition of Safe Schools—a program that aimed to create more inclusive spaces for students who were intersex, sexuality and gender diverse—in NSW in 2017 was one such structural barrier. Another has been Mark

Latham's legislative attempts in NSW this year to make learning about, and identifying as, queer more difficult within the education system—evidenced through the Education Legislation Amendment (Parental Rights) Bill 2020. Notably too, the heteronormativity underlying these political forces isn't ahistorical. Numerous queer and Indigenous writers have talked about heteronormativity as a colonial construct (Farrell 2020; Henningham 2019; Moon 2020), and of the gender and sexual diversity existing in Australia since before colonisation (Henningham 2019, p.103; Moon 2020). For instance, in an article in *bent street 3*, Mandy Henningham discusses how, 'sistergirls in particular have long been part of communities since before colonisation' (Riggs and Toone, 2017 cited in Henningham 2019, p.103). Drawing on the work of Anthony Baylis (2015, cited in Henningham 2019, p.103) she notes this is barely documented in dominant Australian histories. By highlighting some of the structural reasons for the dominance of heteronormativity in Australia, I aim to draw attention to the need for conversations around the articulatory possibilities for queerness. Beyond simply grappling with whether someone is queer or not to assess their suitability for a job, I argue that people's journeys to or away from queerness are significant, as they provide a complex account of the ways colonialism and heteronormativity shape peoples' identities.

Conclusion and recommendations

While I do have a personal preference for queer people occupying paid queer diversity roles, given the way lived experience can be enormously beneficial to this work, an important ethical case can be made for non-queer people doing this labour. For instance, as Charlie stated, sometimes it can be appropriate for straight, cisgender people to do this work when queer employees are exhausted by the effort of queer education. Beyond discussing the significance of positionality for this work, it is important to reflect on the accessibility of queer identification, and the structural barriers that work to reinforce heteronormative lifeworlds. What I hope to stimulate in this essay is a deeper reflection on the implications of hard and fast rules about the expected identity of paid queer diversity workers, and to bring to light a conversation about the role of allies in this work that I have not seen substantively explored in writing in the Australian context.

While I have scrutinised the role of identity in paid queer diversity work in this piece, I turn back to Annese's article, which highlights the need for ongoing work to improve the representation of difference in paid diversity roles (Annese 2018). Ways in which this work could be progressed include greater institutional reflection on *who* occupies paid queer diversity positions. For instance, this could occur through examining the role requirements or hiring practices to see if people with tertiary qualifications are preferred for diversity roles, as this can favour subjects with middle and high socio-economic backgrounds. Such a bias could subsequently prevent some people with lower socio-economic backgrounds from being hired. This possibility is problematic, due to the financial struggles faced by many marginalised members of the queer community, and given that skills or lived experience may make someone perfectly qualified for the job. Secondly, enabling researchers from within or outside organisations (such as myself) to speak with workers can enable invaluable feedback on the effectiveness of queer diversity efforts, and the appropriateness of allies doing paid queer diversity work. Indeed, perspectives like Charlie's are incredibly insightful about the boundaries of allyship. Thirdly, positive discrimination in hiring practices for paid diversity workers could be helpful. My experience looking for work is that generally people who have past experience with a role are looked on more favourably in the hiring process for the same type of position. This means the characteristics that Annese highlighted—being binary, white and able-bodied—get recycled, and there is no opportunity for a break in the pattern. Positive discrimination in hiring for roles—for people with specific marginalised identities who also have the required skills and experience—is one method for disrupting the status quo. Through these recommendations, and outlining what is politically lost and gained by allies doing paid queer diversity work, I have facilitated nuanced and complex conversation on the significance of identity for paid queer diversity efforts.

References

Annese, L 2018, 'Those paid to promote diverse workplaces are rarely diverse themselves', *The Sydney Morning Herald*, December 23, viewed 20 July 2020, https://www.smh.com.au/lifestyle/life-and-relationships/those-paid-to-promote-diverse-workplaces-are-rarely-diverse-themselves-20181220-p50ngb.html

Australian Human Rights Commission 2015, 'Resilient Individuals: Sexual Orientation, Gender Identity and Intersex Rights', Australian Human Rights Commission, viewed 15 October 2017, https://www.humanrights.gov.au/our-work/sexual-orientation-sex-gender-identity/publications/resilient-individuals-sexual

Business Queer 2019, 'Corporate rainbow-washing: the truth behind awards and accolades', *Archer*, 3 October, viewed 14 October 2020, http://archermagazine.com.au/2019/10/corporate-rainbow-washing/

Business Queer 2020, 'LGBT+ corporates: unsafe workplaces are winning awards', *Archer*, 30 July, viewed 14 October 2020, http://archermagazine.com.au/2020/07/unsafe-workplaces-are-winning-awards/

Cheung, AS, Ooi, O, Leemaqz, S, Cundill, P, Silberstein,P, Bretherton, I.,Thrower, E, Locke, P Grossmann, M and Zajac, JD 2018, 'Sociodemographic and clinical characteristics of transgender adults in Australia' *Transgender Health*, Vol. 3, No. 1, pp.229-238.

Cohen, C 2005, 'Punks, bulldaggers, and welfare queens: the radical potential of queer politics?' in EP Johnson and MG Henderson (eds.), *Black queer studies: a critical anthology*, Duke University Press, Durham and London, pp.21-51.

Education Legislation Amendment (Parental Rights) Bill 2020 (NSW), viewed 12 October 2020, https://www.parliament.nsw.gov.au/bills/Pages/bill-details.aspx?pk=3776

Equality Australia (2020) 'Inequality magnified: submission to the Australian senate inquiry into Australia's response to COVID-19', Equality Australia, 9 June, viewed 8 October 2020, https://equalityaustralia.org.au/eacovidsubmission/

Farrell, A 2020, *GCST2607: Bodies, sexualities, identities, Week 6: Aboriginal queer identities and decolonial queer approaches*, lecture presented on 30 March at the University of Sydney, Darlington.

Filmer, J 2020, 'Infrastructures of intimacy: queer (re)configurations of cultural space' PhD thesis, The University of Sydney.

Henningham, M 2019, 'Still here, still queer, still invisible' in T Jones (ed.) *bent street 3: Australian LGBTIQA+ arts, writing & ideas*, Clouds of Magellan Press, Melbourne, VIC, pp.98-105.

Innis, G 2014, 'Dealing with disability discrimination: our destiny is in our hands', presentation to Access Arts conference, *Graeme Innis*, 28 October, viewed 14 October 2020, https://graemeinnes.com/2014/10/30/dealing-with-disability-discrimination-our-destiny-is-in-our-hands/

Moon, H 2020, 'Brotherboys and Sistergirls: we need to decolonise our attitude towards gender in this country', *Junkee*, 20 July, viewed 8 October 2020, https://junkee.com/brotherboy-sistergirl-decolonise-gender/262222

Nonno and Aroosa 2018, 'A QPoC manifesto: fighting for invisibility in a world that loves to talk' in M Pallotta-Chiarolli (ed.) *Living and loving in diversity: an anthology of Australian multicultural queer adventures,* Wakefield Press, Mile End, SA, pp.185-193.

Olsen, K 2019, 'Hiring bias and employment barriers for trans and gender diverse people', *Star Observer*, May 13, viewed 8 October 2020, https://www.starobserver.com.au/news/national-news/fixing-the-system-hiring-bias-and-employment-barriers-for-trans-and-gender-diverse-people/182062

Price 2013, 'Tony Abbott, minister for women? No thanks', *The Sydney Morning Herald*, September 19, viewed 15 October 2020, https://www.smh.com.au/opinion/tony-abbott-minister-for-women-no-thanks-20130919-2u179.html

The University of Sydney Business School, Diversity Council of Australia and Australian HR Institute 2018, 'Benchmarking diversity and inclusion practices in Australia', *Diversity Council of Australia*, viewed 22 July 2020, https://www.dca.org.au/sites/default/files/benchmarking_di_practice_2018.pdf

Waters, L 2014 'Why Tony Abbott should resign as Minister for Women', *Daily Life*, May 23, viewed 14 October 2020, http://www.dailylife.com.au/news-and-views/dl-opinion/why-tony-abbott-should-resign-as-minister-for-women-20140522-38qu9.html

Hannah Gillard is a non-binary writer in their final year of PhD study. They have blogged for a community legal centre and written for *Archer* Magazine. Hannah performs doctoral research on LGBTQI+ workplace diversity and lives on Wallumedegal land.

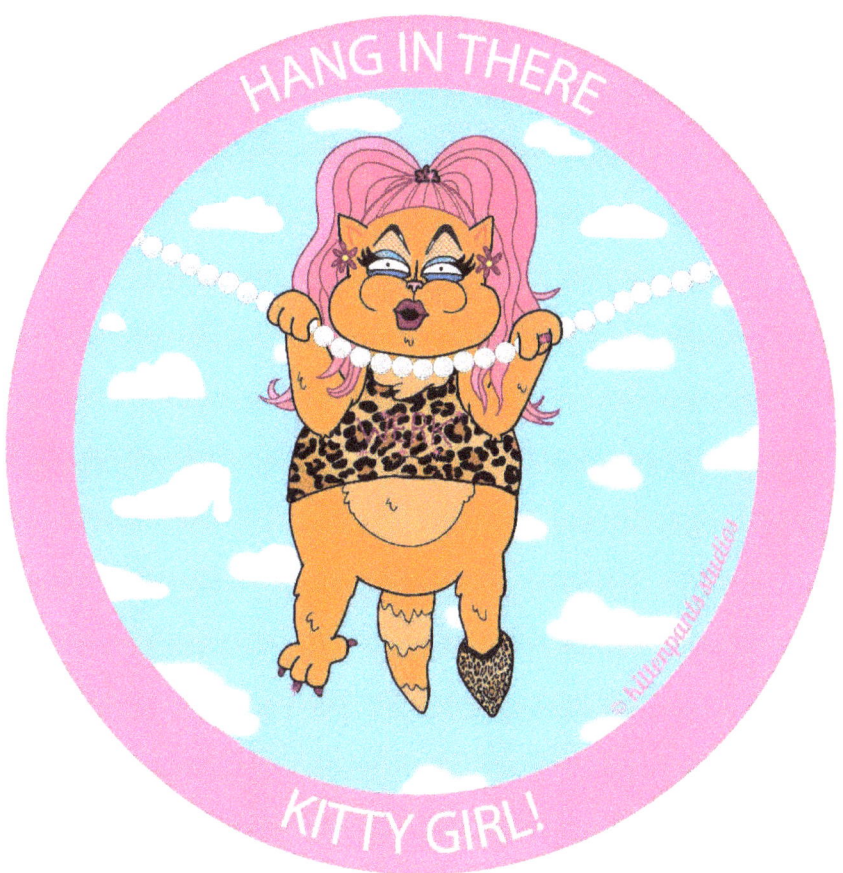

Mel Simpson—*Kitty Girl!*

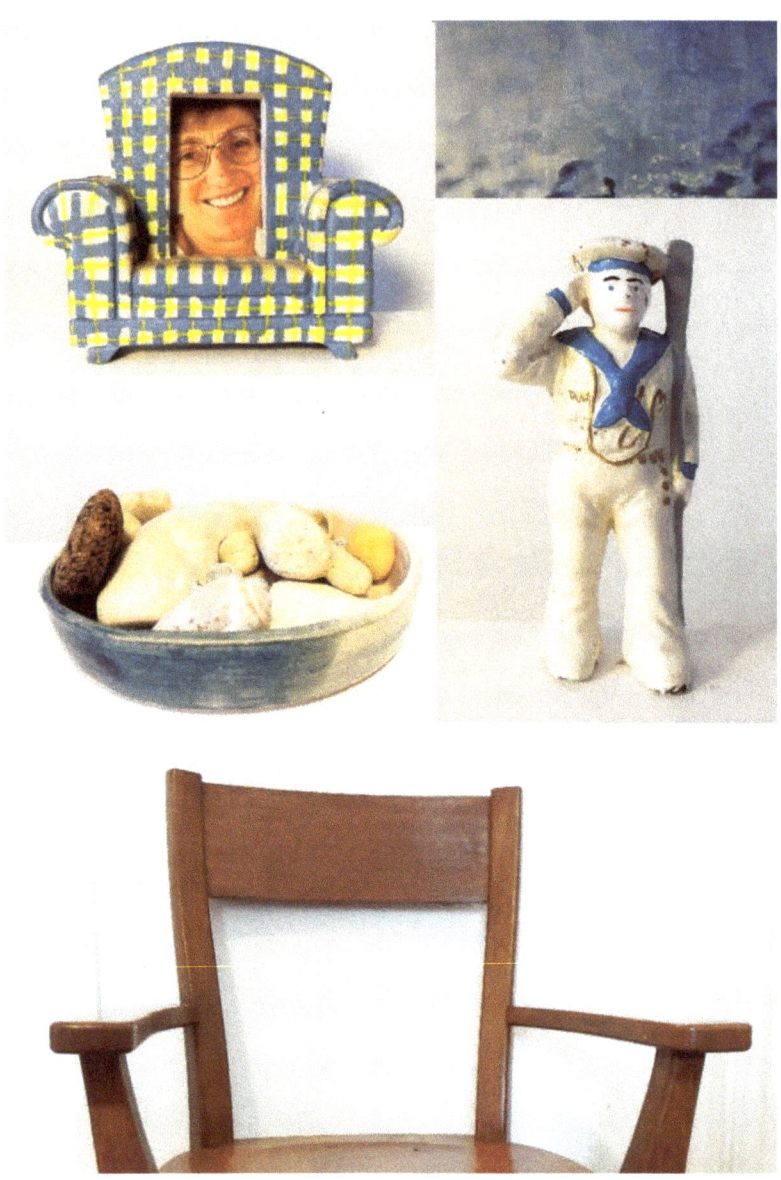

Clockwise from top left: Softwood and resin frame, gingham vinyl covering, 10cm high; detail, painting by Cate Phillips, 2016—acrylic paint on paper 900mm x 500mm; Cast iron sailor, 900mm (h), iron, lead paint, 1950; Redgum handmade chair—60cm seat height, 1.1m back height—35kg; Plate of stolen rocks, periwinkle and limpet shells, unidentified seed pod

A SHIFTABLE MUSEUM
Max Hayward

Real museums are places where Time is transformed into Space –
Orhan Pamuk, *The Museum of Innocence*

Photo frame

There are sentimental mementos that people carry with them through life, as they move from house to house. These objects survive new boyfriends, girlfriends, sharehouses, working holidays, sicknesses and affairs; they are part of the shiftable museum of which we're the curator. It's a warm feeling of familiarity when you pack your things up in yet another stack of carboard boxes and you're reacquainted with these things that consciously, or subconsciously, you've held onto like old acquaintances that you keep bumping into at the supermarket. 'Oh, what are the chances of seeing you here again?!' you might say.

A photo of a deceased grandmother is something you'd expect most people to cherish. Grandmas are of unique significance in a child's life—they tend to be more relaxed with lollies or fizzy drinks, they have most leisure time so are more enthusiastic about games, movies, talking to animals—but for boys who loved the Spice Girls and witchcraft they were even more important. Grandma completely indulged my rambling opinions and penchant for wands and capes from the day I could speak. We wrote letters to each other, and drank a lot of Coke, and walked endlessly up and down riverside footpaths. We didn't see each other as much when I moved to the city, but I still saw her most times I ventured back to the country until she died.

The photo frame that holds a snapshot of grandma—who looks tanned and vibrant with cropped hair and enormous glasses—is truly silly. The portrait I carry around of this cherished person from my first twenty-seven years of life, is encased by the model of a cartoonish giant chair, the type you'd see on a children's show. If you didn't know our rapport, you'd think it was completely tasteless. But the ugly chair I carry around, with grandma perennially grinning and floating above its cushion, embodies our relationship: filled with magic, questionable style choices, and eccentric storytelling.

Chair

East Gippsland—Gunaikurnai country—is a landscape that was once dominated by massive eucalyptus forests that stretched from coastal wetlands to high alpine plains. Over the past 150 years, many of the valleys and river flats in the region have been cleared for farmland, but the remaining bush still dominates the psyche of the locals. Deer hunters stalk their prey at night in the rocky hills, day-trippers hike trails, firefighters backburn, and forestries still (legally and sometimes illegally) log tracts of native vegetation. The bush still feels wild, and something that everyone, to some extent, wants to control. It's not surprising then, that my grandad spent much of his life preoccupied by wood. He worked in forestries, as a volunteer firefighter, and earnt a living from making innumerable wooden signs, trestle tables, and chairs for local schools, national parks and town councils.

The procurement, management and use of wood became, as a consequence of grandad's livelihood, a family obsession. I remember playing in the sawdust of his workshop, running my hands against the smoothness of a freshly sanded chopping board, thinking that it was the best scent and texture imaginable. Grandad made a wooden rollaway bar for my parents, and everyone was in awe of its rich colour and incredible weight. He made bits and pieces out of various species of eucalyptus—a major condition being a wood's density. Later in life, grandad painstakingly created furniture for many of his friends and family, as a kind of parting gift as his carpentry workshop wound down. Everything had that trademark smoothness, those deep shades of red and brown, and with that (sometimes overwhelming) heft.

Grandma was less of a wood connoisseur and more of a firebug. Her modus operandi was to burn anything that wasn't living or useful. As a family we would have lunches on hand-crafted seats around a wooden table, then venture out to the paddock and watch a bonfire explode and crackle. Grandkids, uncles, aunties, sons- and daughters-in-law would gather transfixed by the flames and smoke, as if watching a sacrifice.

My grandad died only a few weeks after we scattered grandma's ashes across the paddocks where we'd once lit bonfires. He chose to be buried, aptly, in a solid wooden coffin.

I inherited one of the last things grandad made—a dining chair with luxurious armrests, a curved back, and the weight of a small horse. It is a beautiful object that looks out of context in my office, which is full of cheap furniture and second-hand books. The chair is a masculine and solid presence in my collection of objects that's both a link to my grandad and the landscape from which I emerged, both as a firebug and lover of wood in all its forms.

Glass painting

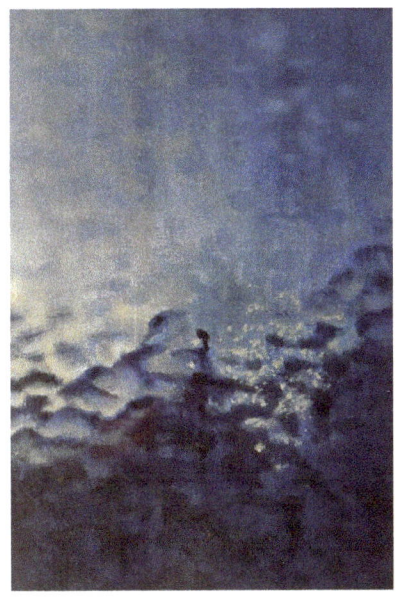

In the house where I spent most of my adolescence, the front door had panels of frosted glass that warped objects in the outside world into dream-like shapes and blurs of colour. Something banal like a recycling bin waiting on the curb, with a yellow lid, could look like an open-winged tropical bird. A passing white van would flash by like a ghost.

The house was always cold, apart from a few weeks from late-January to mid-February, and the garden around it was generally sodden. My mum, brother and I had shifted from the dry high country of fast-east Victoria to the low, wet hills of West Gippsland when my parents separated. And although we made a home in this place near the train tracks, and I did love my strange room with bright orange walls and an enormous built-in-robe, the mid-century house on King Street always felt slightly haunted.

I saw a photo of an old work colleague's painting on Instagram five years ago, and it reminded me of apparitions dancing in frosted glass—a spectrum of dotted and wavey blues with glints of yellow of white, dancing across the surface. I was taken back to the old house and that cold hallway, the sound of an approaching train, and I could see myself wrapped in a blazer and tie, leaving for school. Now, when I look at the painting, I still have that same sense of nostalgia, with a tinge of melancholia, about those uncertain years as a teenager, watching the world unfold through a pane of frosted glass.

Cast iron sailor

When I left home for uni in the Big Smoke, I became swept up in the swirling excitement and improvisation that comes with simultaneously 'coming out' and coming-of-age. I lived in a share house, drank goon nightly, and had an anaemic diet of mi goreng noodles and the occasional carrot. While I was so distracted by this new lifestyle, my little brother left for our dad's farm, and mum departed the house of my adolescence, for a road-trip around the UK. After six weeks abroad, she returned to a new job in a place I'd never heard of—Port Albert.

Sitting on a deep natural harbour on the South Gippsland coast, Port Albert is one of the oldest towns in Victoria. It was established as a shipping station for natural resources—gold, wool, beef—in the mid-19th century. At the time, the area was a far-flung outpost of the British colony of New South Wales, and also the site of horrific massacres which almost eradicated (and entirely dispossessed) the local Gunaikurnai people. Angus McMillan, a Scottish pastoralist, was both an explorer and mass-murderer [i] who enabled the establishment of European-style agriculture in the area, and he agreed that Port Albert was the perfect place for exporting goods. Today, some of the buildings from that 'frontier' era still remain, but there's little evidence of McMillan or the shadowy history of what's now a quaint seaside town.

Mum lived in large brick-veneer house down a gravel street and on the edge of a morass. It was one of those places with a surprising layout—small rooms adjoining bigger rooms, with seemingly random corridors wedged in different directions—and smelt vaguely of swamp and old cigarettes. In hindsight it was probably a dreary place, but I enjoyed visiting. My sense of *home* was abstracted by living in a Burwood share-house with ten other people and paper-thin walls, so I embraced its oddness. Mum did mention that I didn't visit enough, but without a car it took four hours, and five methods of transport to get there (walking, tram, train, bus, mum's car).

Apart from a swish seafood restaurant newly perched on the historic Port Albert Wharf, mum's favourite part of the town was a café-museum-gift shop in a weatherboard building, straight out of a Wild West movie.

'The coffee is OK,' said mum, 'but the things you can buy are amazing.'

The eclectic objects for sale included knick-knacks with 'Live Laugh Love' scrawled across them, giant spiky shells, antique fishing equipment, $20 hand soaps, and a vast collection of figurines—fat ladies in bathing costumes, elegant birds with exaggerated steel legs, and earnest-looking sailors. We spent hours looking through everything, and I ended up buying a postcard.

Mum later shifted to a modern townhouse on the foreshore—objectively nicer than the brick-veneer place, but without the spooky charm—and eventually left South Gippsland entirely. That Christmas she gave me a cast iron figurine of a sailor saluting. It was a romanticised and somewhat queer figure from a yesteryear that never existed in Port Albert. The figure was more representative of the randy Navy officers in *On the Town* than Angus McMillan's Port Albert. When I look at it on the end-table now, I see it as nothing to do with the town, sailing, or that expensive gift shop—it's simply a gift from a mother to a son, both of whom are improvising in their new lives.

Plate of stolen rocks and shells

As a little boy, I spent a lot of time searching for rocks in riverbeds. The Tambo river curved around the farm where I spent my first twelve years, and its flow—whether dried up or flooding—was a source of constant conversation at the dinner table. Back then, I was less interested in the health of the environment than the health of my rock collection, so my main interest centred on the accessibility of bone-white quartz, glittering pyrite and blueish stones that all looked like precious gems if the water was clear and shallow. I scooped them out of the river with all the fervour of a prospector who's stumbled across that long-sought gold nugget.

Over the years I filled up milk crates and boxes of rocks, each of which looked luminous in the water, but less special once they'd dried out. If I had a longer attention span, perhaps I could've reassessed the collection every now and then, but I was a regular kid that loved everything new and shiny. So, the rocks quickly just became habitats for spiders in the bungalow. Dad still has a box full of them—untouched for twenty years.

I was more selective with shells, probably because I started to search for them as a teenager, when building sandcastles had become a little embarrassing. Shells were usually smashed up along the Victorian coast, perhaps because of the storm-prone Bass Strait, but the occasional lustre of mother-of-pearl, a delicate fan shell or spotted cowrie did beckon from the sand. I hid my artefacts from excursions to the beach away in a shoebox, and tried to ignore shells I saw when boogie boarding with friends. I was afraid that my enthusiasm for such tiny, ornamental objects could shatter any semblance of masculinity.

Shells and rocks, in a way, became a commodity in my family, like cowries once were around the Indian ocean [ii]. Mum would give them to me, I would display them, and talk about their rareness with anyone who'd listen. I would take them from national park beaches (don't tell anyone) and smuggle them through customs. I gave them to past boyfriends, who found them a puzzling thing to receive. I took photos of them and shared on social media.

I keep a plate of shells and rocks on my set of drawers at home. They're beautiful specimens from Vanuatu, Cape Tribulation, Wineglass Bay, and the Gippsland coast. The plate is made by a Melbourne ceramicist. The object as a whole is incredibly bourgeois, but now, aside from memories of holidays, and of a wide-eyed kid who found glamour in digging riverbeds, it serves as a document of cluelessness.

I didn't have a sense of shell collection as being potentially problematic—how taking something from another's ancestral country could be ignoring Indigenous peoples' links to the land—until I had an awkward conversation with my current boyfriend:

'I have a shell for you!' I said.

'Oh, nah, it's not from my Country,' he said.

Now, I can't help but think about that awkward moment and reassess why I have the need to collect and store these objects at all.

I still have the shells and rocks, but now they have a slightly different function. While being pretty, they spark a recognition that, whether they're in national archives or in the autobiographical museums we create for ourselves—our homes, our Instagram accounts—our emotional attachments to objects are subjective and exist in a wider, postcolonial world.

These shiftable, shifting museums we create about and for ourselves are a projection of who we were, who we are and who we want to be. I'm not a reality TV-level hoarder (yet), and I am definitely not Marie Kondo; but I think everyone could benefit from carrying a few things through life—not necessarily a heavy wooden chair or platefuls of rocks—that remind us, as individuals, that we're all built from a million jigsaw pieces of experience, some of which are awkward, bland, messy, or wavey-blue like frosted glass.

Notes

Grandma in a (ridiculous) photo frame. Location: high on the bookshelf in our office.

Grandad's extremely heavy chair. Location: shifts between the lounge room and office (still unsure about where to keep it).

A painting of frosted glass. Location: leaning against the wall, collecting dust. Cast iron sailor. Location: underneath my monstera on an end-table in the kitchen, next to a smiling Buddha.

Plate of stolen rocks and shells. Location: on top of a chest of drawers, next to my collection of hand creams and 'Hummusexual' badge from *Téta Mona* (Lebanese restaurant in Brunswick).

i Mahoney, Ciarnan. (2019) 'The Scottish explorer who became the butcher of Gippsland' *The Guardian* (accessed October 5, 2020) https://www.theguardian.com/australia-news/2019/mar/08/the-scottish-explorer-who-became-the-butcher-of-gippsland

ii Litster, Mirani. (2016). *Cowry Shell Money and Monsoon Trade: The Maldives in Past Globalizations.*

Max Hayward is a Melbourne-based arts marketer, writer and events coordinator. He is also a true crime podcast tragic, hopeless at crosswords, and makes mean margaritas. You can read his film reviews in Lindsay Magazine and a selection of his short stories and essays at I'll do it today. His short story *The Return* was the recipient of 2nd prize at the 2020 OutStanding Stories Competition.

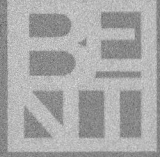

POETRY

Rob Wallis

Percy Haynes Has A Rare Win
1935

Dressed as a woman
because it made me
feel good about myself,
and anything for a lark,
I went window shopping
in Melbourne
then went to the pictures.

Oh the romance
of being Ginger Rogers
as the dashing Fred Astaire
swept me around the dance floor
in *Top Hat*.

Ever on the alert
two detectives followed me
home on the tram
and arrested me
at the gate
in front of the neighbours.
The judge, bless him,
threw the case out.
If a woman, he argued,
could wear jodhpurs,
he saw no reason
why a man
couldn't wear a dress.
I could have kissed him.

A Policeman's Report
1939

Usually we don't know the person
whose done themself in,
but this one was different.
Turns out that this bloke
was Jack Dale, the famous
American singer and composer.
We found him dead
in a St. Kilda flat, a suicide note
next to the body.
To whom it may concern
it began, then he mentioned
the three people in his life
who mattered the most, who he'd lost
to death,
to marriage,
to his own unfaithfulness.
But no names, no pronouns.
Without these people, he said,
I have nothing to live for.

'Truth' had a field day.
70 Pound A Week Star Whistler's
Queer Note Before End.
Readers knew what they meant.

Rob Wallis's fifth collection, 'Caught Jesting', was published by Birdfish Books. His poems
have appeared in various magazines and anthologies both in Australia and overseas. He has
won the John Shaw Neilson Poetry Award and the W. B. Yeats Poetry Prize. He has been
shortlisted twice for the Fish Publishing International Poetry Competition, Dublin, the
Bridport Prize, UK, and the ACU Prize for Poetry.

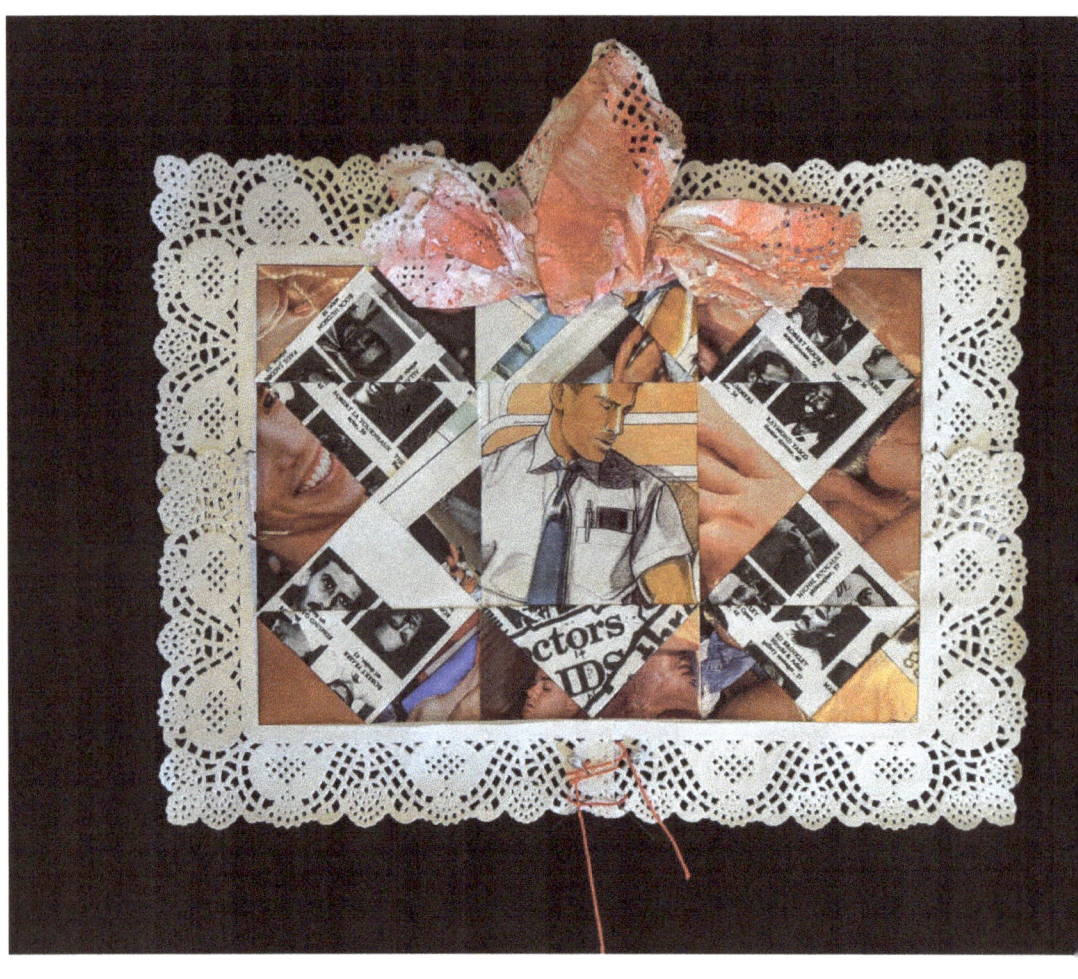

Henry von Doussa—AIDS doily

I'VE BEEN THINKING A LOT LATELY ABOUT THE
RESIDUE AND ONGOING TRAUMA FROM HIV/AIDS
IN THE GAY COMMUNITY. THE IMAGE IS A
MECHANISM FOR GRIEVING, REMEMBERING AND
RECOVERY. MAKING THIS ARTWORK TOUCHED
EACH AREA.

Henry von Doussa is a writer, artist and regular Bent Street contributor from Melbourne.

Leila Lois

Last light

'There is a coherence in things …' Virginia Woolf—*To the Lighthouse*

I've made a tradition of chasing sunsets
all the distal way to the lighthouse,
through the blushing last breath of day,
to watch as the tall ecru tower
ignites a shawl of light
through violet dusk.

I see the candles my mother placed
in our bay windows lashed with sea-spray
& think how love is like a shining ruby,
while tides drift, sunlight fades.

Fog

You read aloud today's
'Did you know' …
'in your dreams you cannot smell?'
and I tell you
how strange, all night
I dreamed
that the air was frosted
so thickly across the city,
mist breathing into everything,
then I caught sight of your face,
fear vanished.
Losing my senses
had never felt so welcome.
The only thing in focus,
were your dreamy eyes,
the rest indistinct,
fog-draped.

Jazmín

'Como un ciego, regresé al jazmín de la gastada primavera humana.' Pablo Neruda

A constellation of fumes and dust
the aureole streets shine
laced with ivy, buildings, lined
with stalls of jasmine
woody stalks, bursting blooms
in stellar hues
vanilla-yellow, opal and white,
sweet, heady
and impatient.
The city, a grand cemetery,
air timelessly glides
past tombs of buildings,
a mingling of flowers, half-dried and pink marble.
Stalked by sunset,
the light begins to fray as
I hold up jasmine to the dusk
and memorialise this day.

Leila Lois is a woman of Kurdish and Celtic heritage, who identifies as bisexual, and who has lived most of her life in Aotearoa. In her poems, Leila explores a personal sense of origin that, like the ocean, binds several landscapes and times, coming back to the idea that a timeless, boundless love pervades. Her publishing history includes *Southerly*, Djed Press, *Right Now*, *Lite Lit One*, Delving Into Dance and *Salient*.

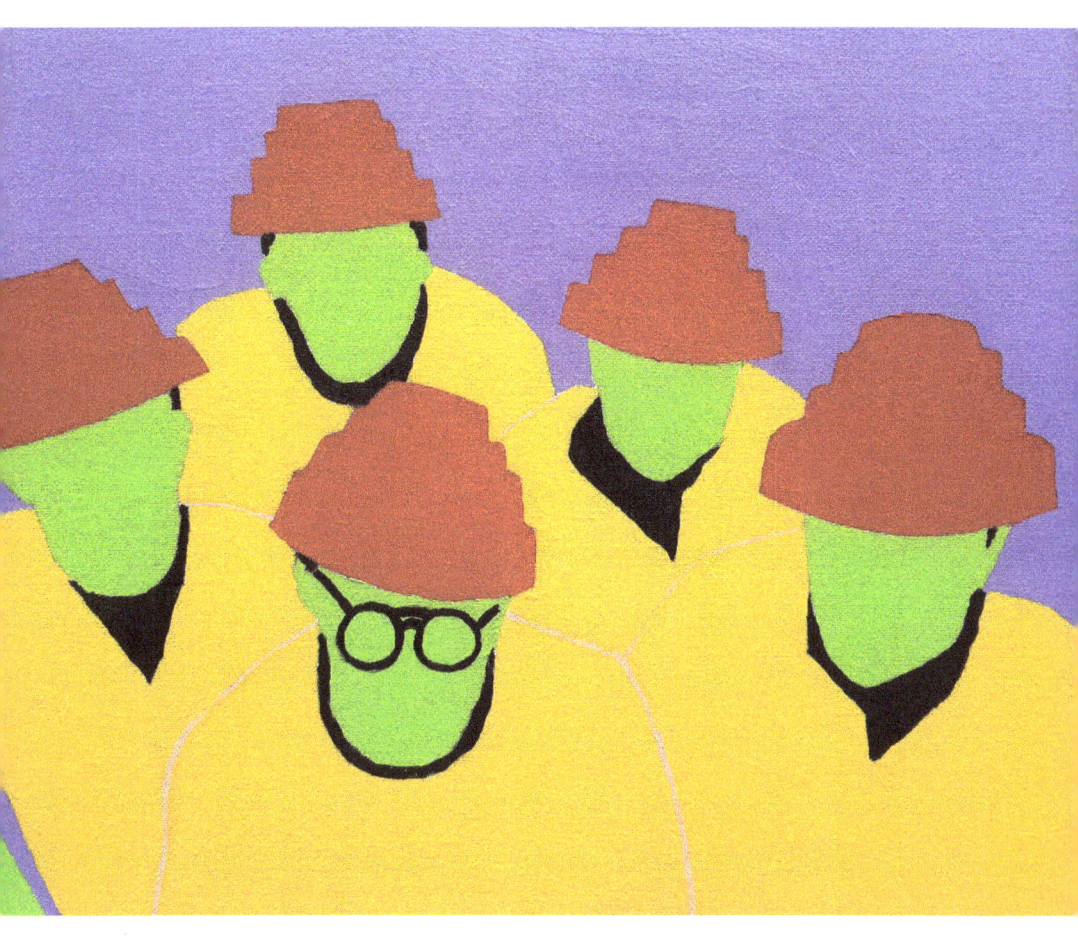

Andrew McNamara—*DEVO*

John Bartlett

Installations

Installation: A form of art, which involves the creation of an enveloping aesthetic or sensory experience in a particular environment, often inviting active engagement or immersion by the spectator.

what the boys are doing in Chaturbate
might surprise their mothers
their range of intimacies bar-coded
for a global market checkout
                         - nonchalant exhibitionists
#cock flash #flexbiceps #nippleplay #assflash
these boys need your dollars and your adoration
and might decide to talk to you
just keep on tipping
if you like what you see
                         - a globalisation
of the hard-on although it doesn't rate
so high in the Economic Complexity Index
                         - solitary boys
DIY
withholding their ejaculations
to boost the Competitive Market
Equilibrium Risk Load
                         - is this what Adam Smith had in mind
by Gross Domestic Product and
will it save us from Recession?
                         - how many million viewers
does it take?

you #beautynthebeast #selfsuckbro #peterbeater
#vanillaguerilla #hunghulk #megahorse

you stand outside
yourself attentive to the lens
watching yourselves watched
this double mirror of Narcissus
traps you in these screens, these cells
of meditation, like monks devoted to

small prayers and genuflections
bodies on display willing to be
pierced with the arrows of our eyes' desires

but dear boys, better
this articulation of your limbs, these installations,
than you carve despair and loneliness
upon your blue-veined wrists
or slip a noose around your necks
in locked garages while the family shops at Safeway

The Songs the Wind Sings

(after Jeremiah 6:16)

You hear them on train tracks
those voices of departure,
the songs of farewell
those rattling door melodies
leaking from abandoned houses
where dog-days transform
into wolf-nights

The wind makes use of
what it will to warn us,
to tell us where the good way is,
so we can walk in it

John Bartlett's poetry has been published in a number of Australian and overseas journals. In June 2019 Melbourne Poets Union published his Chapbook *The Arms of Men* and Ginninderra Press has just published *Songs of the Godforsaken* and *Awake at 3am*. He is the Winner of the 2020 Ada Cambridge Poetry Prize.

Mark Anthony Cayanan

This long piece—intended to be an aggressive display of candour, its persona's penchant for self-aggrandisement couched in specific historical and material conditions—is a love poem. Its starting points include *Death in Venice* by Thomas Mann, as well as a book by Primitivo Mijares; a biography by Ronald Hayman; an essay by Massimo Pigliucci; fiction by John Cheever; news/feature articles by Mohammed Al-Mosaiwi, Helen Coffey, Joyce Ilas, *Esquire Philippines,* and *The New York Times*; novels by Ben Brooks; and poetry by Anne Carson.

Ben Ben Ben Ben Ben

The narrator who foretold my life says passion is like crime
both welcome the weakening of society because they can profit off it

A month has passed in the novella and the locals are dying
as though thinking of you could make cholera a sunset backdrop

The barber who trims and darkens my beard says I've no fear of the disease
my personality plagiarised from my favourite characters, all magnetically staring out into the void

I think I'm alone because I manage romance
with a girlish evasiveness that's a front for sexual frigidity

When a man's already in front of me, too loose, the wanting slips off
my mind scrambles ahead to the ride home and Tim Tams before bed

I'm being facetious though not entirely incorrect
I pine for life-altering tenderness but prefer it in the abstract

Outside St. Mark's I feed on impatience like the other pigeons
or like the sweet medicine death-smell of Venice I wait in ambush

≈

More than wanting the reward I want to be the reward, the boy
who knows his beauty but not its magnitude, bending over a prie-dieu

I wish to be in a situation where I could say Am an attendant lord
though I'm pretentious I haven't gone beyond the required reading

The one dénouement of all plotlines I repurpose for what you think of me is
in retaliation I write poems about impossible men with hairs on their backs

Sad Ben, sarcastic Ben, Ben who wakes at noon and pees while waiting for his tea to steep
and sighs loudly as he writes and microwaves burritos for brunch

You're Tadzio plus adult acne and the threat of a paunch and an open invitation to destroy me
though I won't die for you yet you're dreamt of the way he is

Your friends keep tagging you in pictures of smoky cafés, face turned away from the camera
I want to step into their bodies or be the thing you're looking away at

Ben of the macho sentences, Ben as bracing as a papercut, as permanent
Ben, you're mainly incontrovertible proof

       ~~~

Mann cultivated a public image of Teutonic reserve
among friends he was prone to nervous trembling and convulsive sobbing

Whenever nervous I replay in my head that scene in Clueless that references Monet
I use it as a conversation starter, it's one of the few insights I have into myself

I borrow Mann's biography from the library to discover why my impulses override my tact
when in his diary he draws a parallel between his sweet tooth and covert desires, he gets poetic

Extra fastidious he writes about his daily walks to the market to ogle shirtless workmen
in his fiction he defends himself when he writes about other people

All I want is to prove I orchestrate my life with the efficiency of a single mother
yeah that's another lie

I'm the videoke singer who licks the corners of their mouth between lyrics
I make every heartache ballad salacious, vaguely offensive, absurd

If in me are anxieties that need unpacking would you want to hear me
if not you then I want them exorcised with everyone's ear pressed against the door

       ~~~

The first time we shared a cigarette, just to connect you said
you preferred brawny men who could suffocate you, I looked at my hands

I congratulate myself for charming you into changing your preferences
never mind your girlfriend

The year you were born, overweight and swishy I had as much potential as a 349 bottle cap
I love you enough to look for confirmation in newspaper microfilms

Erap was the comic relief in the vice-presidential debates, needless to say he won
funny things stupid people say grabbed headlines 28 years ago, as they do now

A woman in her 20s was found stuffed inside a suitcase
she wore green basketball shorts, a cord around her neck, and a baby tee

Bakit Ako Mahihiya was showing at Ali Mall, not sure if it's a remake of the 1976 film
some days your beard's still scratching against my cheek, Ben

When I was born a man died from a cigarette he flicked at a bunch of balloons
do you know that a bunch of balloons is called a festival

      〰

I feel weird whenever your novel refers to a Southeast Asian
had to put it down when the Thai girl on the webcam plays with her nipple

At 16 I offered my married neighbour a blowjob
just because summer took too long and it seemed an important thing

You've gone over the age of Keats when he died
not enough time has passed for me to leave myself behind, fervently I giggle at your jokes

I've begun dating younger men, I'm embarrassed about it
I rely on Korean moisturisers to camouflage the fact

Before you're 30 your dishevelled pompadour will transition into a combover
Aged-out Asian Twink isn't a porn category, it's why I don't upload nudes to Grindr

Wouldn't you say we're perfect for each other
we deserve a maisonette in the suburb, we'd take turns vacuuming the carpet

You'd write your books and by 7:30 I'd set the table
for each other let's be someone's dreams, outside dailiness marooned forever

      〰

Love makes Aschenbach realise how much he neglected his looks
his intelligence made him assume beauty was an unnecessary capital

Translators differ on Aschenbach's lipstick shade
Appelbaum and Heim: raspberry, Luke: cherry, Lowe-Porter: strawberry

The point is he gets a horrible makeover, the kind you never see in romcoms
the point is it gives him enough hope to magnify the obligatory disaster

My role models are either abject homosexuals or doomed women
why don't you ask yourself what that reveals about you

Walking into a room I pretend my hand isn't mine and turn on the light
then recoil in dismay at my undisguised face, puzzle that one out

Aschenbach concludes his hope by eating lukewarm strawberries
he continues to stare longingly at the water before the epidemic bests him

Because hope has turned me into a bat inside a cave, I make screeching noises
still essentially alone though the acoustics are much better

∿

The one time I asked about your girlfriend after your fourth lonkero
you said Sometimes you wake up next to a person and wonder why you're there

I've never experienced the luxury of being so bored you have no choice but to stick it out
this is a hint, Ben

Meanwhile I'm always dishonourable from a distance you won't bridge
poets can't soar upward, only commit extravagances, says Mann

And in the end hunger for a new naïveté, the severity of wanting only the feeling itself
for encouragement I curate a Spotify playlist of pathetic indies

When I run errands in Cubao everyone bops terribly to it as we do to fear
I want to keep sighing your name while I'm in the back of a Grab

Today I think about newly elected senators and keep all the doors locked
a man who's beside himself, says Mann, dreads becoming himself again

You've moved to Bulgaria, no longer sober you go drinking with the ballet dancers
are you finally single again, why haven't you declared your intentions

∿

Just so Tadzio remains untouched by the epidemic and the worshipper's fearful awe
Aschenbach considers telling the boy's mother to flee Venice

In Aschenbach's dreams his fear is a brutally insistent flute
when a heavenly VO shouts The foreign god, Mann drops a brick into a beaker of water

In a field stands a gigantic wooden dick, worshipped by satyrs
this chapter-five dream is an orgy or a buffet or yet another unsubtle contrivance

In my mind Gloucestershire is your neighbours climbing up the roofs of their semi-detached
it's 2007 and being a teenager with drug issues you go back down for your bass

But a three-foot flood's just another August afternoon to us
and by us naturally I don't include you

I pretend to be so used to horror I make off-colour jokes about it, that's my aging persona
like Mariah I contort my boxy body into sultry poses

I fold a frozen lake into my luggage before separately we leave
out of your lyric curtness I engineer elegiac caesuras, slightly lurid and regretful

      ~~

Smooth-skinned boys grabbing onto he-goats, Aschenbach's dreams
are Nick Joaquin dreams, the boys goad the goats

For Joaquin smooth skin isn't so much an indicator of youth as a given
hands tugging down my thermals, you already know this

Our post-coital talk would've covered random topics
the Hollywood starlet who honey-trapped the former president and then survived

In the recording you could hear Marcos begging for a blowjob
reason gives way to violence, the headboard bangs against the wall

Dovie Beams wipes the saliva off her underboob, he asks if she enjoyed it
no matter how white you are there's only one answer to a dictator

Eventually he tires of her and she wouldn't have it
she takes the tenderness in his letters and builds a press conference out of it

In her final years she has a golden pool installed in her Beverly Hills home
she dies free of him on the eve of Rizal's death anniversary

      ~~

Mann says art is a war, a struggle people can't keep up for very long
I hope for the rest of my life to be as privileged

In Berlin you'd be the best person to keep drinking dinner with
you'd nurse a beer on the subway, I'd match your repartee

Everywhere cigarette butts wedged between cobblestones
I scuttle past streets that smell of piss and I'm flung to Manila with you, would this city do

I worry about the Philippine fishing boat rammed by a Chinese vessel
then get distracted by my hair collecting on the shower grate

I want to fly out to where you are, gallivant, order unpronounceable drinks
nothing but a backpack with underwear, mouthwash, your books as proofs of devotion

But as you know I'm a middle-middle-class citizen of a poor country
between you and me lie a hundred-dollar visa fee and a plane ticket

Spontaneity is a gift of the lucky
I have to retreat back into my low-cost longings

〰

I show Jov a video of you singing Like a Virgin
I cover my mouth when he says The British have bad teeth, no

Sir Thomas Rich's School added a swimming pool in 1966
the potted history of your school says it was closed in the '80s but reopened in 1995

On Wikipedia's list of nationally significant events is a teenager who died
from drinking too much water while on Ecstasy, you were three and six months and 10 days

You got yourself a writing career at 17, fuck higher learning
at first I went straight to envy, now I wonder what it says about your inner life

You showed me your KS5 band covering The Pogues, thank god you outgrew that phase
instead you're always in a puffer jacket, through my window you can hear These Days

I enable my self-absorption, I'm silly enough to think it makes me interesting
I make obsequious bows, apologise to the world and my betters

I have to open another website to figure out what potted means
though I'm not dumb I don't know English

〰

Aschenbach knows his last few days are his last days
the city government disposes of the sick, each one floating away like The Lady of Shalott

Professing love to someone who says it too easily is the second most exciting carnival ride
impertinent to stop a man who's about to jump into a river, says Wilde

I deal with chronic depression through pathological self-mythologizing
or I sleep a lot, watch the same series until heart and soul I'm Kelly Kapoor

I don't ask but I wonder if you're still somewhat hot
if I press your jacket to my nose are you still your special odour

Wherever you are come back from the bottle shop, shake the snow off your boots
out of your stories I've built a house we wouldn't want out of

Don't you like editing your sentences until they're basically just verbs
I have so many verbs to give and so smash three plates, startle a cat for emphasis

I'm true as a Ponzi scheme and assembled from defence mechanisms
but let me be the most compelling version of myself with you

♒

Love's a wheel rolling downhill, said a poet back when jeepneys were a new invention
I especially enjoy fresh tread marks decorating my cheek

Mann offloads his gay shame onto his characters, makes the kyphotic music lover kill himself
ambition was his antidote to self-disgust

I write long poems about shame, they're decent-sized flats
if enough people tell me how brave I've been I'd at least have use for it

I consider being funny but I only bring it out
when kindness, an offshoot of my need to be universally liked, proves ineffective

Since I was 14 it's been my dream to be the person someone masturbates to
at what age does transformation stop meaning various other possibilities

What is the cure for shame, my shame indisputable as the mole on my nose
I'm one of my lesser faces, Mann excised his by disfiguring Aschenbach

I check in on him, collapsing on the beach
and having depended on him for guidance, of course I end up thinking Why not

♒

After years of erotic austerity comes abandon, in Mann as in Freud this means oblivion
punishment unretractable as academic tenure

Before it arrives Mann finally calls Aschenbach delusional
with Apollonian arrogance reasserting his moral ascendancy

And the world enters a new politeness, shame discarded like last millennium's plastics
like the unlicensed gondolier in chapter three, I try accepting disappearance

Ben, though I'm afraid of living as myself I don't want to be unafraid

Mark Anthony Cayanan is from the Philippines. They obtained an MFA from the University of
Wisconsin in Madison and are a PhD candidate at the University of Adelaide. Their third poetry book,
Unanimal, Counterfeit, Scurrilous, is forthcoming from Giramondo Publishing in 2021. New work has
appeared or is forthcoming in *Sporklet, The Margins, Overland, The Spectacle,* and *Lana Turner.* They
teach at the Ateneo de Manila University.

Bron Bateman

Kintsugi

I leave our bed to go to the toilet
I am tired and sated as I pee and wipe myself
with care, my vulva tender from having you inside me.
I mouth your sweet name, over and over,
like the words of a song I know off by heart.

After all these years together
our bodies are still a miracle to me. Making love,
the soft   O of your mouth
against my skin, uttering fragments of nonsense
as I let you in, the silken scissors
of my legs around your waist,
ankles hooked in the small of your back,
your voice and my voice, both,
caressing one another in the chill, winter air.

I return to the bed,
our resting place among the blankets
where I opened to every
curve and dip and press of you.
Your hand against my chest, I
pepper it with kisses, cradle it tenderly,
then open my mouth against your neck,
lap at the cooling salt of your skin,
Our warm breath shines golden in the darkness
as joy and sleep take us.

Blue Wren

Think of a bird,
think of how it died,
its small-boned self, smashed
against your kitchen window.
one solitary delphinium blue feather,
and a tiny smear of blood and flesh
that you will clean with newspaper and ammonia.

Think of a bird's frail body sinking into hollow bones,
still but for the breeze that stirs its thinning feathers.
Think of teams of ants, think of flies
laying maggots into the small cave of a belly, picked clean.
Think of your child finding this bird, or what is left of it,
a scrap of faded blue at her feet. She looks up at you,
expecting like last time, a shoebox, and a cloth.

Some words spoken.
Some kind of ritual.
But you are out of words.

It is late in the afternoon,
she needs a bath and pajamas
and something to eat before bed, and you are tired.
Tired of how they come at you,
their small dark bodies falling
like kamikaze out of the sky,
almost one a week,
to smash their fragile skulls against
your deadly, transparent panes of glass.

Fishing with my Father

That Sunday afternoon,
the two of us, fishing from the rocks.
Standing just clear of the black moss
at the water's edge, the grey striations of a fish
flopping in my hand, as I tore the hook
from its mouth, under his direction:
gentle, gentle. No need to tear it.
Under the matching grey of an Albany sky,
I hunched against the wind in my jeans, and
fishing jumper, stiff on the front
with fish guts and whale-oil.
I flung my burley and whale-oil mix
as far as I could into the inky water,
a prismatic slick like petrol in the wake, mirrored by
the sleek silver bellies of the skippy in the bucket.

As he took his serrated knife, and twisted his hand,
spearing the fish I'd just caught through its eye,
he told me about a friend of his,
with more money than sense,
who fished in cashmere sweaters.
My father clucked his tongue,
scrubbed his hands together,
and stood up, tall compared to me.
They were all the colours of the rainbow.

Bron Bateman is a poet and academic. Her first collection, *People from bones* (with Kelly Pilgrim) was published in 2002. Her second collection, *Of Memory and Furniture,* was published by Fremantle Press in 2020. She lives in Perth, Western Australia with her wife and daughter.

FOLLOWING PAGE: Cat Cotsell—*Pink Duke*

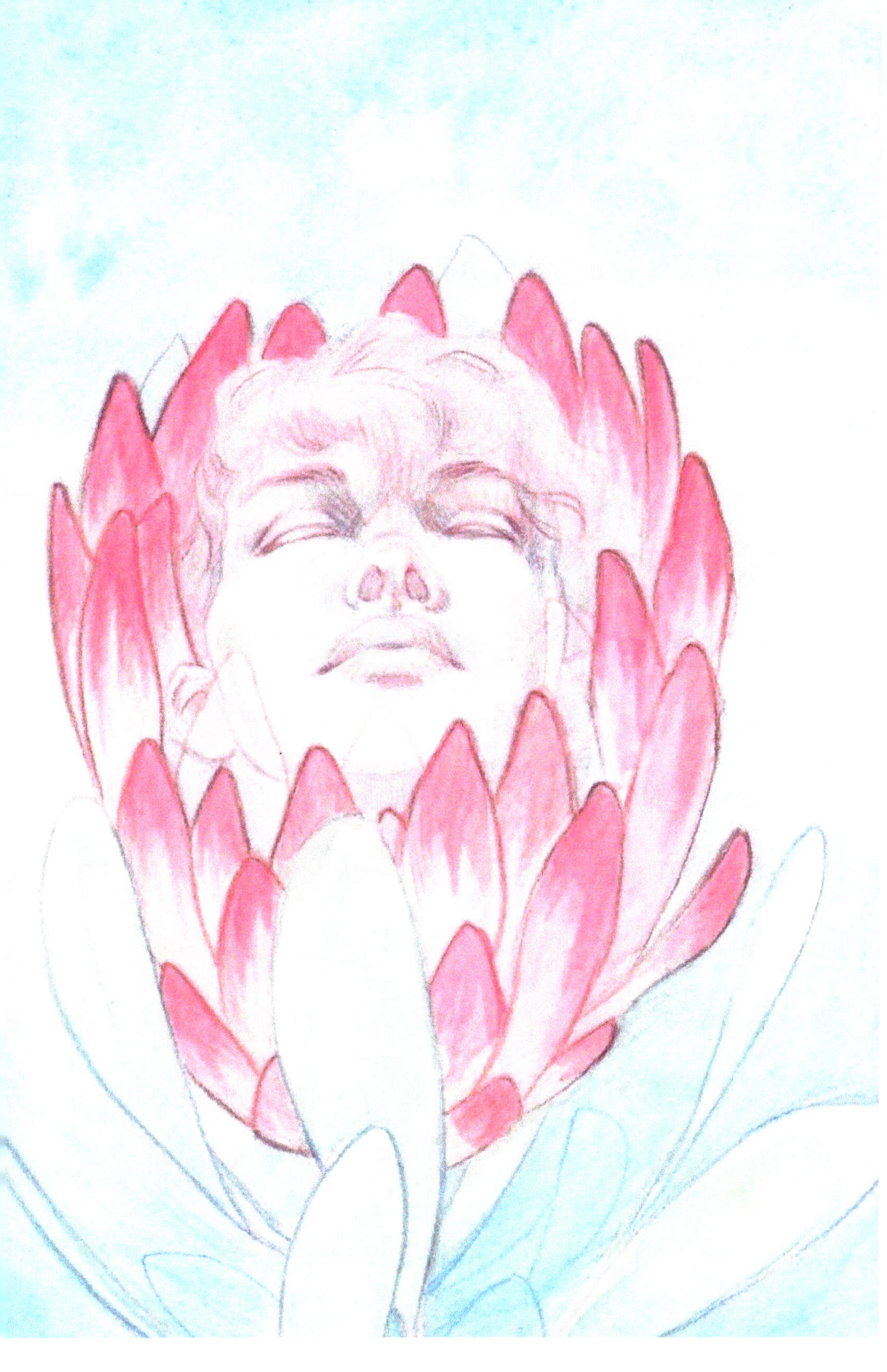

Cat Cotsell

None of your bucking fizziness

'I just think you're confused.'
I know you are
but what am I?
You're not getting any hints
from looking down my shirt.
I just think that –
It's just funny how –
I just want to say –
You can't just—
It's just my opinion.
(I live in an unjust world, but you Just)
'You can only have XX or XY chromosomes'
says the guy who last took science
in high school.
All he has to do is
read the wikipedia page
on chromosomes.
All I have to do is
read every book, every paper
shove a Masters in my own queerness up my arse
comprehend and be ready to comprehensively defend
the nuanced and delicate interplay between what
science knows and what science does not yet know
the subjectivity of culture and identity and
grasp fully the concrete biology.
All I have to do is
all the stuff it's unreasonable to ask him to do
check his every unchecked fact
answer his squirming invasive questions
about my body, my hypothetical trauma
cross every box on his list while patiently
letting him dehumanize me with his 'opinion'
and respect his right to spit on me
and, in the end,
to Just Disagree.
All I have to do. All the shit
I have to do.

Why are you so defensive?
Here's a thought:
All you have to do is
treat me
like
you would treat
a housecat.
'What's her name?'
'Catrick Swayze.'
'Oh, his, sorry. Cool name.'

Courtship Ritual

I'm dressed to the nines, to kill, to impress
upon you the impeccable silhouette of
the wide-eyed owl, unforgettable
svelte as a white ghost alert on the fence,
a startlingly serious familiar little alien.
But the unmoving is part of the charm and I
want to strut,
a grey pigeon head bobbing in the sun
turned out in wings flashing turquoise,
gold, rose, rainbows refracting on a
rugged round grey peasant,
provincial but not unpleasant,
I want to look how trendy ghosts
wish they looked.
You make me crave to be
effortlessly fancy, not by design
but organically, a stunning accident of
natural selection, because no bright god
could invent something like a toucan,
who can, bless his heart, with a
beak like a space age bike handle
somehow occupy the forest gallery wall
of a work of living art, up against
birds of paradise, that's the kind of
confidence I aspire to, thanks to you.
I just want for you to think I'm
weirdly graceful, be momentarily
stalled by me, that's all,
the way I am when you
wobble, turn your head and tilt it like that,
like you're up on stilts and keeping an eye out
for stealthy cats.

Cat Cotsell is a nonbinary panromantic creative generalist. Their writing can be found in
Bent Street, qommunicate's *Hashtag Queer* volume 2, and cicerone journal's Canberra
anthology *These Strange Outcrops*. They also illustrate as Cat Hesarose.

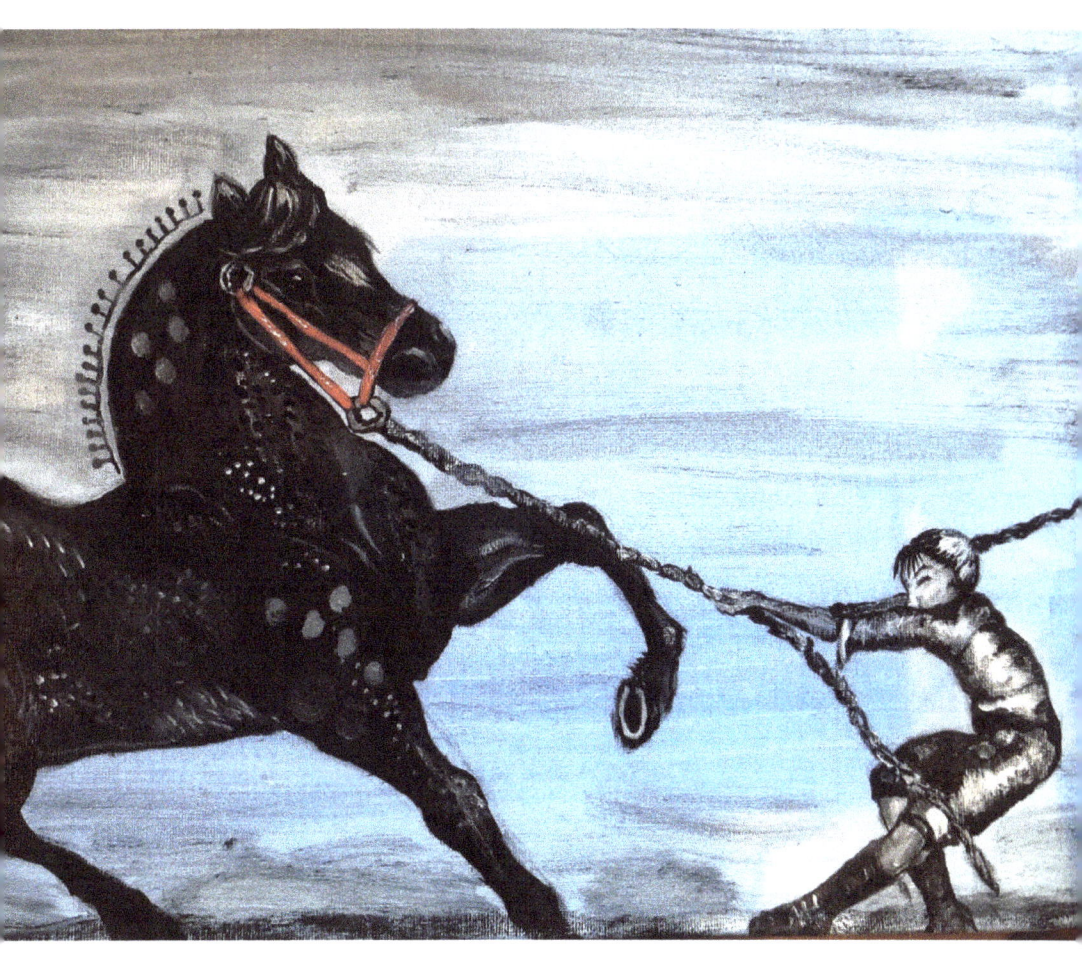

Jennifer Power—*Come into my patch of blue*

Adele Aria

Known

I hate the labels
You've made available for me
Non Something
Something Diverse
Person of Not Like You
Off the right path
Off centre
Of Something
All it says
Is Distinct from easily accepted
Different from preferred
and palatable

But
Consume my image
Devour my body
Ignore (my) protests
Regardless (our) humanity
Use me to frame your argument
Hold up (your) products
Shape y(our) ideas

I perform
With your language
Of Words, Clothes, Manners
I am Masterful
I will never be Master
Because I am not man
Nor owner
Of me in public

Even my traumas
Carefully dripped out
Coffee pressed
Milked into whiteness
Sweetened with language

Served like I am
Conveniently small
Easily contained

Wrangled into a vessel

I'll pack back into the cupboard.

Fiercely Independent

Trying on other people's bodies
Looking for love
To plug up the holes
Of scars that
Are secretly wounds
Weeping tears
I never cry

Witnessed by anyone
I fear losing
Are snack-size
Candy bar versions
Of history
To make a semblance of
Getting closer

Adele writes non-fiction and poetry with occasional forays in short fiction. An advocate for human rights and social change, they draw on their studies and personal experiences of complex trauma, domestic violence, disability, and queerness to explore the politics of existence and identity, and the ways in which we integrate personal and shared histories. They have been published in international and Australian literary and academic publications. A bisexual genderqueer person of colour, Adele is grateful to be living and writing upon Noonga Boodjar.

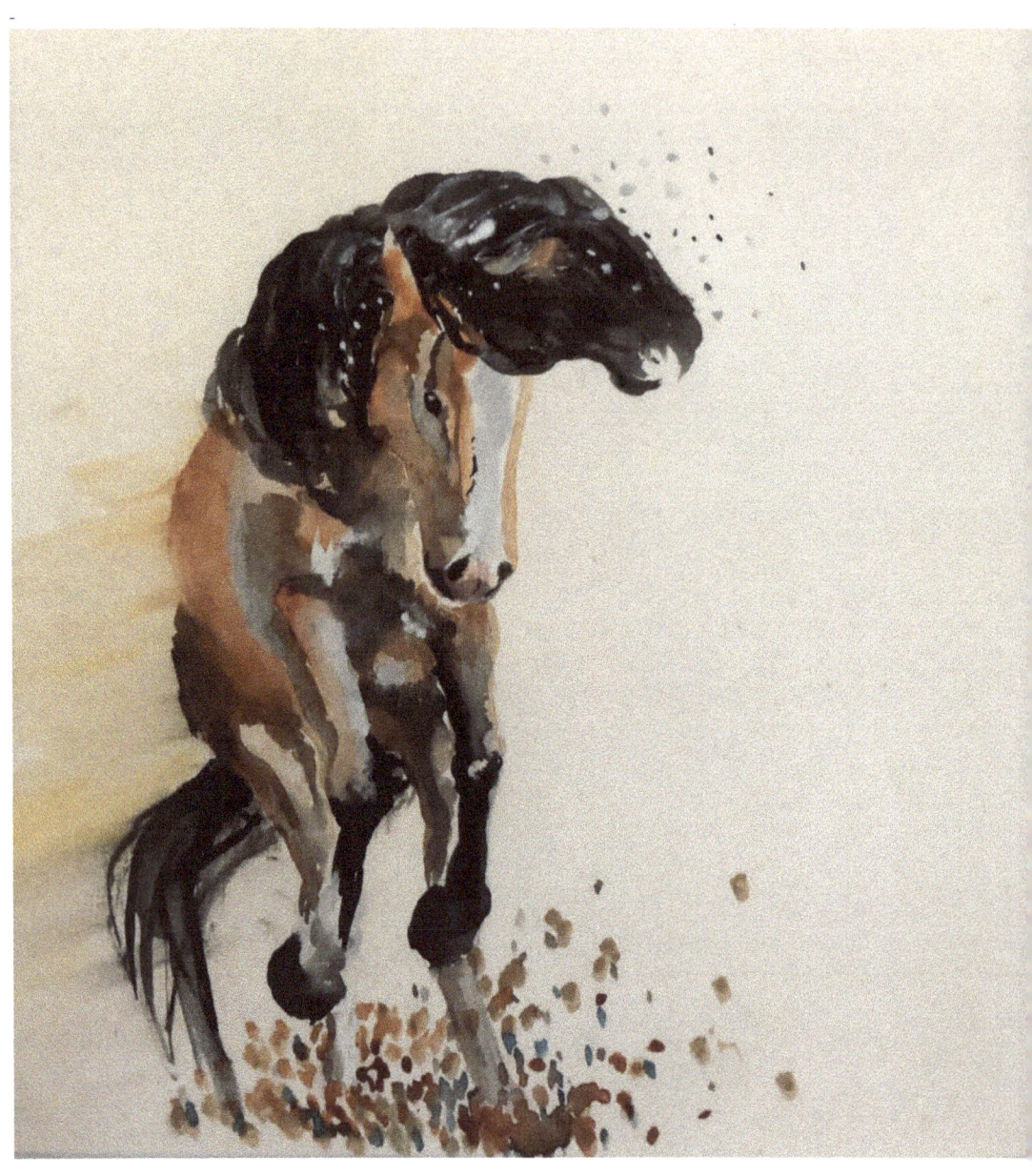

Jennifer Power—*Negotiating freedom and constraint in 2020*

Michele Saint-Yves

Melbourne Street

First the hour.

Lying depleted, shed.
In a hotel room guarded by card slot time.
In a building of glass and steel,
on a street of ivy lined innuendo,
coffee filtered coercion and terraced terror.
In a city seeming sweet and vulnerable yet defensive:
cornered by drought, threatened by light, armoured
within a mushroom cloud of subatomic chaos.

I felt her before I saw her
dust made its way in her cut-out shapes
musk spittled her outline upon my skin
dusk scuttled her contours' shadows on liquid walls
 lust of liquor, sweat, scorched tar librettoed her ego
I snuffed her in by increments;
thimbled particles of promise.

I refuse deserts. Mountains. Forests. Gorges. Lakes.
My life doesn't unfurl, meander, unfold—snail paced.
Not lived on unpasteurised produce, fresh air,
organic moments.
It's pixellated, high octane, insatiable image driven—
moment consumed next forgotten.
I remember not the names of countries
and constellations.
Out there.

But in here, in this horizonless city, I feel the ocean.
Feel the swell:
smell oxygen, taste salt, touch what swims within.
She is here.

In here, Room 703:
between her legs,
on her surface all quivering with gulls

in my belly,
through the fluted purple coral of her throat
by her drowning breath,
in the song forming as a villanelle in my head
in sonic waves,
that lash my tongue's tip then pound elsewhere
at high speed frequency—breaking light
I can see.

Through her eye's slit, a crescent moon of enigmatic light peeps—halfway
between life and exaltation—
and in holding sight of me,
stars draw in their panting fires.
Entire civilisations implode
in the dying constellation of her face.

In this: the last hour.

Route 251

'I sing because I'm happy, I sing because I'm free,
His eye is on the sparrow, and I know He watches me.'
Never any other day, other time.
Never another bus, street. Nor stop.
Only ever: Sundays. 09:36. Ferryden Park, Kilburn, Wellington Square.
Always with this song.
Not with bags. Nor market trolley.
Nothing to shield from white sun,
nor hydrate in blue heat.
Just the hymn.
And always kerb-side. Front, window set.
Ticket redundant.

At the stobie superglued poster from post-Twin Towers
right on cue: *'Don't Be a Lert. Be a Llama.* Ha ha ha!'
Her bun-bird's nest of dry straw, copper wire, brillo thread threatens to
cliff fall
save the polka-dot-synthetic scarf.
Her tissue thin cheeks are caked in bubble-gum-pink blush,
as per ventriloquist dummies.
Her rheumy fish-bowl eyes are shadowed in cupcake-blue-icing,
like Les Girls dancers.
Her fish bone frame bends feebly, as if broth-soaked
but pot's now dry.

'The beauty of a woman is not in the clothes she wears,
the figure she carries or the way she combs her hair.'
Her dress, nylon with florid print, splutters beneath
cardigans and cagoules from op-shops'
bargain basement bin.
Pointless to a contrarian, haltingly she carries herself
stockingless, in silver-lurex sandals
that maybe used to fit.

Khaki bus shelter graffiti pukes: *'Feminists walk amongst you!* Ha ha ha!'
No one ever sits near.
Nor talks to her though she talks non-stop.
With iPods, iPhones, Kindles they don't even listen.
'If you're not careful, the media will have you hating the people who are
being oppressed and loving the people who are doing the oppressing.'

I tune in.
Her tone a feast belying her anorexic physicality.
This is what I pick up:

She would have been found smoking cigarellos
with Collette in dapper-duds
kissing under lamplight on Rue de Pigalle
and later manequinned for Saint Laurent.

In search of her ashen love shot
by Sherman in Manhattan.

And in the space of fixation, ends up here
at world's edge.
All expectations spent.
Where love's loss and time's mistake rendered her
a 1970s pastiche of Miss Haversham.

She says we can visit her past
at the Tate in 1998, Pompidou in 2002.
For as Collette says—mine and hers:
'*By an image we hold on to our lost treasures,*
but it is the wrenching loss that forms the image, composes, binds the
bouquet.'

Welly Square stop is here.
Bus mimics passengers' collective sigh, as she drops
like browning petals to teeter in the gutter's grate.
Turning, she primes her palms,
Von Trapp kids' farewell song poised.

This time, in her pause, I proffer:
'*What is forgiveness?*
And Sufi replied:
It's the fragrance that flowers give
when they are crushed.'
And glass doors squish shut at her gasp.

Black Saturdhaze

A slot. Five fingered fit.
Recycled pieces of pulped wood are sleeved
dropping at dawn
to go West.

A day lay in the dark
when the moon was to turn on its other side
emptying its millennium ashtrays
           on to Earth.

A day in cinders
when weeks of gutter gripes and trash talk
went up in flames
           falling to Earth.

A day in mortar
when cracked caches of granite
pestled molten steel
pockmarking Earth.

A day in diaspora
when woman and wallaby
collided pitch perfect
turning Earth.

A day in eclipse
when the black eye
seered hope blind
           blackboxing Earth.

And from this day
in this backburn of time
a letter lies.

All I left you.
All that's left
of me.

In the only thing
left standing
in the town that stood here.

Australia Post's box.
'Fire engine red' they call it
even to this day.

Michele Saint-Yves is an Adelaide-based writer who lives with disability and primarily writes
for performance—stage, screen and poetry. When able, she loves swimming in wild water
places, dancing in the rain and delving in to the rabbit hole of lesbian web-series.

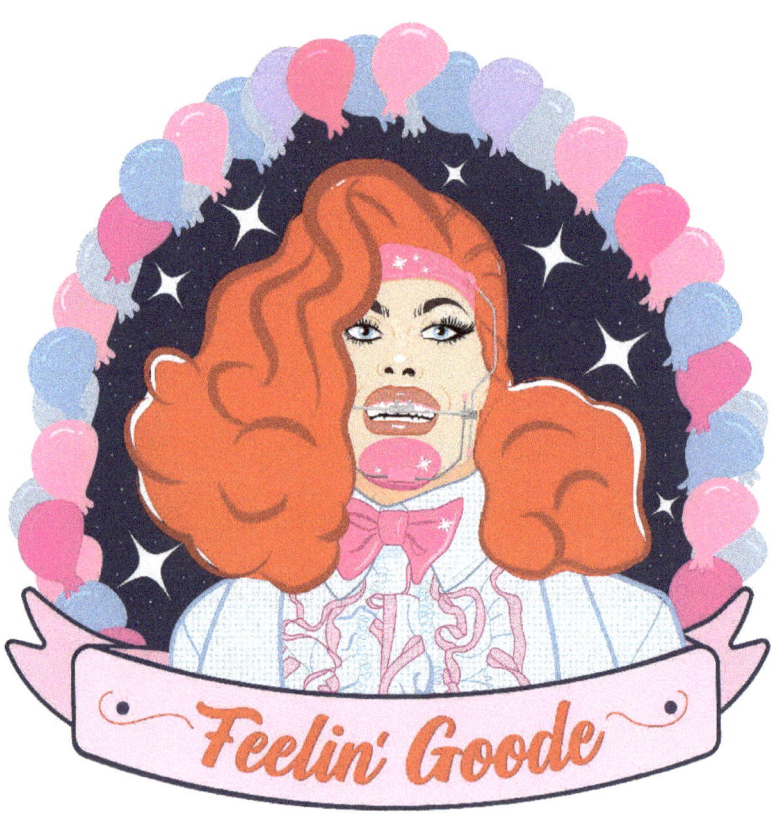

Mel Simpson—Feelin' Goode

Gemma Rose

The Colours That Appear When You Hold Pointed Corners To The Light

I wanted to be alone in her company
I fell into the parts I hated in his
I hesitated every time I kissed her
I kissed him effortlessly
When I felt strong I didnt call him
When I loved myself I called her
When she touched my leg I flinched
I hardly held her eyes
Every feeling was full of hesitation
Anxiety crept in and I naturally pushed her away
We were plagued by stagnant kisses
Ones asking us to kiss deeper
We don't like new love
Even when it feels so much fuller
She was bewitching and beautiful
But she never had a chance because she was too new
And it's so much easier to settle
To accept lukewarm love

So I kissed him for months full of dark blue nights and stars we never
watched and stars that hardly shined
And the moon never became full.
And when I fell asleep I felt comfortable.
But I didn't fall in love

And I over thought every touch of my fingertips. and I analysed every
movement of her lips. and I saw pink clouds in the night sky.
And love became something I had to piece together.

And love became an aged wine and honest truth not lies of forever. and my
heart beats too fast.

So I walk away.

but no love that's easy is worth having.

Courages kisses and risks taken and professing love to the one who may not love you back.

At the risk of losing everything.

To see salmon pink stars in the night sky.

To when you fall asleep learn how to fly.

To have 50 kisses of hesitation before you know its heaven and fall in.

Deep in.

Its scary.

Its meant to be scary.

Staying with someone you don't love fuck that's easy.

He can confidently touch every part of your body.

and I'm terrified to.

But excited too.

And darling all the best love is worth waiting for.

I don't need to love you forever but I can choose to.

Take your time.

Fall into that perfect night sky count the shades of acrylic paint on both our fingers. Count the clouds that sparkle in the rain. Learn to see rainbows again. Learn to choose the path for you. Learn that you are the painter and you can paint your sky blue. Not live in his shadow. You can choose to love the angel.

The road that isn't easy

Is golden.

Like that sparkle in your eyes that I sometimes see shine

Before he dulled it

Let's talk salt water. And fall in love in lavender bath water
And heat our bodies next to crimson fires
Let's count fallen leaves and climb tall trees and fall in love together
To candle light
moon light
The stars will shine
As sunflowers grow towards the sun
And on mildew grass our guts will belly laugh
And love grew feathers and halos tonight

Gemma Rose is a young queer writer residing in Adelaide, currently coming to the conclusion of her degree in creative writing at Adelaide University. Gemma facilitates a community poetry event called 'Tatenda' to promote healing through story telling and connection in these uncertain times. In the last fringe festival she starred, produced and directed a show titled 'slowly but surely' with an entirely queer and female/non binary cast. She spends her free time with her dog, writing a poetry/prose life writing novel and volunteering for feminist radio station 'pink rabbit'.

Zachary DB Smith

Fuck men
At least I'm trying
But lying comes quick—must come with the dick

Must be a two-for-one deal on that shit

Did I suspect? Not so much
I always lacked insight as such
Always lacked that Midas touch
Mine was more like a curse
Where gold reverts to something worth
Less

The truth behind a lie always hurts

And just when I thought I had no more torches
To carry, here comes this guy and he forces
Me to consider my limits—he's gorgeous
And sort of scary; could this twink be
The first canary down my
All-too-eager coal mine?

God, his lips are a gold mine
And in my dreams, he's all mine

In my dreams. It's all in my head
My alchemy—my talent—is gold into lead

When I'm at my most hopeless
A hole in me opens
It's a cavern and it's ravenous
Devouring the hope I've found
And then, *their* voices resound
Echoing up, telling me
Who I really am deep down
Fuck men
Who made me this way
Who'd pray for their knowledge
Instead of just acknowledge I might be gay

My self-image was transmuted
And tarnished by men
But I will not be made worthless again

My truth hides behind the mask of a lie
But it's a mask I can take off any time
And beneath it is nothing but glittering
Twinkling gold

Zachary is a genre writer and poet based in Adelaide who, as a former coordinator with Writers SA, has built a deep love and connection to the South Australian writing community. His current project is a fantasy novel based in themes of queer identity and self-realisation.

Shivani Preston

A letter for a friend

I miss you. I think about you every day you know. Why the fuck did you have to do that? Why did you leave? You left everyone behind. I wonder if you knew of the pain you would leave behind, would you have still done it?

I wish you were still here. I want to volunteer with you. I want to drink with you, dance with you, laugh with you, cry with you. But you are gone now. You are unreachable. Unattainable.

I hope that you are in a good place now. Somewhere where you can smile and be everything that you could possibly be. I wish you could see me now and see all of the amazing things that I'm doing. I wish you could see how much I've grown since you left.

I dream about you sometimes. You seem happy in my dreams. Peaceful even.

We planted a tree for you. It would have been your 28th birthday that day. I made your favourite cake. The chocolate banana cake that I used to bring into TAFE for you. I remember you tried to make it one time but you refused to let me try it because it wasn't as good as mine. I guess I will never know …

Sometimes I just cry, thinking about the immense pain you must have been feeling. I cry for the other people who are hurting because you are gone. I cry for my beautiful friend. The sister I always wanted, who is no longer here. But you live on in my heart and in my memories. Every day I will strive to be more like you.

And maybe one day, at the end of the road, I will see you again.

Shivani is a young queer artist, writer and musician who lives in Adelaide and is studying arts at university. They are involved with many creative groups and projects, and they are a valued member of Adelaide's queer community.

Heath John Ramsay

He Who Shall Be Named

I've made a recording
of me screaming your name
with ear-splitting ferocity
ROGER CUNNINGHAM

An anguished, wretched scream
which perfectly encapsulates
the depths of my suffering and despair
ROGER CUNNINGHAM

My Savage Soundbite™
will be permanently lodged
inside your bloodless brain
ROGER CUNNINGHAM

Amygdala Armageddon
Operation Limbic Whiplash
Self-esteem, I'm gunning for you
ROGER CUNNINGHAM

Retributive Justice™ software
in cataclysmic concert
with your emotional undulations
ROGER CUNNINGHAM

Now **every time** you crest
toward a feeling of happiness or pride
my Atonement Audio™ activates
ROGER CUNNINGHAM

So that you immediately suffer
at tremendous volume
an articulation of pure misery
ROGER CUNNINGHAM

By none other than myself
your original victim
HEATH JOHN RAMSAY
Roger Cunningham

Your Umbrella

Sex in the city after film class
you weren't who you pretended to be
but I didn't mind
you were cute and bashful
hungry and nervous

So many noodles!
I'm drowning in an ocean of Mi goreng logos
you take me by the hand and lead me to a bedroom that isn't yours
then, glory of glories
you ask if you can take off my shoes

We jostle for position
the race is on
by crikey you are determined
but wait, just a moment
come closer and give me your face

Post coital glow and candour
horizontal rain pelting the windows
our own private carwash
a roving silhouette of raindrops dance across your torso
Well isn't this nice

Bear hugs and chuckles in the hallway
a quick sting of sadness behind my eyes
we both notice we're holding hands
a reluctant slow dance
towards your front door

You offered me so much more than your umbrella
but this tone-deaf fool politely discouraged your kindness
promises, promises
I'd like that, stay safe
one final kiss in the Kingdom of Noodles

It felt exquisite to be alive in our carwash
but now, a plague of *if onlys*
the Fail Whale stole you from me
my Noodle Prince

Heath John Ramsay, actor, sub-average singer, private dancer, pop culture glutton, former colourist at *Elevation Hair & Beauty* and Enrolments Advisor at *The Phoenix Institute* (raided by the Federal Police in March 2016) enjoys french knitting and *Murder She Wrote*, and is currently reading *Balancing Act: The Authorized Biography of Angela Lansbury*.

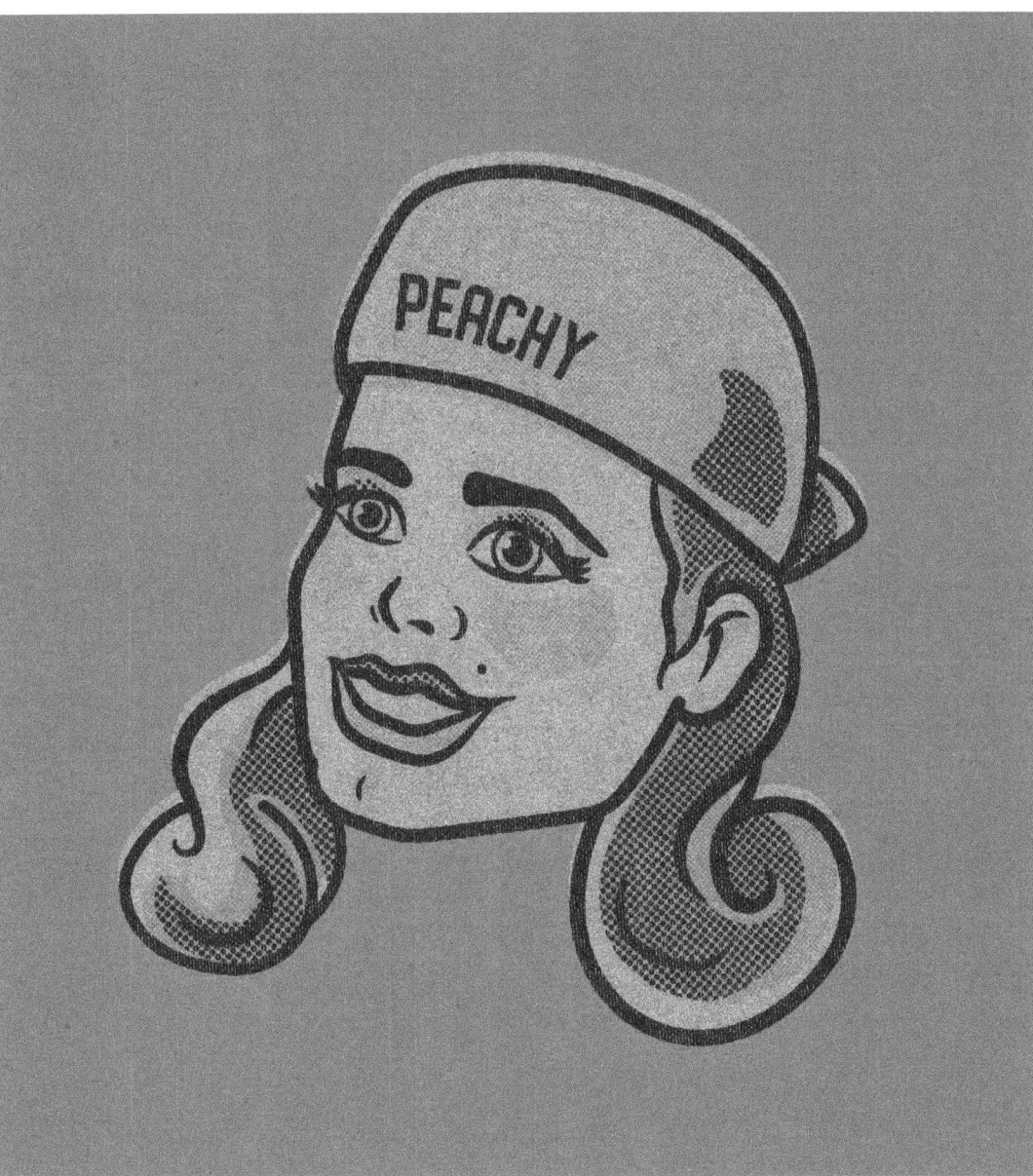

Mel Simpson—*Geena*

Penn O'Brien

1)
This is a love poem.
Which in itself is not revolutionary, but maybe it should be.
This is a queer love poem,
To someone who is hesitant to call themselves lesbian.
Who is worried about taking up too much space in a space others believe is not meant for them.
But this poem isn't about the others.
It's about us.
Detailing how we fit together,
Intrinsically and through hard work.
Open and honest communication making a garden of my tongue,
Growing flowers with which to adorn their hair.
We are not two halves of a whole.
Each of us too much our own person to ever be incomplete.
We are creatures of the universe.
New and old,
Full of stories and stardust.
I swear I can see it shimmering in their galaxy eyes
And glowing from the constellation freckles on their face.
They are radiant.
Permanently lit by the light of the sun.
Golden.
Gaze upon them.
As much a goddess as Athena and Aphrodite.
Still, we are human.
Perfect and imperfect in the truest way.
Houseplants with complicated emotions.
Brains full of chemicals and bodies that don't quite fit us right.
But together we are trying.
Their arm draped over my stomach, my knees curled against their thighs, our fingers woven together.
My heart does not know love in the way others claim it is meant to,
But that will not stop me from loving them with every fibre of my imperfect being.
And as truly as I know this, I know that they love me too.

2)
I breathe in poetry,
Feel it diffuse through my lungs,
The words clinging to my red blood cells.
I don't know how to get them out
But it won't be through my skin.
I'll keep my blood where it belongs,
So I try to use my lungs instead.
Push the words back out into the air,
Attempting to get the metaphor of my body just right.
Because the only way I can handle it is in the abstract.
Separated from my self.
Always fracturing fun house mirror, never whole.
Pin it through the chest,
Make it sit still on the page for long enough for me to trace its outline.
Like it isn't a shifting amorphous thing
That distorts into something new and differently horrific when I turn away.
It is at once too large and too small.
Not enough skeleton and too many bones.
Too much space and too many organs.
See me dissected,
Cut open and stitched back together.
Monstrous.
But even that monster was made in the image of beauty.
Written by a woman to prove a point.
But I am not a woman,
Despite how this body presents me.
But I am No Man either,
So who has hurt me?
Blinded me to the truth of my body.
That it and I are one in the same.
This rickety house that I have inherited.
Unable to move so I'm left renovating.
Knocking down walls and dragging in new furniture.
Filling it with life and love,
So that it can be a home instead of a cage.
I grow houseplants in my bedroom to remind myself that some things are counting on me to live.
This would be a metaphor if this were a poem and not a confessional.
Chest spilling open to reveal cracked rib and fluttering lung.
How else to rid myself of this toxin?
Cutting venom from the wound

Is not how you cure a snakebite.
My body may never be just a body until I am gone, and it is sodden with earth and earthworms.
But until that day,
I will pick up the pieces of the mirror,
Careful not to cut myself,
And I will look at my body,
And finally see my reflection.

Penn is a young queer writer originally from Renmark in regional South Australia, and most interested in writing poetry and for theatre.

Stephanie Russell

Thanks

Have you ever known the full compass of pain and passion
when the wicked one steals from the depths cloaked in darkness
takes you unawares
challenges what you know to be right and true
strips you bare
takes all you hold good and dashes it on the ground in front of you
and you fall in the mud and filth
screaming
flailing
don't let me fail
don't let me
something dies inside you
charred and twisted
burned forever
but somehow you hold onto a shred
you hold on with a strength you thought you never had
till she pulls you free
and casts you on a salt-washed beach
and through the tears and flaming curses
she sees the glimmer still there inside you
and thanks you for it

Stephanie is a transgender female, but only for the last five years, 'so I am still learning. I love writing, and I am secretary of the Kensington & Norwood Writers' Group. I have written short stories for many years, and more recently I started writing poetry.'

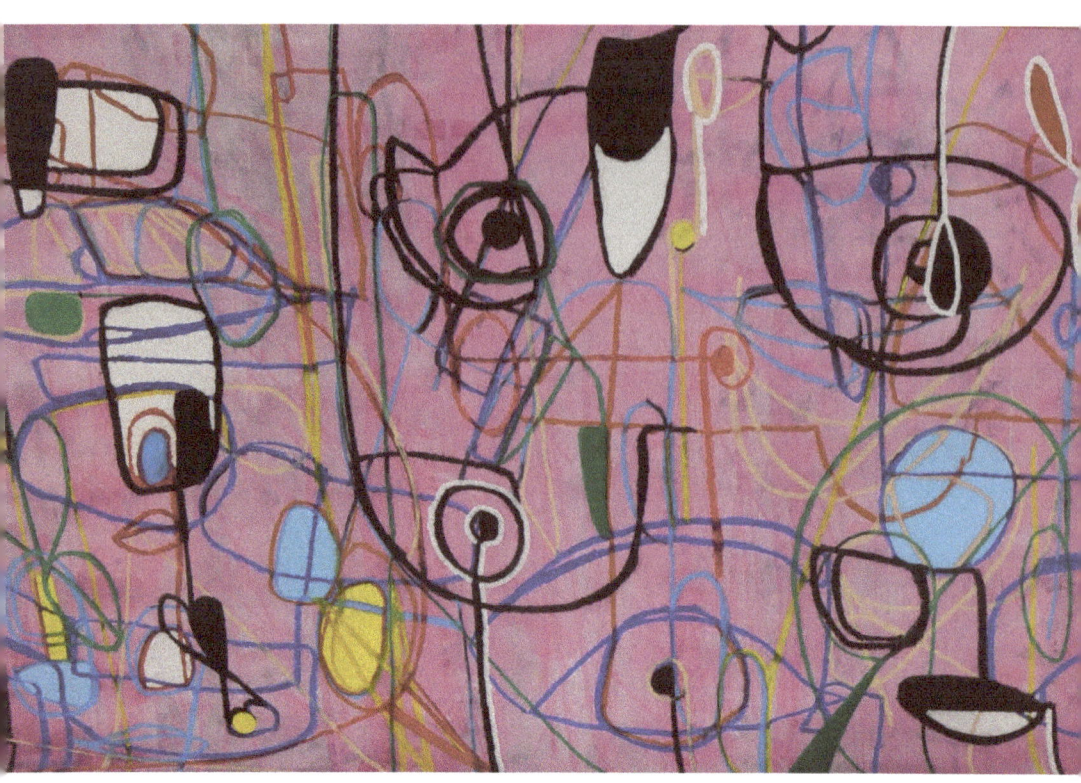

Frank Bonnici—*Surrounds*, 800x1100

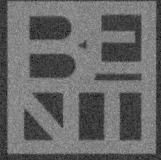

FICTION

ARCHIPELAGO
Jan Prior

A client you've mentioned many times calls at our home. Unusual. You usually go to his office in the city.

'So this is Alice,' he says, dropping to his haunches in front of the child I've come to think of as our daughter. His eyes are almost level with hers. 'Hi Alice. I've heard so much about you.'

For a while I keep myself busy in the kitchen. I peek my head around the corner of the studio. Three heads swing in my direction.

'Coffee?'

'Roland, this is my housemate, Rachel.'

You're not looking at me. You're smiling at him.

Black Audi Roland.

I wait. You have already texted that you will be late, but 1:37? Headlights sweep slats of pale light across the curtains and disappear. The roller door clunks up and then comes down. The key is in the lock, a tiny snick, then the front door closes. I turn on the bedside light and hunch up.

'I told you not to wait up,' you say.

You drop your handbag on the chair in the corner. You sit on the bed beside me and tug at the scarf around your throat. My hand lies on the top of the sheet. You enclose it within yours. You bend your head as if you might be about to murmur a prayer, a benediction, a condolence. Soft and grave, you look up. 'There's something I have to tell you.'

You sit at a corner table of the café in the shadows. When you see me your face lights up. You stand and move towards me with your arms out.

'It's so lovely to see you. I wondered if you'd show.' I'm still holding my plastic smile, and you put your arms lightly around me and we air kiss. You seem thinner than I remember.

We order coffee from a boy with brio and a shaved head.

'It's not really about Alice,' you say. 'I thought you might refuse to come otherwise.'

How would one more lie make any difference?

You fiddle with a white paper napkin. 'I told Mum and Dad about you and me. I wanted to get some honesty into my relationship with them.'

Ha! Rona and Doug getting their Hillsong heads around that revelation! 'How did that fit into the divine family plan?'

'Oh … you know … they pray for me …' You give me that grin, the crooked one with the rueful tug at the corner of your mouth that used to melt me. 'In spite of what I've told them, they still can't seem to get their heads around why I left Nathan. So when Roland appeared …'

'Oh goody. A stepdad for Alice.'

You pick up the napkin and start to twist it into a pretzel. 'I've been seeing a counsellor.' You clear your throat. 'Not letting people know that you were my partner … I couldn't admit how unfair it was to you.' You suck in breath and your gaze slides away. 'Nathan's a great Dad, and Roland's a good man. I hurt them badly, as I hurt you, Rachel.' You move to the shredding stage. 'I wanted to see you to apologise. You deserved better. Much, much better.'

A clot forms in my throat. 'Enough,' is what I would say if I could get the words out.

'I was really happy with you, Rach, particularly in the beginning, in spite of what you might think.' You reach across the table and grip my hand. 'I really was in love with you.'

Christ almighty, show me some mercy. Strike me deaf now. Make me leave before I say something stupid.

You give a little self-deprecating laugh. 'I only ever fall in love with women. I can have sex with men, but I can't fall in love with them. And after a while I don't even want to have sex with them either.' You pick at your fingernails. 'It's a pity I didn't realize that sooner.'

Our lattes arrive. You fiddle with your coffee spoon even though you don't take sugar.

Deflect, deflect, regroup. I clear my throat. 'So how is Alice?' How will I bear to hear? How could I not ask?

Your eyes burn. 'She was happy when Roland left, but she's still angry with me for sending you away.'

'But we told her I had a job transfer—'

'She knew what was happening. You know Alice.'

A laugh seeps out of us in small grimaces.

Your face softens. 'What's your situation now, Rach? Do you have someone special in your life?'

I am in a wind tunnel. Whoosh whooshing. I try not to think of my unit, my empty cubicle, the lifeless air when I come home at night. 'I live alone.'

I'm lost, the ground is slipping away, I must find a handhold, something to halt my slide towards the precipice.

'So, do you think we could—'

'It would be a dead cat bouncing.' My own words reach out to save me.

'What's that supposed to mean?'

'It's the idea of a dead cat being struck by a car and leaping into the air as if it's still alive, and then falling back onto the road. Totally dead.'

You flinch.

I am not the sort of person who says things like that. Am I?

Gathering your bag, you stand and nod in the direction of the cash register. 'I'll get this,' you say and stride towards the counter.

A premonition of the shame that would haunt me if I let you go in this way jerks me to my feet. I call out to you. You turn, hesitate.

'Please come back.'

Eyeing me suspiciously, you make your way back to the table. I tell you in an outpouring of violent emotion what I hadn't recognised in myself until that moment—how grateful I am that you and Alice had been in my life. How much I'd missed the life that we once had.

When we part we hold one another so closely that I can feel your heart racing.

'Nathan will be bringing Alice back on Sunday afternoon,' you say. 'Why don't you come over?'

The front doorbell rings.

You open the door and Alice shrieks: 'She's here! I can see her car!'

Nathan stands behind Alice, pink backpack in hand.

'Hey Alice! Wait! Give your Dad a hug!' Nathan says. He sees me and momentarily his jaw sags. 'Err ... Hello, Rachel.'

'Hi, Nathan.'

Eyebrow raised, he hands Alice's backpack to you. Alice pulls away from him and sprints towards me. 'Don't run, Alice!' you call after her.

I drop to my knees. Alice scrambles over me in a whirlwind of blurred limbs. I drag myself up from the scrum, and she rises with me, refusing to let go. I laugh and make my way crablike down the hall, with Alice still hanging off one leg. I lift her up.

'I knew you would come back,' she croons into my neck. 'I missed you— I missed you so much, Rach. I wanted you to come home. Every day, that's what I wanted.'

I murmur sounds into her ear, kiss her hot, flushed face.

Your gaze bores into mine with both anguish and pleading. I can't expunge four years of my life as if it never happened. Gently I try to unwind Alice's limbs from my torso.

'Steady on, you little boa constrictor,' I say, laughing to cover my tumult of feeling. 'Come and show me your drawings.'

Reluctantly she releases me. She slides down my legs to the floor. She grabs my hand, and skipping ahead, drags me down the hall to her bedroom.

You follow, and as Alice leafs through her drawings and paintings, slip your hand into mine and squeeze.

'And this painting's from when I got lost,' Alice says and holds up a wrinkled sheet of foxed paper scrawled in charcoal. 'You put my name over the loudspeaker, and I had to wait for you to get me. Your face was all red and blotchy!'

'That's such a long time ago, sweetheart. How could you still remember?'

'I remember everything we ever did,' Alice says.

'Surely not everything,' you say, looking worried. Shouted words behind doors. Arctic silences at breakfast. Alice would not have forgotten those.

'I was so relieved I wanted to throttle you! You gave me a terrible fright.'

Alice smiles smugly and pulls out the next picture.

Over Alice's head, you and I exchange a look of joint appeal, helpless witnesses to such innocent faith.

'Why don't you stay for dinner?'

At the kitchen bench Alice beats the goo for the corn fritters. Under your supervision, she fries them to a point beyond sludge but before incineration. I scavenge in the fridge and make a salad. You pour two glasses of white wine and we sit down to eat.

Alice twirls a donut shaped fritter on the end of her fork with an air of triumph and satisfaction. She takes slow bites and looks at me sideways as if she thinks that I might disappear again. You look at me that way too.

With a mixture of slyness and apprehension, Alice says: 'Will you read to me before bed tonight? Or I can read to you. I know a lot of new words.'

'Like what?'

'Ithmuth,' she says through the gap in her front teeth.

'Ithmith?'

'I-S-T-H-M-U-S,' she says benevolently.

'Goodness. Do you know what that means?'

'Actually, I am quite clever.'

'Modest, too,' you say, placing a hand on dark springy curls.

'So, do you know archipelago?'

Alice shakes her head and I try to explain about chunks of land that somehow got separated from the mainland. I know little about geography, even less about the strange and compelling dream that I seem to be floating in. But Alice is real. She bounces up from the table and runs down the hall to return with an A3 sheet of paper and a handful of marker pens.

She bites her bottom lip and looks up at me. 'How many islands are there?'

'As many as you like. They're a group, that's the thing.'

She selects a different colour for each Rorschach blob, then fills the surrounding ocean with cavorting whales and dolphins. 'You can have this for your house.'

'Thank you. I'll put where I can see it every day.'

You refill our glasses.

'If you have too much to drink you aren't allowed to drive,' Alice says.

'Who told you that?'

'Roland. But he always had too much to drink.'

'I'm not going to have too much to drink.'

She looks at me and purses her lips. 'That's what Roland used to say too.'

Now this.

Already birds are about their business, twittering and chirruping. I lie here with my heart banging and wonder if the best thing to do would be to rise and silently leave. Your fingers sneak across the sheets.

'Are you going?' you say.

'I'll come back to visit Alice. But not like this.'

I have a sense of heaviness, of harbouring a reservoir of feeling that could drag me under. We are separated by a wide channel that I cannot swim against. I have tried, but that deep, passionate attachment has ebbed away, washed up.

Out of the watery light: 'Can you forgive me?' you say.

Something's rising up, or maybe falling away. Dark currents have swept me far beyond your reach. You cannot haul me back. I remain flotsam. Adrift.

'There's nothing to forgive. It's just what happens sometimes.'

I want to tell you that whatever it is that you miss, will surface again one day with someone else. Try not to dwell on last night. Be okay for Alice.

I have no right to say these things.

One tiny island has been submerged, that's all. Many are left.

Jan Prior writes contemporary women's fiction. She has been self-employed as a screen printer, a picture framer and house renovator, and is still a practising visual artist. In 2019, she graduated from Queensland University of Technology with a BFA in Creative and Professional Writing. Jan identifies as lesbian, and lives in a small country town near Brisbane. She gets lost anywhere else.

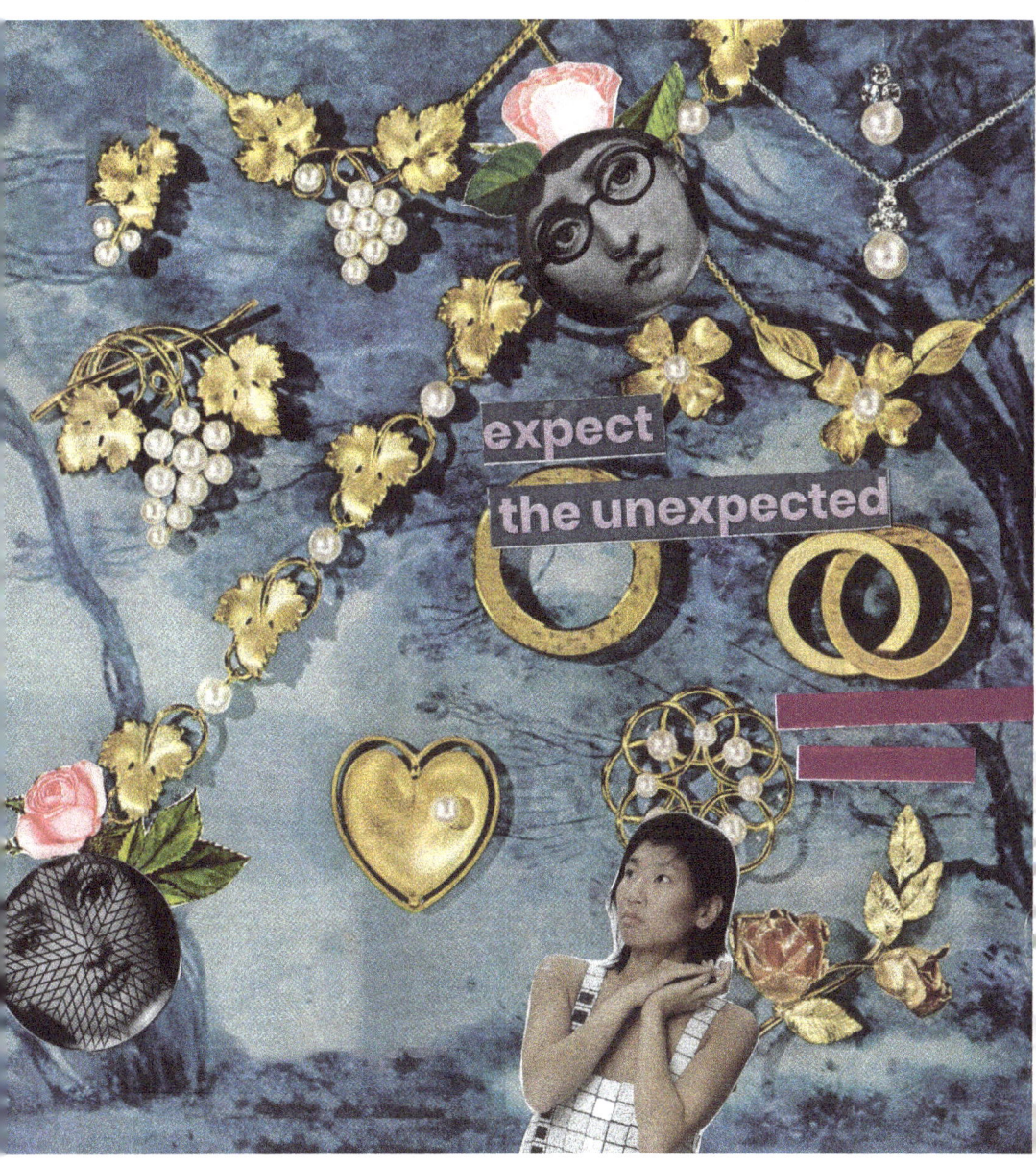

Firdhan Aria Wijaya—*Expect the Unexpected*

TELLING
Zachary Pryor

Mum is driving as fast as she can. We're three hours out of Melbourne, on our way to Bright, though our reason for travelling isn't so colourful. Nan lives there, and she doesn't have long. My eyes are heavy as I drift in and out of sleep. Cold June downpours have drenched the roads, lending a miserable air to the countryside. A truck barrels down the freeway and kicks up the rain—it looks like we're driving behind water nymphs.

'Almost there,' Mum says and changes the playlist. The familiar clap and jingle of Whitney wanting to dance with somebody flows from the speakers. This melody always gets my toe tapping, only this time it causes me to think.

Five years ago, standing in a nightclub, intoxicated from too many vodka lemonades. A boy I was interested in from my class at University had urged me to come along to an eighties night. In fear of being poked and prodded, I had spent my high school years too scared to attend parties. As that gangly guy with a lispy voice, I'd been an unwilling target for the cruel taunts of youth. I'd only been out to my friends for a few months and I'd never been to a 'gay bar'. The place itself represented something of a holy grail—the promised land. Upon entry, men dressed in heels and fairy-floss coloured wigs greeted me, the venue shrouded in smoky haze and lambent light. We danced and danced, surrounded by inebriated men. We ended the evening walking down the street holding hands. The sky stained light blue and a puff of wind lifted his hair. I faced him and had my first kiss.

A few months after flirting with disco I told my parents. We sat in the living room drinking cups of tea.

'I like men.' I said. As the words rolled off my tongue, it felt like I was leaping out my seat with the fabled song by Diana Ross chiming overhead. I thought Mum and Dad would freeze like children who had done something wrong. Instead, Dad smiled. Mum cheered.

'We always assumed. You never showed much interest in girls. Do you remember? One of our favourite activities was getting ice cream after school and you only ever wanted the male server at the milk bar to scoop yours.' Mum then gave me a hug.

After ripping off that parental band aid, my news became easier to share with anyone willing to listen. It became part of my identity: Henry, brown hair, brown eyes, homosexual. One day, standing in line to order coffee when asked my name, I said I was gay.

'Okay Gay, well here's your latte.'

There was still one closet that remained: Nan. Turning to Mum one day I said I wanted to tell her. When I was fourteen Nan had once said something flippant about the 'pansy' boy next door who pranced around in a dress—that comment took hold like a root. She'd lived through a different era. But I resolved myself that this was my news to share. Not Mums, not Dad, not anyone else's. Mine, alone.

Mum supported me. 'She's alone up there and you haven't visited in a while, she'd love to hear from you and see who you've become. You know she's getting doddery, so better late than never!'

While growing up, we spent our family holidays in Bright. I loved being there when I could stomp on the golden leaves and watch my breath turn silver. Taut and regal, Nan would watch me from the kitchen window, with one arm curled around a mixing bowl. Her baking was famous throughout the town, but so was her irascible temper. She once told off three children for walking too leisurely past her house.

As I got older, I made more excuses not to visit. Sport at school, study at University. Until it just became avoiding her to save from confessing my not-so-secret secret. Several months ago, I visited. Driving up, I rehearsed over and over what I would say.

My car crunched against the gravel as I pulled into her driveway. Nan was sitting on the porch, nose down in a book. Her mop of pewter hair had thinned since Christmas and she struggled to give me a hug.

'Henry, about bloody time you visited,' she croaked, and I followed her through the front door. 'I'm always going down to Melbourne. It's good to see you here at last.'

The sweet and acrid scent of oranges wafted through the house as she pulled out a cake from the oven. She lost her grip on the tea towel wrapped around the tin and *smack!* The cake fell to the floor and splattered everywhere.

'Jesus. These old bones. Everything is falling apart.' She said as her face turned pink. I guided her to a seat and rushed around scraping splotches off the floor, then made us some tea. The elixir that somehow makes everything better.

This was my moment. I handed her a cup, sat down across from her and took her hand. It was soft but veiny like a map, and her verdant eyes twinkled in the diminishing afternoon light.

'Nan, I'm gay.' I whispered. 'I was too scared to tell you.'

'That's why you stayed away so long? You foolish boy.' She leaned over and gave me a kiss on the cheek.

The triumphant shrill of Whitney finishes. I jerk awake. I remember Nan dropping the cake, the crumbs on the floor, yet I remained mute—I didn't tell her. My cheeks are wet, thinking of her lying supine in palliative care. What if we get there in time? My heart skips several beats and I bite my lip, watching the countryside turn into a muddy watercolour painting.

Another song with trumpets blasts from the speakers.

Zachary Pryor is a New Zealand writer, painter and change manager living in Melbourne on Wurundjeri land. He writes short stories, flash fiction and is currently trying his hand at writing a novel about a relationship gone wrong. He tweets at @ZackJPryor and posts what he reads on Instagram at @literature_lad.

OPPOSITE: Frank Bonnici—Mixed media on paper, 1205x850

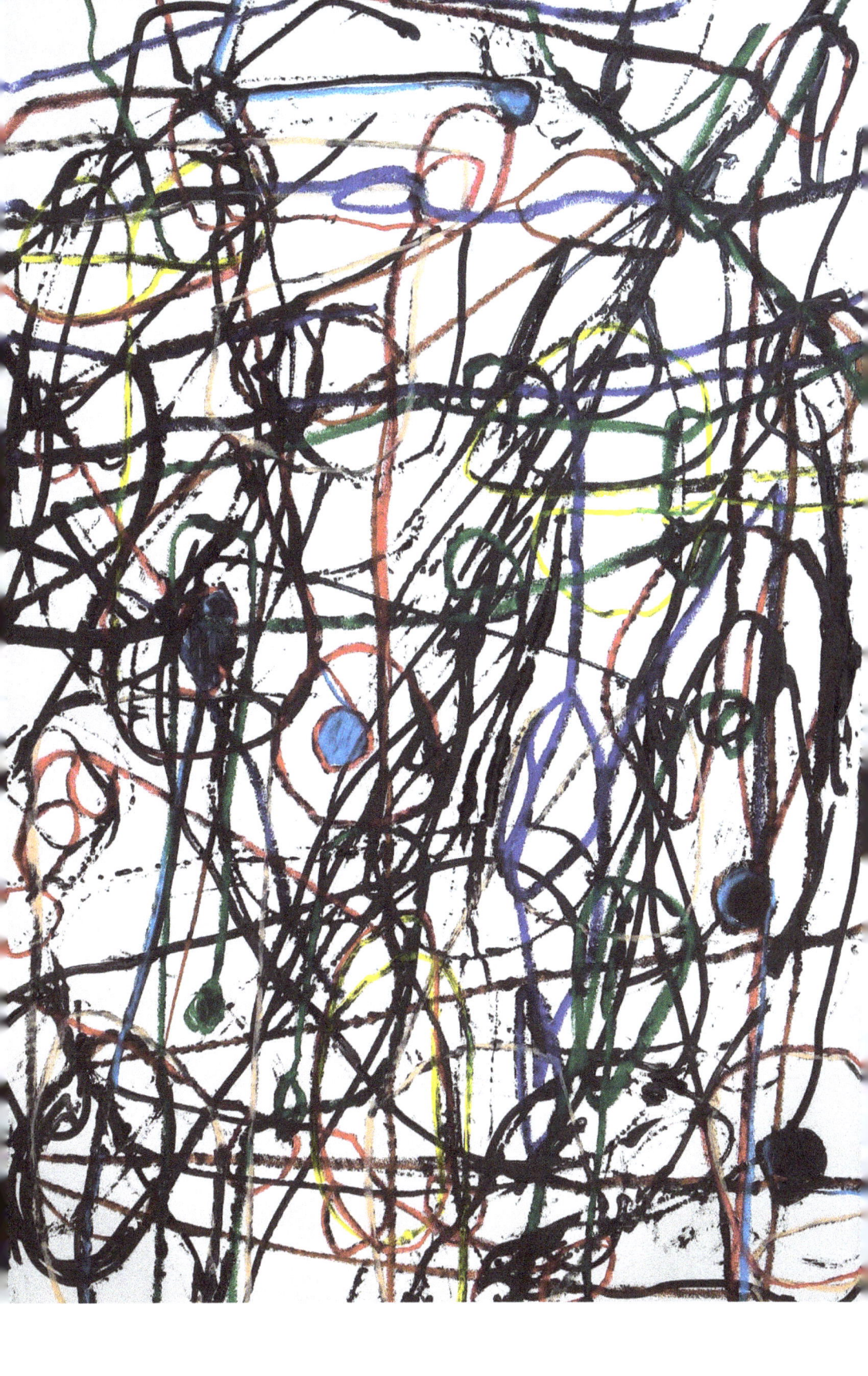

THE WATERS OF JORDAN, AND THE WATERS OF BABYLON

Andy Murdoch

A chapter from a recently finished novel

I make a mistake when I get off the *caique*. Or—'mistake' is what I'll call it, a day or two later, in my diary. But probably it isn't a mistake. Probably it's totally subconscious. I get off the *caique* and I follow all the bright young things down the beach, past the umbrellas and the sunlounges and the overweight Americans and the svelte Scandinavians—the Scandinavians seem to understand the importance of sun protection, the Americans not so much. I follow the bright young things to the western end of the beach—no umbrellas, no sunlounges, just a bar or two in the hills behind—and it's only when I've laid out my towel, taken my shirt and shorts off, slathered as much of my body as I can reach with SPF15+, only then, as I'm lying on my towel, gazing at the water, wondering about a swim, only then do I realise, looking away from the water, then trying not to stare, looking back at the water, only then do I realise that the bright young things I've followed down the beach, many of them ridiculously handsome Germans, have laid out their towels and then stripped off their togs. They're all naked. All of them. Pretty much all of them.

Bright young things. I haven't read much Waugh at this point, and I'm pretty sure he doesn't use 'bright young things' in *Brideshead*. But still, that's what I'll call them, in my diary.

Bright young things.

I'm standing on the banks of the Avon River. No—not *that* Avon River. No Shakespeare has ever graced these parts. I'm standing on the banks of the Avon River, not far from Brinjibup, near the foothills of the Great Dividing Range, and in front of me are a dozen, maybe twenty people—family, friends, fellow churchgoers who've bothered to make the effort on a chilly October Sunday morning. The minister stands on the stones to the left of me, Ross to the right. Ross and Molly. It's weird that it's them. They hate each other's guts. But that's not important today, because today—today—

I'm dressed all in white. White shirt, white trousers—well. Beige. White sandshoes. White underpants, because I don't want coloured ones showing through once my beige trousers are wet.

Because today—

Today I'm getting baptised.

The first time I saw the waters of the Mediterranean it wasn't from a beach on Mykonos. It wasn't even from a Greek island—or a beach. Or Greece. It was from Malta. It was on Malta, walking from my hotel on the coast to Valetta, past all the little fishing boats with the evil eye painted on their prows; and then, later, gazing out over the sea from the top of the city's fort. They were amazing moments, those moments. But the actual fact—You Are Looking At The Mediterranean—didn't really strike me until a day or two later, on the other side of the island. I was standing on the Dinghli Cliffs, and the sun was an hour or two off setting, and it hit me. *You Are Looking …*

'In *The Odyssey* Homer uses a word to describe the colour of the Mediterranean which does not translate well into English,' I wrote in my diary the night after I'd stood on the Dinghli Cliffs. 'The translation we read at uni uses 'wine-dark', but the translator notes this is not all that satisfactory. He's right.'

It's frustrating, reading that diary all these years later, that I don't at least make a stab at getting the colour right myself.

The waters of the Avon River are not wine-dark. We've chosen a shallow stretch, for obvious reasons. Wide too, the banks either side lined with stones washed smooth by the centuries. Still, while the worst of the spring floods are gone the snow is still melting in the mountains above. The water flows fast. Fast and white.

'It'll be cold,' Ross whispers. 'We'll need to be careful. The rocks'll be slippery.'

The minister has been contemplating the river, but now she turns, throws her arms in the air. 'Brothers and sisters!' she calls, and she's loud. And yeah, she's a she. Molly. That's one of the reasons Ross hates her guts. *I do not permit a woman to teach,* Paul wrote to Timothy. But this is the Uniting Church. Ross is a Baptist, technically, but … anyway. 'Brothers and sisters in Christ!' Molly calls. Though if I'm honest she's not that keen on all this. A dribble of water from the font in the church in Flynn—that should be enough for me. But oh no, Andrew's been listening to all this nonsense from Ross and Joy and now he wants to be baptised in a river. Full immersion. Silly boy.

Although I can tell she's actually kind of excited. Just quietly. Kind of loving it. Molly's never done this before.

'Welcome,' Molly says, 'and thank you for coming out so early on this chilly Sunday morning as we prepare, by the act of baptism, to acknowledge and affirm Andrew's commitment to his Lord and Saviour Jesus Christ. As he says goodbye to his old life and welcomes the next we stand here as one, witness to his love of our Father. And what a glorious setting for such a rebirth!' she says, and she throws her arms up again, sweeps them through the air, spins on her feet, three sixty degrees, taking in the wide, shallow, rocky valley. 'I think, without too much imagination, we can see ourselves on the banks of the River Jordan, each of us about to be plunged into the water by John the Baptist himself.'

Yeah. *Totally* loving it.

I slathered as much of myself as I could. As much of myself as I could reach. I could've asked, I guess. I reckon one of those hot naked German guys would happily have rubbed some SPF15+ into that patch of my back, in between my shoulder blades, that I just could not reach. Well—not happily, perhaps. I'm sure one of them would have been prepared to, grudgingly, maybe, if I'd asked. I'm sure they'd have thought nothing of it.

Or—what if—what if maybe one of them did in fact think something of it, after all? And not something bad? What if one of them might have been *more than happy* to rub some sunscreen into my skin?

I'll never know.

And it's what I thought of it that was the problem, of course. Even without it actually happening. That was the problem.

The waters of Superparadise Beach aren't wine-dark, either.

There were plenty of people in the water further up the beach, back towards where we'd got off the *caique*. There were plenty of svelte Scandinavians and overweight Americans frolicking in the water. But down our end of the beach—well, not really 'our' end, just the end of the beach on which I had somehow found myself—there was, fairly conspicuously, no one in the water. The guys around me were stretched out of their towels, some chatting with friends they hadn't seen, perhaps, since last year. Occasionally one would wander casually along the edge of the water, blissfully, nonchalantly willing us to believe he didn't see himself as he was: a Teutonic Adonis.

But no one was in the water.

And I wondered if there was some etiquette on gay beaches, if there were rules about who got in the water first, or when. I was worried I'd maybe break the rules. I wasn't sure I wanted to be the first in the water.

They weren't really all German. There were a couple of guys near me speaking something that sounded like Spanish—it wasn't German, anyway. I'd learnt German at high school, and it definitely wasn't German. I'd learnt a bit of Italian at high school as well, and it didn't sound Italian but it sounded more

Italian than German so I thought maybe it was Spanish. There were a few Americans among the Germans and the possibly Spanish guys, although they weren't fat. Although, to be fair, neither were all of the Americans up the other end of the beach. Most of them, though.

No English accents, up our end of the beach, No Australians.

Except me.

I don't know why I was worried about getting in the water first. Breaking the rules. I'd flown halfway round the planet specifically planning to break the rules. I was on Mykonos because it was the gay island. I was on Superparadise because it was the gay beach on the gay island.

But I hadn't really planned to follow all those bright young things down to the gay end of the gay beach. No, I really hadn't.

And I didn't want to be the first in the water.

It will work. It will. I know it will work.

I will be plunged into the water and my old self will die, my old self will be washed away by the melted snow of the Great Dividing Range and it will wash into the Gippsland Lakes and out into Bass Strait and I will come up out of the water and I will be free, cleansed, renewed, reborn.

Ross and Molly and I walk into the waters of the Avon. We turn to face those who have gathered on the river's shores. Molly begins to speak. I don't listen to her words. I only know that I have to say yes to her questions, and then I'll be free.

That's how it works. That's what the Bible says. That's God's promise.

I stand in the waters of the Avon River and I know this. It is God's promise. I have walked into these waters and I know it is true. I know what will happen. I do. It will work. It will, I know it will work.

Molly asks me one last question and I say yes, and then she and Ross place a hand behind my shoulders and a hand on my arms and they lower me into the water.

I am under the water.

It will work.

It will work.

I am fifteen years old.

On Superparadise Beach I'm twenty-five and kind of pissed off, to be honest. Kind of frustrated. I mean—well, yeah, in that way too, but right now I just want to get in the fucking water. Because it just looks so good—not wine-dark, not that at all, more sort of, I don't know, ice-blue or something, which might not sound real alluring but on a Greek beach in late May with not a cloud in the sky and no shade it's looking pretty fucking alluring to me. I can think of nothing finer right now than getting off my towel and walking into that water, but—

But.

A few more of those Teutonic Adonises have done their thing, wandered along the water's edge. There's a couple—I assume they're a couple, maybe just friends, perfectly tanned, subtly muscled arms draped across each other's generously muscled shoulders, generous, uncut cocks lazily slapping against one thigh, then the other, under immaculately trimmed pubes as they lazily, louchely make their way along the sand. One of them puts his toe in the water and withdraws it immediately, laughing. '*Zu kalt! Zu kalt!*' he cries, and half the beach laughs with him. And then they go back to their towels, and lie down, and no one gets in the fucking water.

And so at some point, after a couple of hours, I say 'Fuck it' and I stand up. I get off my towel and I look around. I maybe don't say the words 'Fuck it' out loud. Like I said, I haven't heard an Australian accent all day. Not even mine. So maybe I don't actually speak, but I stand up, at least. I haul myself off my towel as nonchalantly as possible, which isn't very nonchalantly, and I look at the sea of male beauty in which I've found myself. Accidentally.

And then I look at the sea. Itself.

'Daft name for a beach,' my boyfriend says as we get off the *caique*. 'Superparadise? Seriously?'

We get off the *caique* and we follow the bright young things down to the west end of the beach. 'There's a Paradise Beach as well,' I say, though I'm pretty sure we've already had this conversation. 'But it's a bit rubbish.' I don't say 'It's not as gay'. 'It's terrible for swimming—there's this horrible rocky reefy thing a few metres out in the water. It's more for preening and, you know, people watching.'

'Nothing wrong with a bit of people watching,' my boyfriend says, looking through his sunglasses at the bright young things as we make our way down to the other end of the beach. Not that we are remotely bright young things ourselves.

And this is a new generation of bright young things. It's more than a decade since I was on this beach. Now there are umbrellas and sunlounges down the gay end, and you have to pay for them—unless you order a drink from one of the bars in the hills behind.

My boyfriend and I order a Mythos each, and we drink a bit. Then we slather each other in SPF30+, and then we drink a bit more, and then we get in the water.

Well.

My boyfriend's toes hit the water and 'Jesus,' he said. 'Jesus, it's so cold. Too cold. Way too cold.'

I roll my eyes. 'Fucksake,' I say, and I walk in up to my knees, and then I dive in. I come up for air and turn around, and he's still standing there. 'Come on in, big boy,' I yell at him. 'The water's fine.'

It isn't, actually. It's fucking freezing. But I am in Greece. I am on a beach on a Greek island. I am on Superparadise Beach with my boyfriend and if you'd told me fourteen years ago this was even maybe a possibility I'd have laughed in your face.

I don't think I've ever told my boyfriend I was baptised by full immersion in the Avon River in the eighties.

'Come on, big boy,' I yell again. And then I take my togs off and I drape them over my head, and my boyfriend hoots. 'Come on in,' I yell. 'The water's fine.'

I come out of the water and I know it's worked. I walk out of the river and I hug people, Mum, Dad, Philippa, Ross and Joy. Colin, cynical, sly, my best friend from school, slaps my back and rolls his eyes. 'Such a crock,' he says. I hug those who've come to see me baptised, leave them dripping the water of the river that saturates me. I'm taken to a home nearby, I shower, change into dry clothes—fresh clothes. It's worked. I know that the Lord has kept his promise.

We go to church in Flynn and Molly preaches a boring sermon but she says something about me and the congregation claps, a little bit. We go home to Tennabra, Mum and Dad and I have lunch together—my favourite, spaghetti bolognese, and even though Dad hates it he has a few mouthfuls because today's special, even though he's not properly saved he knows that today's special and he has a few mouthfuls of that wog stuff, that's what he calls it. And then I go for a walk along the creek, I come home, I do some homework, Mum and Dad and I have some tea, we watch some telly—that documentary series about South America, how rude is that?—and then go to bed.

And it's worked. I know it's worked.

The next morning I get on the bus to school and I know.

I look at Declan—blond, beautiful Declan, who gets on a stop or two after me on the way into Flynn—I look at Declan, the one the kids call poofter. I look at Declan, and someone calls him poofter, and he looks at me, and I look away, and I look at Declan, and I know.

It hasn't worked.

The Lord hasn't kept His promise after all.

I half-expect a communal clutching of pearls. 'What's the strange Antipodean doing?' I imagine them saying to themselves, although of course they can't possibly know I'm Antipodean because I haven't opened my fucking mouth all fucking day. Unless of course I did in fact say 'Fuck it' a few seconds ago, and I'm pretty sure I didn't. I expect an intake of breath—'Doesn't he know how this works?'—but there's nothing. I look around, standing next to my towel, and—they couldn't care less, as far as I can tell.

Although who knows. Maybe that's one of the rules as well.

I stand at the water's edge. It is cold, actually, but I don't care. I take a step, and then another. The sand shelves swiftly. I look over my shoulder—just the once. No one cares. I smile, and turn back to the cold, blue water, and I dive in.

Andy Murdoch is a Melbourne-based writer and journalist. *The Waters of Jordan and the Waters of Babylon* is a chapter from his recently completed novel, *Whatever the F*ck I Want.*

WELCOME TO THE GALAXY
Suz Mawer

Shafts of moonlight illuminated the white dome of the observatory. The little girl clutched her aunt's hand and dragged her up the path towards the entry. Struggling through the early evening humidity, her aunt gave a little resistance at first. Then with a cheeky laugh, she let go of her niece's hand and ran ahead.

'Come on Lily! Don't you want to see the stars?' she goaded. Lily scowled and picked up speed, bulleting up the path and catching up swiftly.

'That wasn't fair,' frowned Lily, 'and now I'm all sweaty.'

'It's 30 degrees babe. You were sweating in my air-conditioned car. I reckon you'll survive.'

An evening treat with her niece was just what Kate needed to feel human again, after a month locked away in her flat finishing the umpteenth draft of her novel, she was ready for the public again. They'd reached the admission booth. Kate was fishing around in her purse for the printed tickets when she caught a look at herself reflected in the admission booth window.

Sweat had caused a slight sheen to her shoulder length blonde hair. She used to be as light a blonde as her niece, but as she'd gotten older, her hair had darkened to an almost light brown, a brown she described as 'dirty blonde'. She brushed an errant strand of hair back off her face and behind her ear, briefly revealing an ear with multiple piercings from the ear ridge to the lobe. Her eyes lingered on their reflected selves for a moment. Sharp, intelligent, ice blue eyes with small flecks of gold peered back at her.

'Not bad for thirty-five,' she thought to herself as she gave her reflection a wink.

Kate looked down at Lily. She was often mistaken for her daughter. At 10 years old, Lily was a time capsule of what Kate had been at her age. Except that Kate had been bit of a loner and Lily was the ultimate extrovert, interested in everyone and everything. This month her interest was the universe.

'Come on, Aunty Kate! We'll miss the session!' Tickets found, and scanned by the attendant, they wandered into the air-conditioned observatory.

Before they could enter the observatory proper, all of the ticket holders were mustered in a small antechamber, walls covered in fact sheets about the history of the observatory. Kate looked around her and wondered how long Lily would be interested in the session before wanting to drag her into a café for a coffee—the very thing she'd promised her sister she wouldn't let herself be bullied into by a 10 year old. She hoped that they could both endure what she expected to be a mind-numbing explanation of star configurations. At least it would be a respite from the final heat of the afternoon.

'Aunty Kate! Are you listening?' She wasn't. 'I said, this is Amica and her dad Leo. Amica is my best friend at school.' Kate noted a bemused smile cross the lips of Amica's dad as he looked from Lily to his daughter.

'Leo is *single*,' said Lily.

'All the subtlety of her Mum,' thought Kate as she felt her cheeks redden and looked at the handsome man in front of her. Her sister Lisa was constantly putting her in embarrassing situations with men, and it appeared that this was yet another of her well-intentioned traps. Kate made a mental note to herself to have another chat with Lisa.

'Nice to meet you, Kate,' Leo extended his hand for a sweaty handshake. Kate immediately regretted it. He held her hand a little too tightly and for much too long.

'Yep. Great.'

'So, what do you do for a living? I'm an architect at Grayson and Associates. The new Cove Tower is one of mine.' Smug.

'That's…good. Not the most environmentally focused design if I remember correctly.'

'Well everyone knows that climate change is a conspiracy. It's crap. Just doesn't exist.'

'Right.' Lily grabbed Kate's hand in the nick of time and gave it a firm squeeze, the signal begging her not to ruin this opportunity.

'Aunty Kate's a writer. She's freelance.' And it was obvious that Lily wasn't quite sure what this meant. Leo raised an eyebrow.

'To him, freelance writer must be code for unemployed lefty loser,' thought Kate, 'but he doesn't look put off.'

Kate smiled uncomfortably. She had hoped that the situation would backfire in her favour. For a long moment no-one spoke. They were drowning in silence when the doors to the inner sanctum of the observatory swung open, bringing with it a gust of air-conditioned coolness. Standing in the open doorway was one of the most beautiful women Kate had ever seen.

She was tall with perfect and unblemished olive skin. Thick, black, wavy hair bound in a neat ponytail. Eyes a mysterious light brown. She wore the standard issue uniform of the observatory guides, but on her it looked tailored for her lithe, long body. Then she spoke. Her voice was a dark melody of sweet honey.

'Welcome to the Galaxy. I'm Samira, and I will be your guide this evening. Prepare to experience the universe.'

Samira. Kate was mesmerised. She knew that the people all around her were chattering away, Leo was even trying to ingratiate himself with her. But all Kate heard was silence. From the moment that those doors swung open, she had not taken her eyes from Samira.

When Samira spoke again, her velvet voice was the only sound Kate heard. She was transported into the galaxy, amongst the stars and swept along with stories. Samira made the photographs of galaxies come alive and told tales of the Maori and the Australian Aborigines, comparing their stories of the stars with the tales from her own South Asian background. She wove stories from science, myth and fable making each a personal journey.

The time flew, and her interplanetary guide landed them from the wonders of the stars back into the observatory. People ambled out of the room. Before she knew she was doing it, Kate walked to the front of the room to introduce herself to Samira.

'That was amazing. I'm Kate. I was wondering if you were doing anything now? Can I take you out for a coffee? I'm a writer, and I'd love to hear more.' She was babbling, but somehow in what she thought was incoherent gushing, she had made her point.

'Actually, this is my last session of the day. I'd love a coffee.' And when Samira spoke to Kate, once again the rest of the room fell silent. It was as though it was just the two of them floating in space. Kate felt her face flush and a distinct lack of oxygen.

'Aunty Kaaaaaate! Can we all have coffee?' Her niece abruptly brought Kate back down to Earth. Leo and Amica stared expectantly.

'Yes. Let's all grab a coffee. Is there somewhere here you'd like to go?' Leo. It seemed as though he sensed competition and was staking his claim.

'How about I meet you at the Observatory café? I just need to change out of my uniform.' And Samira smiled at Kate. Kate knew in that moment that there was no hope left for her.

*

The Observatory Café was not as spectacular as the observatory itself, but Kate didn't care. As she waited, Kate wondered if Samira would be interested in her, the girls loudly discussed the latest fashion magazines, and Leo did his best to impress.

Leo had just reached out to put a hand on Kate's knee when Samira glided in. It was impossible, but she was even more attractive than Kate had remembered. She was now wearing jeans and black sneakers with a light blue V-neck t-shirt. Nothing special, but on her it was spectacular. Kate leapt up, knocking Leo's hand away.

'You made it! What can I get you? Coffee? Cake! Would you like some cake?' Amused, Samira grinned, and it was like the light of a billion stars reaching through the blackness of space to find Kate, and only Kate.

'No cake for me, but a peppermint tea would be good. Actually, why don't I grab it? I won't be long.'

'I'll come with you. I did promise to pay.' And with a shared smile, they both meandered to the front counter.

'Why don't I grab that tea takeaway? It looks like you have a situation here with your partner?'

'Oh, no! I've just met him.' Kate clutched at the opportunity as she saw it slipping away from her.

'I'm here most days, feel free to pop in any time. We can grab that coffee then?' Kate was rendered mute. She nodded in disappointed agreement, her mouth dry.

And with that, Samira was gone. Kate dragged herself back to the table.

'She's not staying? That's disappointing,' smirked Leo.

'Yeah. And I should be getting Lily home. School tomorrow Miss—your mum will kill me if I don't get you home soon. And do not tell her about the coffee.'

After dropping Lily home, Kate felt restless. She drove around in the warm heat of the summer night, turned off her air-conditioning and rolled the windows down so she could feel the warm night breeze. How could she have made such a fool of herself? Samira was probably straight.

'You really need to get out more,' Kate berated herself and before she knew it, she found that she'd driven herself back to the Observatory car park.

There was one other vehicle at the far end of the parking bays. A small yellow hatchback was parked perfectly near the grassy area in front of the observatory. On the grass behind it, on a red tartan picnic blanket lay Samira. She was on her back, her head pillowed by her arms, gazing up at the stars. Her hair flowed out around her like a black halo.

Kate leapt out of the car, composed herself and calmly walked over to Samira. She didn't want to startle her. About to speak, her mouth was inexplicably dry.

Samira made the cold silence as warm as the night air with one sentence: 'Why don't you join me?'

Kate dropped down on the rug beside Samira and lay down on her back, facing the stars. It was a perfect, humid night with a clear sky full of a billion pinpoints of light. As she gazed at the night sky, Kate was torn at what to surrender to—the night sky or the beauty of Samira? She fought the urge to turn and stare at Samira, to lose herself in her star speckled eyes. It was a fight that she eventually lost, and when she turned to look at her, found Samira lying on her side, appraising Kate.

'Did you know that by the time we see a star it's already old or dead? We see it in its youth as it's simultaneously dying of old age somewhere far away.'

'That's a cheery thought.'

'My point is, how lucky are we that we get to be present with each other at this time simultaneously? It's a million to one shot that you would find me at the Observatory. Then you drive back and find me here tonight? That's got to be about a billion to one.' Again Kate was dumbstruck.

Samira reached out and gently took Kate's hand in hers.

'You're cute. It's not often someone tries to pick me up at work.' Samira whispered. Kate's face reddened.

'Was I that obvious?'

'And now you're even cuter,' purred Samira as she took Kate's face in her hands and kissed her.

Samira smiled with the warmth of a supernova. They lay back and once more appraised the sky for what seemed like aeons, safe in each other's orbit.

Suz Mawer is a writer of prose, poetry and script. She has had articles published by online Arts Journal Audrey Journal and voices a podcast of her short stories ('Modern Myths & Legends'). Suz recently made her public debut as a poet reading some of her material for the 2020 Mardi Gras program at Kings Cross Theatre.

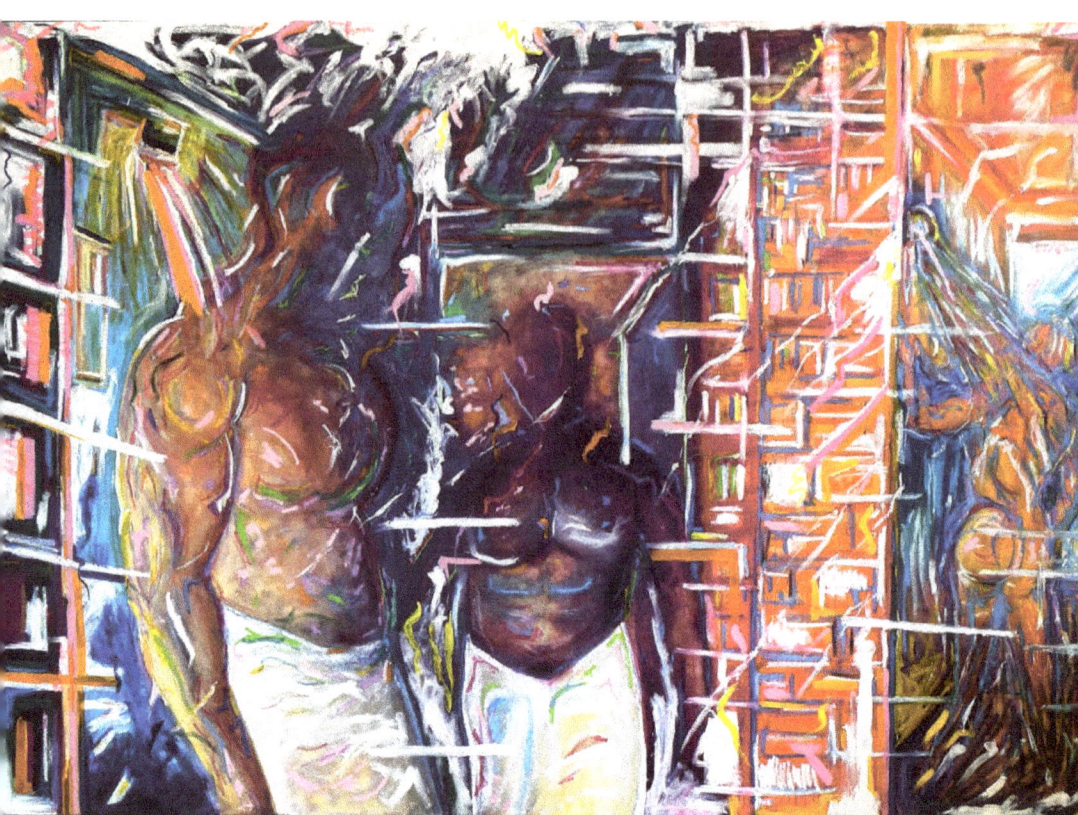

Zachary Pryor—*Bodyline*

TRUE NORTH
Peter Mitchell

Twenty kilometres south of Murwillumbah on the Greyhound bus to Brisbane, Brad wakes and gazes out the window, a frown rippling his forehead. *Did I make the right decision? Should I be on this bus right now?* His night of sleep honeycombed by restlessness, his eyes are veined with blood, the edges gritty. He sits up and rubs them with closed fists.

He leans left from his seat and looks through the front window. The Pacific Highway is a meditation of straight-blue metal. He looks right and scans the horizon. The tip of the sun is just visible, a fire-orange curve peeking above the line of earth and sky.

The bus slows, stopping at a set of lights in Tugun on the southern end of the Gold Coast. In the distance, tall hotels and apartment blocks spike the skyline. He rests his head, the seat upholstery a firm support. The sun is now a large, orange-red orb.

Brad leans forward and stretches his arms in the still air. The tightness in his upper back and shoulders eases with the lengthening of his muscles, reminding him of the uncomfortable seat. *Next time, if there is a next time, I'll fly up to Brissie.*

A solitary car is parked on the left-hand side of the freeway, its alarm shrieking, the hazard lights blinking. The sound triggers a recollection with his ex-lover, Phil.

I've rung to see how you are, reassured Phil.

Yes, said Brad, at least you've rung. He swallowed hard. Even if it is after two years.

But mate, said Phil.

The two words hung in the tight silence.

You were the one who threw me out.

Twenty seconds gathered more tension.

Remember?

Yes, but you … said Brad. His shoulders slumped, his words fading into the hollowness of the telephone lines. By that time in their conversation, he was sitting up, his left-hand cupping his face, his stomach knotted with guilt, anger and inadequacy.

But I'm only ringing to see how you are, repeated Phil.

Hmm. Brad sighed.

Phil offered a weekend in Brisbane where he lived. As recompense, he said. All expenses paid. On me. Phil's voice by then was honey-smooth.

Brad recollects some of the braids of anger and guilt dissolving. *Anyway*, he thought at that time, *it's the middle of winter and its been eighteen months since I've had the warmth of another man's body next to mine.*

A religious advertisement stands beside the freeway. He reads an aphorism about the lord promising atonement. Call this number. Another detail from their phone conversation crosses his memory. Phil said he'd rung to atone for some of the things he'd done to him.

An uneasiness tethers Brad to a reality check. He considers the possibility of history repeating itself. *Is Phil the genuine article? Or simply a conman?*

The bus turns left onto the South-East Freeway.

During their relationship, Phil had travelled to the United States for three months. The Paul Hogan movie, 'Crocodile Dundee' was screening at the time. Australians were the flavour of the month. Phil had flattened his vowels, his voice as plain as a milk arrowroot biscuit. Brad remembers Phil's brittle laughter as he recounted stories of gullible Americans thinking he was from the outback with his Akubra and R. M. Williams boots.

Ascending a small hill, the freeway curves left then right, snaking up the incline. On both sides of it, Nerang spread in square-shaped grids. Brad faces the front again, his view over the top of the seat in front of him, his right forearm resting on the window ledge. The suburban streets blur like a movie in fast forward. In the large, rear-vision mirror next to the driver, Brad notices the reflection of a second man in a bus uniform. Earlier in the trip, he'd seen the man staring at him for long seconds.

The bus ascends another hill and stops at a set of lights. He settles into his seat, closing his eyes. His hindsight returns to a weekend at Rainforest Lodge near Mount Warning. He and Phil were walking to the summit on a warm morning, the air damp and perfumed. They had stopped at a rest area overlooking the caldera. Phil decided to walk to a nearby lookout; Brad remained on the seat, admiring the view. Twenty minutes later, he was startled awake by Phil's whistling. They resumed their walk. A blond surfer passing them several minutes later.

Brad swings his legs angrily back onto the seat, his back square against the armrest, his eyes glaring out the window. He flicks through a travel brochure to distract himself. On the inside page, there are addresses of hotels in Brisbane.

The bus stops at a shopping mall in Logan City. Pedestrian rampways criss-cross the air above the bustops. Several passengers disembark, two hailing a taxi. The third, a man in his early forties, hugs and kisses his female partner, their two children jumping up and down on the spot with excitement.

Brad sits up, his eyes plains of blue ice. The last day of their relationship projected onto his memory. For hours, he had questioned Phil about the surfie, asking him about his recent case of gonorrhoea.

I haven't fucked any other blokes, Phil had asserted.

Brad considers staying at a pub as an alternative to the planned weekend and places the brochure in his overnight bag. He notices movement down the aisle in his peripheral vision. The second bus driver chats to an elderly couple eight rows from Brad's seat.

That's a long face, a voice suddenly says from his left.

Oh, says Brad, half-turning.

The second bus driver smiles at him. Brad half-smiles too, a little shy at the sudden and unexpected attention. It's just boring emotional shit, he says.

The bus driver shrugs his shoulders. Do you mind if I sit here? He points to an empty seat opposite Brad's.

Yeah, sure, says Brad. He lengthens his smile.

Where're you from? asks the bus driver.

Sydney.

And travelling to?

Brisvegas, answers Brad.

The bus driver leans forward over the armrest. Anyway, he says, I'm Allan. He leans across the aisle a little further, holding out his right-hand to Brad. Al to friends, he adds.

Hi Al, says Brad, shaking Allan's hand. Mine's Brad. *Hmm, a firm handshake. I like that in a man. Phil's wrist was always so limp.*

Have you been to Brisbane before? Allan leans back in his seat.

No, this is my first time. The soft upholstery embraces Brad's broad back too.

Have you come up for the weekend?

Yeah, I've come to see the sights. He pauses and considers his options. *How long am I staying? Will I mention Phil?* He decides not to. Yeah, Brad repeats, I'm definitely staying the weekend and maybe for a few days after that.

Oh, great, says Al.

Phil wakes, exercises, breakfasts and showers. In front of the full-length mirror, he turns side-ways. *Not bad for forty-four.* He winks at himself. Back in his bedroom, he dresses quickly, grabs his car-keys and throws them into the air, catching them with his right-hand as they fall tinkling.

He drives his sleek, black Mazda 300ZX from New Farm to the Roma Street Transit Centre. He locks his car and looks at his watch. *Fifteen minutes to spare*. He crosses Roma Street, his eyes fixing on the sex shop sign one hundred metres away. *Enough time for a quick squiz*. Browsing the shelves, he gazes at black dildos and flicks through a copy of *Honcho*. A young blond man walks into the shop. Phil misses the moment when the bus carrying Brad pulls in.

The bus stops in a bay at the transit centre, the passengers disembarking. Several minutes later, cases and overnight bags island the parking bay. Brad looks at his watch a second time as he waits in the bright sun, his mouth a thin line, his overnight bag at his feet.

Phil rushes back across Roma Street. He looks at the blond's phone number, pushing the piece of paper into his jean's pocket. In the distance, he sees luggage spread out on the loading ramp. He hurries into the lounge area and looks around. He walks back outside, puzzlement furrowing his forehead.

A taxi rushes past, the back of Brad's head a brown blur. Phil stands on the spot, his face a canvas of surprise, words stuck in his throat.

Brad sits in the back of the taxi and takes the brochure from his overnight bag.

Where to? says the cabbie

Oh, says Brad, the gay pub. He folds the piece of paper with Allan's phone number on it into his wallet.

Which one? The cab driver looks into the rear-vision mirror. There are several gay pubs in Brissie now. The cab zooms along Roma Street.

Shit, says Brad. He looks up from the brochure. Sorry, I didn't know. He scans it again. I'm not really sure which one. Do you know which is the best?

The Sporties seems to be popular.

The Sporties?

Yeah, the Sportman's Hotel, says the cabbie.

Okay then, I'll try that one.

The Sporties, says the driver still staring into the rear-vision mirror. Sure thing. He winks.

Brad leans forward and smiles. He admires the cab driver's muscled legs.

Noticing Brad's gaze, the cab driver smiles too. Sporties is the oldest gay pub in Brissie. There's no bullshit about it.

Brad nods. So it's the genuine article, eh? he says. Remembering Phil's astonished expression he smiles at his ironic comment, a warmth blooming in his chest.

It has drag shows and trivia nights and you can play pool there if you like.

You seem to know it well, says Brad.

Yeah, says the cabbie, it's my regular watering hole. The cab turns into Albert Street. The drag show on Saturday night is a hoot. It's my favourite.

Uh-huh.

Here's my business card, says the cabbie. He hands it over the driver's seat. If you need a cab anytime, ring the number and ask for Joe Calvatori. He winks into the rear-vision mirror a second time. And maybe you'd even like a beer? Joe half-turns, his left-elbow on the top of the front seat. He raised his eye-brows as if speculating the possibility.

Thanks, says Brad. I'll definitely keep the beer in mind.

Joe looks straight ahead, concentrating on the road.

Brad slips the card into a side pocket of his overnight bag. He settles into the back seat, a cool breeze blowing through the open window. *Bloody hell! There's gay men everywhere in Brissie.* He enjoys the freedom of the currents of air ruffling his hair, his head resting on the headrest.

So it's like an old-fashioned pub? says Brad.

The cab pulls into the gutter. Yep, says Joe.

I'll ring you about the beer. Brad passes Joe the fare.

Great. Joe nods and smiles. Until then.

Let's go to the Mine Shaft, says Joe. 'It's the backroom bar downstairs.

Um, says Brad, okay.

The two of them descend the flight of stairs to the basement, pay five dollars at the door and walk into the dim bar.

Two pots of VB, orders Joe to the barman. He hands Brad his beer. They stroll to a corner of the bar, Brad gazing around it in wonder.

What's out the back? he says.

The backroom.

Yeah, I've heard about backrooms. I've never been to one.

Are ya serious? says Joe. His voice rises in surprise.

Brad nods over the rim of his beer.

Shit! Joe raises his eye-brows. Well, it's my duty, mate, to show you around.

Fifteen minutes pass as they play pool. They finish the pots of beer and leave the empties on the bar. The two of them walk around a corner and down a narrow hallway. Near the end, they stop, their eyes adjusting to the blackness wrapping around them like thick blankets.

Brad hears the clang of belt buckles hitting the cement floor and loud moans orchestrating the thick air. *This is the first time I've ever done this. Hmm.*

Come over here, mate, says Joe, his tongue embracing Brad's receptive mouth.

An eon later, the two of them stumble out the door laughing.

That was fantastic, says Brad. Pleasure sapphires his eyes.

Great, says Joe. What are ya doing tomorrow night?

How about the night after that? counters Brad.

Done, says Joe. I'll ring ya. He walks down Spring Street to his taxi.

Brad stretches, his arms reaching for the dome of ink-night. His imagination soars to the heavens, his mind's eye picturing his body floating on feather stars, pointing true north.

Peter Mitchell is the author of the poetry chapbooks, *Conspiracy of Skin* (Ginninderra Press, 2018) and *The Scarlet Moment* (Picaro Press, 2009) and crafts poetry, short fiction, memoir, literary criticism and a range of journalism.

GONE
Sharryn Ryan

It was during the lockdown that the idea first came to her. Everyone had a
pandemic project. Virginia decided that finding Gail would be hers. After all,
Gail wasn't *lost*, merely living her life somewhere else. She assumed.

There'd been no goodbyes, there wasn't time. But twenty years. They
could talk from one side of the world to the other as if they were old friends.
They could even Zoom. *How very Jetsons*, Virginia thought, smiling at the
memory of her favourite cartoon. Since the pandemic she'd become an
expert on Zoom, even though she didn't have a clue really how it worked.
Just like electricity.

There had been others afterwards, but Gail was Virginia's first. Not that
Virginia had ever told her that. It seemed too significant, too much pressure
on both of them. Whenever friends talked about their first love, it was
always how sexy they were, how luscious. But those weren't Virginia's
words.

'She was older. Kind of wise. And so smart,' she'd always add, but
Virginia couldn't really know that. After all, the whole thing had only lasted a
couple of months, and Virginia was always unsure when to start counting
anyway. She'd been sitting on the other side of rooms for weeks before they
finally met. One night, feigning indifference, she'd even stood within
touching distance of Gail, talking with someone else.

She could feel heat coming from Gail's direction, and wondered if others
could feel it too. Or whether they were as overwhelmed as she was to be
near someone who surely was another species, another type of being
altogether? How else to explain Gail's face and that magnificent smile, that
luminous skin and those eyes, green, sparkling emerald.

But it was the first time they danced that Virginia really knew. When she
felt Gail's hand on the small of her back she thought *oh god, I'm gone, I am so
gone*.

Her search was surprisingly easy. Virginia liked to be organised. She
started a file (*Gail*) and saved all her research. After a false start on Google,
she landed on the idea of the UK electoral roll. All she had to do was pay a
small amount of money and she had three months access. She knew the
town Gail had lived in back then, so she started there.

She was surprised at the information she found. There were twenty-four
Gail's living in the same town as her Gail. Once she'd excluded those too
old or too young, she found her, living in a house with a woman of a similar
age, both of them directors of the same company. She wondered if it was

the woman who had appeared on that last night, the night when a friend, seeing Virginia's devastated face, had pulled her aside.

'C'mon Ginny, wasn't it just a fling? Gail and her partner have been together forever. They came over separately from London. Some project or other that had to be sorted over there. Thought you knew.'

Virginia couldn't remember anything after that, just Gail's face when they bumped into each other in the loo afterwards. Gail grabbed her hand and whispered, 'oh God … I think we've lost everything,' before disappearing out the door.

After her success with the electoral roll, Virginia soon had the phone number of Gail's business. All she had to do was ring the number. She stared at the screen.

'Yes,' the nice man at the other end had confirmed, 'Gail did travel to Sydney … a few years back, now … I'll let her know you called.'

Virginia agonised over the second call—*don't want her to think I'm a stalker* she'd said to friends. Ha ha. In the end she rang again, a week later, but even as she entered the numbers she knew that nice people tend to be reliable too. She hung up, realising she'd never be able to say to Gail *hey, we didn't lose everything, here we are talking.* Then it occurred to her that just like electricity or Zoom, she didn't really have a clue how Gail worked either, and probably never did.

She did a final spell check, saved her research, and folded her computer away. She stood up to go and make a coffee, but stopped. She sat down and opened her computer again. There it was, the *Gail* file. She hit delete, twice.

Sharryn has a Master of Arts in Creative Writing from UTS, Sydney. She has been published in *Southerly, The Law Society Journal* and *Grieve,* and was the winner of the OutStanding Miniature writing competition in 2020. She lives in the Blue Mountains of New South Wales.

*

bent street

www.ingramcontent.com/pod-product-compliance
Lightning Source LLC
Chambersburg PA
CBHW040953170526
45159CB00014B/3118